Bill Crosby

BOOKS
by Carl W. Drepperd

PIONEER AMERICA
ITS FIRST THREE CENTURIES

THE A B C'S OF OLD GLASS

HANDBOOK OF ANTIQUE CHAIRS

AMERICAN CLOCKS AND CLOCKMAKERS

FIRST READER FOR ANTIQUE COLLECTORS

THE PRIMER OF AMERICAN ANTIQUES

In collaboration with
Lurelle Van Arsdale Guild
NEW GEOGRAPHY OF AMERICAN ANTIQUES

Drawn by Earl & engraved by A.Doolittle in 1775   Re-Engraved by A.Doolittle and J.W.Barber in 1832

BATTLE OF LEXINGTON.

1. *Major Pitcairn at the head of the Regular Granadiers.*—2. *The Party who first fired on the Provincials at Lexington.*
3. *Part of the Provincial Company of Lexington.*—4. *Regular Companies on the road to Concord.*—5. *The Meeting house.*
at Lexington.—6. *The Public Inn.*

The beginning of the United States of America—the Battle of Lexington
—re-engraved by Amos Doolittle and J. W. Barber in 1832. Ralph Earle
made some quaint and curious drawings of the battles of Lexington and
Concord which Amos Doolittle engraved on copper plates, published at
New Haven in 1775. Doolittle engraved the Battle of Lexington, a view
of the town of Concord, the battle of North Bridge, Concord, and the
southern part of Lexington. He advertised these prints for sale at a price
of six shillings per set plain or eight shillings colored. The originals are all
close to 12 × 17½ inches in size. All of these are now excessively rare
pioneer engravings. The view here depicted in exact size is from the colored
plate engraved to accompany Barber's *Historical Collections of Connecticut.*

Pioneer America
Its First Three Centuries

CARL W. DREPPERD

Garden City, N.Y.

Doubleday & Company, Inc.

1949

Contents

I   WHO AND WHAT IS A PIONEER   1

II   THE HOMES OF THE PIONEERS   12

III   IRONS IN THE FIRE, OR HOW THEY COOKED, AND WHAT   25

IV   GUNS, TRAPS, SNARES, AND HOOKS   37

V   TOOLS, IMPLEMENTS, AND MACHINES OF AGRICULTURE   48

VI   ORNAMENTS AND ELEGANCIES   57

VII   JEWELRY   80

VIII   MACHINES AND TASK-EASING DEVICES IN THE DOMESTIC AND SOCIAL SCENE   85

IX   PHILOSOPHICAL, MATHEMATICAL, AND SCIENTIFIC ANTIQUES   91

X   AMUSEMENTS, DIVERSIONS, SPORTS, AND PLEASURES   97

XI   PEOPLE, PERSONALITIES, CHARACTERS, AND QUEERS   107

XII   TOYS   116

XIII   MASTERPIECES BY NOBODIES   136

XIV   RELICS OF FIRE PROTECTION   148

XV   SIGNS OF THE TIMES   156

XVI POTTERY, CHINA, AND PORCELAIN 164

XVII TINWARE, PEWTER, BRITANNIA, SHEFFIELD, AND SILVER 178

XVIII FLOWERPOTS, STANDS, AND GARDEN PIECES 192

XIX LIGHTING, FROM BETTY LAMP TO ELECTRICITY 199

XX EDUCATION 216

XXI QUACKS AND CURES 226

XXII STOVES AND HEATING 232

XXIII PIONEER FURNITURE 243

XXIV WOODENWARES 269

XXV FOR THE FOIBLES AND FRILLS OF MAN 279
PARTIAL CHECK LIST OF OCCUPATIONAL SHAVING MUGS

XXVI BUTTONS 293

XXVII TRANSPORTATION—PERSONAL, PRIVATE, AND PUBLIC 300

XXVIII TOOLS 308

Pioneer America

Its First Three Centuries

CHAPTER I

Who and What Is a Pioneer

WE SHOULD have one clear idea in our minds before plunging into the amazing pool of antiques which survive as concrete relics of the social history of our American colonies and the federation that became our United States of America. The thing we should get straight is the real meaning of the term "pioneer." To be a pioneer is *to have* a certain state of mind that can best be characterized as full of faith. To be a pioneer is *to be* at liberty to indulge in constructive contemplation. And to be a pioneer one must have freedom of action; freedom *to do*. Thus to be a pioneer is to have, to be, and to do.

It may well be that he who first said "the exercise of faith is a triumph over common sense" was decrying faith and its exercise. Faith, however, is a triumph over what we know from everyday, common experiences within our own lives. But the simile ends right there. Faith gives us experiences beyond our previous ken; faith turns our vaunted common sense into super-sense, into uncommon sense.

Everything of value ever done within the history of our country, colonial and federal, was done by people of no greater intelligence, no greater physical courage or endowments, or no better social position than their compeers elsewhere on the face of this earth—except that our pioneers had a kind and quality of faith which, for want of a better word and searching analysis, we have called the American spirit—the spirit of enterprise. One thing appears to be quite certain: This country of ours, since its first permanent settlements, has endowed a greater percentage of people with the pioneering state of mind than has any other country at any other period in world history. There must have been popular distribution of this state of mind in ancient Greece but something happened to crush it. Ancient Carthage must have had some of it and lost it. Rome had it and also lost it. It would seem that *having* wealth and power, as such, is a threat to the pioneering state of mind, while *getting, doing,* and *acting* are its chief attributes and its major charms. The nations which lost the pioneering state of mind fell, as nations. The pioneer-minded peoples of the nations which fell, if they survived, exercised the pioneering state of mind elsewhere and under different circumstances.

This is not a work of philosophy. Neither is it a book about specific pioneers as individuals. Rather, it is a book about what many pioneers did and what the pioneering state of mind caused most of our people to do, from the days of Jamestown and Plymouth Rock down to the Centennial Exposition of 1876 and the Columbian Exposition of 1893. Within that span of time hazardous navigation changed to steam, the world moved from illumination by candle and fat lamp to gas and electricity; transportation and communications became swift, safe, and sure; and a group of puny, weak colonies was transformed into a nation that is today the world's greatest economic power. The pioneering state of mind, largely in America but sprouting from here to other lands and people, sparked most of this miracle. However, the greatest success secret of all seems to have preferred residence here.

That secret is common wealth creation—the creation of wealth in which all people share. This is not done in government mints by the printing of currency and the stamping out of coins. Neither is it done by political chicanery or by the exercise of ideologies which preach the equal division of all property. It is done by production, which requires employment, and making that employment really gainful by the simple expedient of paying the employees up to 85 per cent or more out of every dollar of production profit.

This sort of common wealth creation is possible only in a country wherein the majority of the people have something of the pioneering state of mind. In countries where only a few have that great asset, production plants are closely held, the workers are not in enjoyment of high wages, and the owners reap the major profits. The fact that in other nations the people have always envied the owners of large properties cannot be denied. Communism, the last refuge of the incurably repressed and of people with inferiority complexes, is proof of this envy turned to blind or scheming hatred. These "socialists" have envied the wrong thing: they have envied the possessions, the outward and visible signs of wealth, and have not emulated the pioneering state of mind that saves money and puts it to work to create common wealth.

In colonial America, under the most trying and difficult conditions imaginable, and under laws, rules, and manifestos imposed by England's politicians and economists, the pioneering spirit sought ways and means of expression in production from the soil, in fishing, wire drawing, bog-iron mining and smelting, and in trade. Men who in England would never have had the courage to open shop as masters, became chandlers, iron smelters, wool card makers, and so on. Men who had been sharecroppers or renters of land from the lord of the manor took up land of their own and farmed it.

At all times, in the colonies, there was a scarcity of laboring hands which, in turn, caused men to consider the use of machines driven by water or wind power. Minds broadened because work and thinking of all sorts had to be done on a broader scale. People who in England had bought but a few candles a week thought nothing of making one or two thousand candles at a time. All of the first efforts were crude, but crudity did not make the effort a pioneering thing. The pioneering mind does not seek crudity to live with and is never content with it. Its every effort is away from crudity, and the move away from crudity is forever an effort to convert luxuries into staples.

There is so much of the formula of our so-called success in this simple fact that we should examine it again and again. The conversion of a luxury into a staple is also the secret of common wealth creation. We need not go back to ancient days to appreciate this. In the year 1900, everywhere in the civilized world, the self-propelled vehicle known as the automobile was a luxury item. Five thousand dollars was probably the lowest price for one. Ten-thousand-dollar automobiles were not unknown. But in America Henry Ford and others pioneered in making automobiles on a mass-production basis whereby the price could be cut in half or less, and thus three times as many people were able to buy cars.

Out of that pioneering idea we developed the American automobile business. With a smaller population than that of Europe, our people soon owned ten times as many cars. We began building roads to accommodate this new form of popular transportation. Today we have eighty-five per cent of all the world's automobiles. Why? Because pioneers built them, converting a one-time luxury into a staple and, in so doing, made cars that other pioneer-minded people could and did buy.

This same philosophy was applied to the making of all of the objects pictured in this book. One luxury item after another was converted into staples for many people by our artisans. When a rush-light holder was a luxury, it was converted into a staple, as were candles, lamps, grilles, iron pots and pans, fire dogs, brushes, windowpanes, barrels, bottles, floor coverings, meat safes, furniture, and buttons. No matter how luxuriously scarce the item in our colonial scene, and in spite of all political and social handicaps, there was determined effort to make it in sufficient quantities to put it into the staple class.

There are some daydreaming economists who maintain that this was just the beginning of that horrible thing, business. They cannot see, and in seeing understand, that the philosophy of business, which is forever converting luxuries into staples, is the truest form of socialism ever invented. It may come as something of a shock to think of our colonies as socialistic. The shock should be located and placed where it belongs. It is the error we have fallen into in thinking that true socialism is complete state ownership in the Marxist-communistic pattern. What we were doing in our colonies was formulating a pattern whereby the people would own everything—including the state. And what the minds of our pioneers were continually striving for, even though blindly, was freedom of the mind and the body of man from state control.

Today every communistic preacher is simply saying to Americans and to the world, "Be wise, go back to the pre-colonial days of complete state control over the people—over you. We will dispense with such titles as emperor, king, Caesar, duke, lord, and prince—we will have only state, presidium, commissars, and police. All of us cannot have luxuries, so we will abolish all luxuries. We cannot all be smart, so we will reduce all men to an 'average.' It will be wonderful."

Every colonist who came to these shores had suffered a taste of that sort of thing, and had an inheritance of it, in Europe. The cream of our crop of colonists were people who had lived through it, won over it, and then came to America to express freedom and liberty in a new land.

Mention the word pioneer in almost any company and say "name three." Chances are, depending upon the geographic locale, that the answer will be the names of men who were frontiersmen—Daniel Boone, Lewis and Clark, Sam Houston, General Sutter, Donner, Brigham Young, et al. Few of us will mention the first clockmaker to set up shop in a new settlement—the first candlemaker, coppersmith, cabinetmaker, brazier, and so on. We seldom, up to now, have thought of the first artist, or the first silversmith, or the first doctor in a new community as a pioneer.

In 1916 there were several hundred thousand pioneers living in well-built houses on city streets who were first to buy a new mechanical refrigerator that made its own ice. Back in 1846 there were several hundred thousand pioneers having bathtubs installed in special rooms in their homes. During the 1890s other pioneers were having their homes wired for electric lighting. Back in the 1790s hundreds of pioneers had wallpaper pasted on their walls. The people who bought these things were pioneers. The people who made and installed them were pioneers.

In the 1750s a map of the province of Pennsylvania displayed a place named Petroleum. Colonel George Washington purchased several thousand acres of land around Petroleum, Pennsylvania, saying, "This rock oil will be valuable someday." In 1857–59 Colonel Drake of Titusville pioneered in drilling a deep well to bring up this oil. Oil refining began. Kerosene, or coal oil, became available for lighting and heating. Several million people had the luxury of brighter lighting at a lower price. The new illuminating oil was at once a staple, not a luxury.

Kerosene oil at a low price fostered the production of millions of low-priced lamps in which to burn it. The pioneers who had developed "camphene," a lighting fluid of highly explosive quality, used the Chicago fire as an object lesson on which to base a smear campaign on kerosene. They issued a colored lithograph depicting the beginning of the fire in Mrs. O'Leary's barn, and stated that the whole fire started because the cow had kicked over a kerosene lantern. "More fires," they stated, "have been caused by this dangerous fluid than from any other cause." In spite of this insidious campaign camphene couldn't compete with the safer kerosene. Kerosene won out and became our number-one lighting source for more than half a century.

As antiques, or near antiques, we have innumerable relics of the pioneering efforts of Americans to produce better lighting for less money. We have the same thing in clocks, pewter and tinware, kitchen utensils, houses, stoves, heating plants, refrigerators, sanitary toilets, rugs, draperies, chairs, cabinet furniture, matches, buttons, jewelry, and many other articles. About the only luxuries still remaining in the American scene are objects of nature which cannot be duplicated in manufacture, such as genuine jewels and precious stones.

Our history is emphatically the history of our production. Simeon DeWitt of Albany wrote in 1813, "The Americans are an inventive people, perhaps more so than any other existing. Without arrogating to ourselves any superiority of intellect, the cause may be traced to our more favorable circumstances, especially to the facility with which a respectable education and comfortable subsistence may be procured and which leaves leisure to the mind to wander through the mysterious, unfathomable repositories of possible things; to the boundless fields of improvement before us, and to the scarcity of laboring hands which acts as a constant stimulus to resort to mechanical powers and every other obtainable aid to supply the deficiency."

DeWitt was not philosophizing. He was commenting upon such things as they were. He, too, was probably unaware that he had touched upon that handmaiden of faith, the willingness to "wander through the mysterious, unfathomable repositories of possible things." In this century, Sir James Jeans, Claude Bragdon, Lucius Humphrey, Thomas Edison, and Charles Kettering of General Motors have said things which support DeWitt and indicate that he had hit upon a great truth. Our later men, all of whom have made great contributions to knowledge, philosophy, production, and invention, agree that *thoughts are things,* and that everything ever invented, and ever to be invented, has forever resided in that mysterious, unfathomable repository of possible things. The epitomization of American success can well be stated thus: We have delved deeper into the cosmic mine of possible things, and the spade we have used is faith.

The same kind of thinking that in 1710 created a revolving basket of iron wire in which to roast a duck before an open fire, and made the basket turn automatically with a clockwork, in 1910 created an automatic toaster operated by electricity. The same kind of thinking that in 1790 made lamp reservoirs to fit in candlesticks to provide cheaper and better lighting without buying an entire new lamp, has been at work in this twentieth century, at Nela Park, making better and cheaper electric lamps for use in existing wiring systems and fixtures.

If this story doesn't thrill you, inspire you, and motivate you to a new, keener, and more positive appreciation of your American antiques, you are not an American in mind or spirit. You want, actually, to go backward, not forward. On the other hand, if you want to live as your ancestors lived, you will not go back to living in an old house, heated by fireplaces, lighted by candles, cooking on ancient stoves and using a cellar for refrigeration. Your every forebear, from 1620 to 1920, would laugh at you for not being a pioneer—for not being among the first to try the new, make something new and better, and make it available to all people for less money. They painted and stenciled walls in imitation of fine wallpaper when they could not have wallpaper for the same money. But when they could get the paper, the painting and stenciling went out of fashion. They painted and decorated floors to simulate floor cloths and rugs, but when they could have floor cloths and rugs they stopped painting floors.

It is no wonder that bootblacks, chimney sweeps, snuffmakers, tinsmiths, and so on became rich men in this country. The pioneering state of mind is not snobbish. It seeks residence in all peoples and when it finds a receptive individual who will use it, it lifts that individual to glory. It has endowed a poor man with the vision of doing something with chicle and making chewing gum popular. It has motivated a nostrum vendor to turn a lard-pail peddling of "pneumonia cure" into a vast drug business. A coffee vendor roasting a bushel of coffee at a time created a business that roasts a thousand bushels an hour. A buttonmaker who laboriously sledge-hammered brass strips into a single die and made buttons one at a time conceived a machine like his arm—a score of machines like his arm—turning out a million buttons a year. His thought became a fact. Another did it with combs. Another with pocket knives. Another with clocks. The great Negro, George Washington Carver, did it with peanuts.

Eli Terry of Connecticut was a clockmaker because clockmaking had been his apprenticeship. But he had a pioneering state of mind. He explored the pool of possible things in clockmaking. He looked at the luxury that was a tall-case clock and said, "Why not make this a staple?" He made as many as three thousand tall-case clocks in one year. Between 1800 and 1820 his fortune turned from that of clockmaker and peddler, with a few dollars of capital, into a neat one hundred thousand dollars. Was that money dishonestly acquired? To say so is nonsense. It was more than honestly acquired; it was acquired under a cosmic law. It was the reward of service rendered to thousands and thousands of people for whom he made clocks at a price lower than a clock had ever been sold before. But Terry was not the only man who profited. Every customer profited; every dealer and every workman in his little factory. They, the workmen, were making more money at their trade than they or any other workmen in clocks had ever earned before. At least six of Terry's workmen started factories of their own and, in his pattern, created wealth in money for themselves and their workmen and in clocks for the people.

So goes the story of the pioneer antiques we now collect. It is the story behind the antiques that is our real social history. It is the pioneering state of mind that must be called the mother of the arts and sciences. What was produced, primarily, was wealth, plus the things which now, as antiques, are artifacts.

Thus we can know there is history of a new kind in everything of tin, iron, silver, or any other metal; in everything fashioned of wood, pottery, glass, or other material; in books, pamphlets and papers, needles, pins, buttons, jewelry, spectacles, toys, scientific instruments, clocks, and watches. Most people today think we had our ideas for the mass production of watches from the Swiss. That is a very modest appraisal and does us credit. But it isn't true. We were the first to make watches on a mass-production basis. The Swiss experts who saw them invited American experts to go to Switzerland and help them set up a similar system. With them it was simply a matter of doing it in the American way or losing the Swiss watch trade, all over the world, to American watches.

This is a picture book. What is said in the first chapter should, for anyone with a thimbleful of imagination, prove that a volume could be written about the history of every single object ever made and offered for sale in this country. There is so much sheer delight in pursuing the history of an object and in analysis of the idea—the thought —that had to precede the thing, that if this book will but inspire one in every thousand Americans to delve into that history it will have done more than a thousand radio speeches by politicians.

The greatest inventions in this country are the documents known as the Constitution and the Bill of Rights. Far, far too many people think of these documents as things created from the whole cloth after the Revolution was won. They were not. They are the sum total of a century and a half of colonial experimenting, of proof of the working of faith, and of the value of the pioneering state of mind. The Founding Fathers didn't "hope" the Constitution and Bill of Rights had the stuff in them to make this nation a success. They *knew* it. Read them sometime. Then reread them. As documents their primary usefulness to you is knowledge that you have liberty of spirit and freedom of action under the laws of the land. You have the inalienable right to possess the pioneering state of mind. You have the right to delve into the unfathomable repository of all possible things. And nowhere else on this earth today do the people of any nation, under any other system, have as much of that right as you have as a citizen of these United States. Even the antiques you collect are your own—and not the property of a police state.

John W. Barber.

House in Medfield.

Our great historian in pictures, John Warner Barber, born February 2, 1798, who began studying maps of the United States when only five years old. Then Ohio, Kentucky, and Tennessee were a part of the Union. Indian Territory and Mississippi Territory were our possessions. Texas was then a part of Spain's Mexico and was known as the New Philippines. The Louisiana Territory was not yet purchased. Directly east of Spain's St. Louis was our furthermost outpost, Kaskaskia, in the Indian Territory. At the southern tip of the Indian Territory stood the village of Old Vincennes. Barber devoted his life, from young manhood, to gathering historical collections and drawing America as it then existed, in terms of the culture we call architecture. Hundreds of cities, towns, and villages—some of them no longer in existence—were pictured by Barber. On this page and on the two pages following are examples of this great historian's work. TOP: Engraving of John Warner Barber sketching views in the Ohio country; the first settlers entering Vermont, the state that was once an independent nation under its own flag, from 1777 to 1791, when it joined the Union; the Sheldon House at Deerfield, Mass., built in the seventeenth century. CENTER: Inauguration of Washington at Federal Hall, New York, March 3, 1789 [not drawn by Barber]; ancient house in Medfield, Conn., built *c.* 1650; Blockhouse at Ft. Plain, N.Y. BOTTOM: House of Red Jacket on the Buffalo reservation, Erie County, N.Y.; Washington's headquarters at Gowanus, Long Island, a Dutch structure built in 1699.

9

TOP: Baldwin House, Kingston, N.Y., where first constitution of New York State was adopted, 1777; Mormon Hill at Manchester, near Palmyra, N.Y., where Joseph Smith got religion and found the golden plates. SECOND ROW: Old Dutch church, Tarrytown, N.Y., built by Frederick Van Cortlandt, 1699; Swiss cottage, Columbiana County, Ohio, 1840. THIRD ROW: Hightstown, N.J., 1840; glass factories at Millville, N.J., 1840. BOTTOM: New Canaan, Conn., 1840; First courthouse in Green County, Ohio, as it appeared in 1845.

TOP: First hotel at Zanesville (originally Westbourne), Ohio, built in 1799; Campus Martius, Washington County, Ohio, built in 1791. SECOND ROW: Home and grave of Simon Kenton, pioneer who preceded Boone to Kentucky, at Mad River, Logan County, Ohio; General Harrison's home when governor of Indian Territory at Vincennes, Ind.; the Minnesota mine, Michigan, 1850s. THIRD ROW: Colonel Bouquet's redoubt at Fort Pitt (Pittsburgh), Pa., built in 1764; William Penn's private brewery at Pennsbury Manor, built in 1682. FOURTH ROW: The old Townsend House near Chester, Pa., supposed originally to have been erected by Swedes prior to 1682; first house built in Bethlehem, Pa., c. 1740.

11

CHAPTER II

The Homes of the Pioneers

IT IS the year 1607. A little ship comes to anchor in a broad river off the Virginia shore. A group of people land. There isn't a single house, hut, wigwam, or other habitable place. Spars from their ship and timber cut from the forest are covered with sailcloth to provide tents. Pots, pans, axes, and saws are brought off the ship. A few men take guns and shoot some birds and beasts; others drop lines and catch fish. A spring of fresh water is located and staked off. The settlement of Jamestown begins. Trees are felled; huts are framed; wattles are woven over the frames and mud is applied. A few men begin making bricks of clay, fire them in the open, and then build a crude kiln for the burning of more bricks—bricks for walls and tiles for roofs. Every meal enjoyed is a matter of catching fish and shooting game. A garden is planted. A field is cleared to raise corn which, to our early settlers, meant wheat.

Then came the first production idea. The native American Indians were willing to trade furs, food, and other things for a peculiar kind of money. Bead money. Wampum. So at the brick ovens the settlers began melting down sand and soda ash into glass, and blowing beads. Strings of these beads were traded for valuable furs. The Indians were not cheated. They valued the beads more than the furs. The brick ovens provided bricks with which to fill the spaces between the frames of newly set up cottages. Thus the first houses of Virginia were built.

Jamestown was wiped out by hostile Indians. But the middle plantations, now Williamsburg, progressed. Better houses were built. More bricks were made. Virginia flourished.

At Plymouth Rock the scene is repeated. A ship lands its cargo of pioneers; tents serve until caves and lean-tos are contrived; then the wigwams of wattles and mud over a framework of timber. What, no log cabins? Not a single one! Wood houses, but not log houses—huts with wooden chimneys that burned down with the greatest of ease.

At New Amsterdam the scene is repeated, but with variations. A free Netherlands is about to set up an extension of itself in the New World and make that extension a trading post of some importance. The first houses on Manhattan were crude timber huts within a stockade of piling. Dutch-type houses of brick were built as soon as possible. Perhaps the Svensons from Courland who became Van Cortlandts, and the Larsens from Sweden who became Van Rensselaers, introduced the Swedish log house on Manhattan.

On the shores of the South River a ship comes to anchor, a ship of Swedish and Finnish pioneers. They look at the standing timber along what we now call the Delaware River, and go ashore with axes, saws, and adzes. They built the first log houses on these shores. As early as 1650 they were using ledge stone in house building. By 1660 they had a brickyard and were building brick houses. Amazingly, these Swedish and Finnish pioneers had the finest, safest, and most comfortable homes of all the early colonists. They had the perfect pattern with which to take advantage of the natural resources of the land. Their log-house construction became the pattern followed in blockhouse and cabin construction as late as the 1880s.

In Virginia, northern Virginia (New England), and in the Hudson Valley from New Amsterdam to Albany progress in home building was marked by the abandonment of small huts in favor of continually better houses. The stone, brick, and log houses of the Swedes were superseded by Elizabethan and Georgian style houses. Pretentious homes, actually manor houses after the English pattern, became the plantation seats dotting the James River and other waterways of Virginia. Royal governors erected miniature palaces. Merchants, doctors, divines, and tradesmen began building better houses, and even mansions. The progress was rapid compared to the times. In the first fifty years of settlement some families erected five houses—abandoning the previously erected ones in favor of ever better ones. Only the Puritans, to whom progress was anathema, remained static within the colonial scene. With all others, progress was the order of the day. Eventually the Puritans, too, caught the spirit of progress.

It is with the beginning of the nineteenth century that the luxury we call modern plumbing entered the housing picture. Just why we and the rest of the world waited so long to put this luxury into our homes and make it a staple is something of a mystery. Queen Elizabeth had a sanitary toilet. Even in her day it was not a new idea. Sanitary toilets existed in Italy in 1400, brought back as an idea by Crusaders. Most of our early "plummers" graduated from the craft of pewterers. There is a most fascinating story buried in this fact. Pewter, on its way out as a metal for household tablewares, was made into ducts, pipes, sink benches, reservoirs, cisterns, conduits, and such. It was easily worked. It was malleable, or could be made so. Water was conducted to houses in lead and zinc piping made by pewterers. Shower baths, bathtubs, and water-flushing toilets were made and installed by men who had graduated from the business of making pewter plates, pots, and other utensils.

The houses of our pioneers—the houses they lived in and the houses they built for worship—are a delightful architectural parade. But within this parade as it actually was and as we have imagined it to be there is much misconception. Most of the error lies in the popular belief that the usual type of pioneer home was the log cabin. This error is committed by radio and movie script writers, advertising counselors, artists, and many schoolteachers. Apparently few, if any, of these experts have taken the time to read *The Log Cabin Myth* by Harold Shurtleff, published by the Harvard University Press in 1939. If any architectural book should be made required reading for all publicists and teachers, all artists and writers, it is Shurtleff's monograph on the log cabin and the houses actually built by our pioneers.

There were so few *log cabins* built before 1800 that the number is hardly worth considering. The Swedes built *log houses*. A few log houses were built in New England prior to 1690, but the log cabin was a late-comer. It seems to have been built largely by Irish immigrants, using either the Swedish or the Alpine style of corner cutting and notching. The Swedish type of log house used squared planks or logs of huge size, making a stout, firm, and weatherproof wall. Most of the nineteenth-century log cabins were made of rounded logs, sometimes peeled, chinked with stones and chips, and daubed with mud to keep out draughts. The better log cabins of this period were made of squared logs, dovetailed at the corners and pinned together.

The Dutch style of architecture characterized, especially in town houses, by stepped gables facing the street or road, was common in the New York and Pennsylvania colonies. There were almost as many Dutch in the Delaware Valley as there were Swedes. Dutch country architecture reproduced, in farmhouses, the Flemish hipped roof and other features delineated in the pictures of this chapter. The Swedes' type of country house, whether of brick, stone, or logs or any combina-

tion of these, was developed in Pennsylvania into what is now mis-
called Pennsylvania-German architecture. Actually there are exceedingly few "German" houses in Pennsylvania. Most of the European
immigrants of importance in eighteenth-century Pennsylvania were
not Germans but Swiss. They built Swiss barns of huge size, and
houses duplicating the techniques often used in the cantons of Basle,
Bern, Appenzell, and the Grand Val.

There was considerable French architecture used in New York
and Pennsylvania. One of the finest remaining garrison houses of
Pennsylvania is the Sellier house, built in Lancaster County in the
eighteenth century but now in Lebanon County. Sometimes called
Zellers Fort, this structure was erected by M. Clothilde Sellier of
Deux Ponts, France. The oldest house in Berks County was built by
Mouns and Ingeborg Jones, Swedes, who settled on the Schuylkill.

Morton Mortonson, grandfather of John Morton, signer of the
Declaration of Independence, built a log house in New Sweden in
1654. In 1698 it was enlarged by building another house of the same
size ten feet away, roofing over both, and having a breezeway between.
In 1806 this breezeway was walled with stone.

During the eighteenth century the architectural style we call
Georgian dominated the town and country-home and church-building
activities of the pioneers. George I succeeded Queen Anne in 1714,
and was followed by a line of Georges, the end of which is not yet.
Because of the stupidity, gullibility, and cupidity of George III, our
own pioneering spirit boiled over. We stopped all building for a few
years and staged our Revolution. After that Revolution, we turned
from Georgian to classic and Greek revival architecture.

To imagine that Greek revival architecture in the United States
was confined to churches and public buildings is another error. By
1810 we were building little houses, barns, big houses, pigsties, outhouses, and backhouses in the Greek revival style. After the discovery
of gold in California, the westward way was dotted with what may be
a completely American style—a one-story house with a false, or curtain front that made it look like a two- or three-story structure.

To say that many people collect old houses is not quite true. Most
people collect but one old house, and live in it. But several hundred
thousand people have done this all across the country, and thousands
of others are now seeking old houses to restore and enjoy living in
with their chosen antiques. The Society for the Preservation of New
England Antiquities has a great collection of old houses. Williams-

burg, Virginia, is a grand collection of restored and rebuilt pioneering homes and palatial structures, inns, and churches.

The following books are recommended to all desiring to study further the subject of American domestic architecture. Certain of our illustrations are taken from these books. Others are drawings from photographs, from authentic reconstructions, and from actual structures standing today.

The Architect, by William H. Ranlett, N.Y., 1853.

Cottage Residences, by A. J. Downing, N.Y., 1842.

Cottages and Cottage Life, by C. W. Elliott, Cincinnati, 1848.

Homestead Architecture, by Samuel Sloan, Philadelphia, 1866.

Rural Architect, by Lewis F. Allen, N.Y., 1852.

A Series of Select and Original Modern Designs for Dwelling Houses, by John Hall, Baltimore, 1848.

The Young Carpenter's Assistant, Or a System of Architecture Adapted to the Style of Building In the United States, by Owen Biddle, Philadelphia, 1805.

The Practical Builder's Assistant, by John Haviland, Baltimore, 1820.

The Country Builder's Assistant, by Asher Benjamin, Greenfield, Mass., 1797.

A Collection of Designs in Architecture, by Abraham Swan, Philadelphia, 1775.

TOP ROW: The Jackson House, Portsmouth, N.H., erected in 1664. Courtesy Essex Institute; The Brother House at Ephrata, Lancaster County, Pa., erected prior to 1750—no longer standing; Wigwam at Pioneer Village, South Salem, Mass. Courtesy Essex Institute. Photo by Weber. CENTER: Sod-roofed cottage, Welsh Hills of Pennsylvania, built by runaway slaves c. 1835; interior of the pioneer wigwam shown immediately above it. BOTTOM: Garrison House in the manner of a French *petit château*, built by Madame Clothilde Sellier of Deux Ponts, France, 1723, rebuilt in 1745 in Mill Creek Township, then Lancaster but now Lebanon County, Pa. Doorway to the basement and spring of the Sellier garrison house. Courtesy Pennsylvania Historical & Museum Commission, Commonwealth of Pennsylvania.

TOP (Photograph): The Henry Whitfield State Historical Museum at Guilford, Conn., built in 1639—from a photograph by H. Alexander Matthews; early lithograph of the same house issued by Punderson & Crisand, New Haven. They feature it as the oldest house standing in the United States. SECOND ROW: Half-timber structure built in 1730, Lancaster, Pa. THIRD ROW: Elizabethan architecture in Pennsylvania. Quaker meetinghouse in Chester County, erected c. 1685; residence of George Ross, Lancaster, Pa., c. 1750; Washington's headquarters, Long Island, c. 1660. This structure is Dutch. BOTTOM: Stone house erected in 1719 by Christian Herr, Lancaster County, Pa.; house of Gunnar Rambo, Philadelphia, built in 1662. Architecture is Swedish. The early William Penn cottage at Chester, Pa., c. 1680 or earlier.

TOP: The new Dutch Church, New York, erected in 1731; view of New Amsterdam, 1651; old Dutch house on William Street, New York, 1648; the old Beekman house at Albany, 1725. MIDDLE ROW: Old blockhouse at Fort Plain, N.Y.; early log or puncheon houses at the first settlement of Roanoke, Va. BOTTOM: Ancient house at Deerfield, Mass.; Log cabin six miles from St. Clarisville, Ohio, 1800; All that was left of the old church at Jamestown before the twentieth-century restoration.

WASHINGTON'S HEAD QUARTERS,
AT NEWBURGH,

TOP: Birthplace of President Monroe, Westmoreland, Va. Note tobacco field in foreground; birthplace of President Pierce at Hillsborough, N.H. SECOND ROW: Ojibway women building a tepee of poles and birch bark; Western log house, c. 1840. THIRD ROW: Swiss chalet in Ohio, built in 1840; the piggery district of New York City, Fifty-sixth to Fifty-seventh streets at Sixth Avenue in 1850; Shaker village, Hancock, Conn., started in 1797. BOTTOM: Washington's headquarters at Newburgh, N.Y., c. 1740; west front of Mount Vernon, the residence of General Washington.

TOP: Pennsylvania farmhouse, *c.* 1750; Tom Moore's Dutch cottage, Philadelphia, Pa., built *c.* 1670; birthplace of Daniel Webster.   SECOND ROW: Tammany Hall and street scene in New York City in 1835; Broad Street, Savannah, Ga., 1860.   THIRD ROW: Houses at Little Falls, N.Y., on the canal, *c.* 1850; Pynchon House, Springfield, Mass., erected *c.* 1660 and pictured as it appeared in 1784.   BOTTOM: Water front of Cincinnati, the metropolis of the West, as it appeared in 1840; building housing the "Rocky Mountain News" at Auraria, Kansas Territory, 1859.

TOP: The Marten Martensen House near Philadelphia, built *c.* 1654; Kickapoo, Kansas Territory, 1856.   SECOND ROW: Log cabin in Ohio, *c.* 1800; Derry Church, Pennsylvania, built in 1720; General Forbes's barracks, used during Braddock's Expedition. Built *c.* 1740 at Lancaster, Pa. THIRD ROW: Revolutionary barracks, New York City. These became the Inventors Institute in 1847; mansion of O. S. Fowler, the phrenologist and publisher. This octagon house of modern design was built in 1853.   BOTTOM: James Buchanan leaving his home town of Lancaster, Pa., for his inauguration as President, 1857; "cheap cottage," offered as modern design in 1842 and guaranteed to cost less than $1,000 to erect.

TOP: Fort Wayne, Ind., 1794. Courtesy Allen County-Ft. Wayne Historical Society; houses at Van Buren, Ark., 1856. CENTER: Model cottage of 1850. Estimated cost of building, $2,000!; under the cottage, the house of Sven Sener, Swedish settler, on the site of Philadelphia, built *c.* 1645; to right, model bathroom of 1840 in the form of a Greek temple; under the bathroom, the Phalanstery near Albany, N.Y., 1843, built by co-operative labor and equitable distribution of profits—the exact opposite of the Soviet communistic idea. Members of the Phalanx were all capitalists. BOTTOM: Jefferson City, Mo., in 1856; house of General Charles Lee, Shenandoah Valley, Va., *c.* 1750.

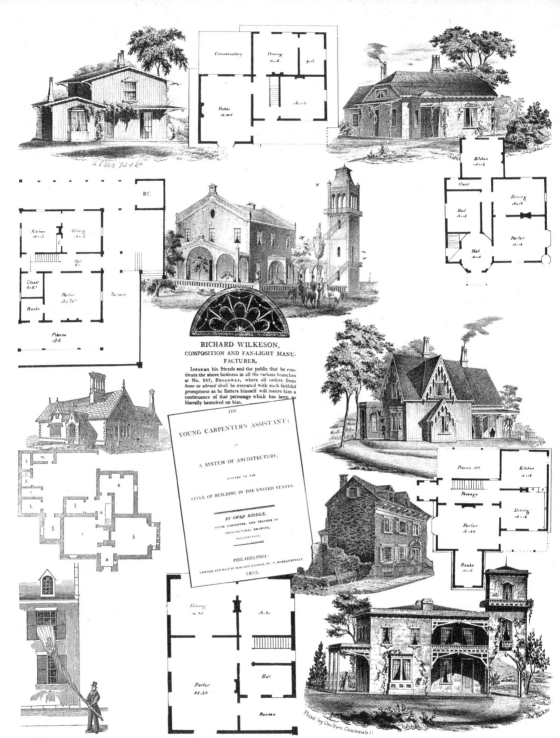

RICHARD WILKESON,
COMPOSITION AND FAN-LIGHT MANUFACTURER,

INFORMS his friends and the public that he continues the above business in all the various branches at No. 267, BROADWAY, where all orders from home or abroad shall be executed with such faithful promptness as he flatters himself will insure him a continuance of that patronage which has been so liberally bestowed on him.

YOUNG CARPENTER'S ASSISTANT;

OR

A SYSTEM OF ARCHITECTURE,

ADAPTED TO THE

STYLE OF BUILDING IN THE UNITED STATES.

BY OWEN BIDDLE,
HOUSE CARPENTER, AND TEACHER OF ARCHITECTURAL DRAWING,
PHILADELPHIA.

PHILADELPHIA:
PRINTED AND SOLD BY BENJAMIN JOHNSON, NO. 31, MARKET-STREET.
1805.

TOP: A pair of cottages of the 1840s. The first estimated to cost $1,800, the second one $1,400.   SECOND ROW: A $3,000 mansion of 1840. There was a sanitary water closet in the tower.   THIRD ROW: Gothic cottage and plan, 1840. Estimated to cost $2,000; advertisement of Richard Wilkeson, 1812, and title page of "Young Carpenter's Assistant," issued in 1805; Gothic cottage of 1840.   BOTTOM: Van Loan's fire escape, 1847. Invented by the postmaster at Catskill, N.Y.   UPPER RIGHT: Birthplace of John Howard Payne, New York City, built c. 1750; a $2,500 mansion of the 1840s.

24

CHAPTER III

Irons in the Fire, or
How They Cooked, and What

IF YOU have doubted that our pioneers were well acquainted with gadgets of all sorts and kinds this chapter, which deals almost exclusively with metallic fireplace and cooking equipment, should dissipate your doubt in one fell swoop. Our pioneers had as many gadgets, if not more, than you'd have if you purchased everything that struck your fancy at the best-stocked emporium of modern household wares. As late as 1845 the catalogue of a housewares store of Philadelphia listed more than 250 items as necessary for a complete kitchen.

We must delve deeply into the history of foods, food preparation and service, into recipes and the analysis of recipes, if we would know the why and wherefore of many items once used and prized around the kitchen fireplace. Stewing, braising, roasting, broiling, boiling, toasting, frying, baking, brewing, candying, drying all called for different utensils and tools. The ancient art of *cury* or cookery was set down in manuscript recipe books as early as the fourteenth century. Apparently it is from cury, the English term, that we derive *curry,* meaning Indian cookery. Within a century after the art of printing was borrowed from the Chinese, who also are said to have invented the art of cookery, cooking recipe books were printed. Today there are perhaps several thousand collectors of cookery books, and even specialized collectors of American cookery books.

Analysis of any early recipe will reveal what utensils the complete housewife had to have in order to prepare the dish. Here is a recipe for "Bursews" from *A Forme of Cury,* printed in the sixteenth century: "Take pork, seethe it, and grind it small with a sodden iron. Add good powders [ground spices], whole spices, salt, and sugar. Make into small balls, dip in egg batter, and fry as fritters." This recipe requires (1) a seething pot, (2) sodden iron and mortar, (3) spice mortar, (4) spice box, (5) salt box, (6) sugar box, (7) dipping or dripping pan, and (8) frying pan. A Bursew was a simple meat ball which we would call a sausage cake.

In all probability the first culinary effort of the pioneers was one-pot cooking. Everything was dumped into one pot and a sort of stew, hash, or New England boiled dinner was the mess. We should not shudder at the usage of the term "mess." In early cooking nomenclature the term meant service, or to serve. "Mess it forth" is the last direction in many early recipes. The first refinement of one-pot cooking was one or more wire baskets in which different meats and vegetables were kept separate in the broth.

Baking various kinds of breads called for numerous different utensils and aids. Not all breadstuffs were oven baked. Much bread was baked for use at a specific meal rather than baked in batches and stored. Spoon bread, now considered a Southern delicacy, once enjoyed popularity in New England and Pennsylvania as oven-baked mush. Pone, now generally called corn pone, although originally baked from wheaten, oaten, maize (Indian corn), and even rye and spelt meals, was baked before many a fire on either a backstone or a sloping baking board. The backstone, originally back hearthstone, was once a slightly raised section of hearth, a sort of partial ledge built across the back of the hearth. Two sides of the fireplace wall acted as natural reflectors of heat to this spot and here pies, bread, tarts, and flams were put to bake. Later the backstone was a large, flat iron disk, ever so slightly dished, either suspended from the crane or supported on a spider.

Among the now quaint and curious things of collectors' interest are all of the early fireplace items used in all forms of cooking and baking. The grocery store wasn't just around the corner from the homes of our pioneers until well into the nineteenth century. The pioneer's grocery store was the kitchen, pantry, and buttery, the spring house, dry house, cellar, and smokehouse. The preparation of almost every food by cooking, curing, or preserving called for many utensils. There were special spoons almost without end, special forms and shapes of knives, stirrers, tongs, et cetera. Some of the items are rare today because they were appurtenances of only the most complete kitchens when originally used. There is pictured a gadget which, for want of a better name, might well be called a baked potato-puller-outer. This utensil is a real work of art. The shape of the bowl is graceful; it is handsomely pierced and exceedingly well balanced. It will pick up a hearth-baked potato in one forward swoop, lift it neatly into its bowl, and enable the user to put the baked potato in a serving dish. Yet, for all we know, this utensil may have had another use.

Up to the time bog iron was discovered and mined in Massachusetts and Virginia in the seventeenth century, iron wares as a pioneer item were precious. In Pennsylvania, shortly after 1700, Welsh pioneers opened mines of considerable richness and began converting the magnificent forest timber of Penn's woods into charcoal to melt the ore. As pioneers, we had many good ironworkers and some few real artist craftsmen in iron. Also, we developed that all-around artisan, the blacksmith, who could shoe an ox or a horse, tire a wheel or iron a sleigh, and make everything from a betty lamp to a smokejack at his anvil. Most of the early cooking utensils and gadgets of wrought and sheet iron appear to have been made by blacksmiths. These same artisans made hinges and other building hardware, turnspits, andirons, cranes, and lug poles. Iron founders cast innumerable pots and pans, although some wrought-iron pans, made by blacksmiths, are among our legacy of pioneer items.

In the following collection of pictures each item is identified and the approximate dates of use given. If a few items are not of iron or other metal, rest assured they are not included in error; they were a part of some fireplace or cooking center. Among these are blanket cranes of wood, huge cook pots used outdoors, and some items partly of wood and partly of metal. The chapter on woodenwares may duplicate a few of the items in this chapter. Very frequently an object in or around one fireplace was also enjoyed in duplicate elsewhere in the house. Our pioneers were apparently far more free from tradition than we of this day and age. They put beds where they pleased, highboys in any room that struck their fancy and, if they wanted a sideboard or lowboy in the kitchen, that's where the sideboard or lowboy was placed.

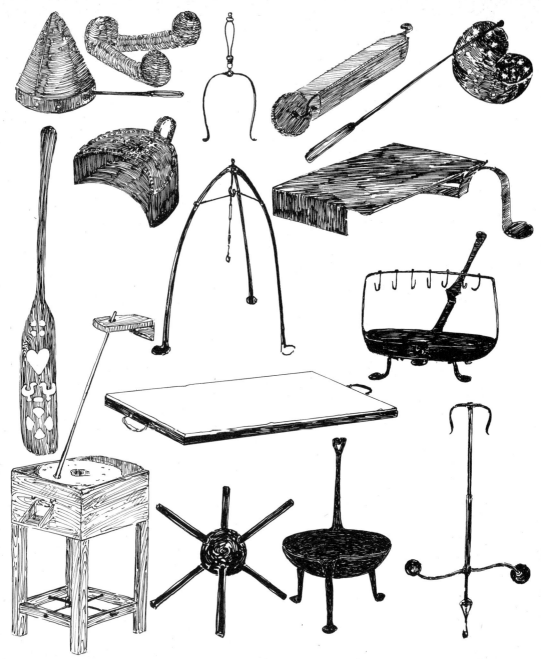

TOP ROW: Curfew to hold fire overnight, 1660–1780; cob iron, to support a skillet or pan amid the embers, 1620–1820; pie fork, 1750–1800; tinderbox with sparking wheel, *c.* 1750–1800; potato scoop, *c.* 1750. SECOND ROW: Dairy oar, *c.* 1650; down-hearth plate warmer, *c.* 1750; brandreth, a tripod holder for pots, 1650–1850; baking iron, 1650–1820. BOTTOM: Quern, a small gristmill for the home, 1650–1850; iron cat. No matter how placed it always rested on three legs and presented three legs pointing upward on which to place a utensil, 1650–1790; footed saucepan, 1660–1800; hanging spit—the heavy balls kept it turning—1680–1800. CENTER: A soapstone griddle in iron frame of a type used from 1650 to 1900; bird spit with drip pan and handle, 1660–1800.

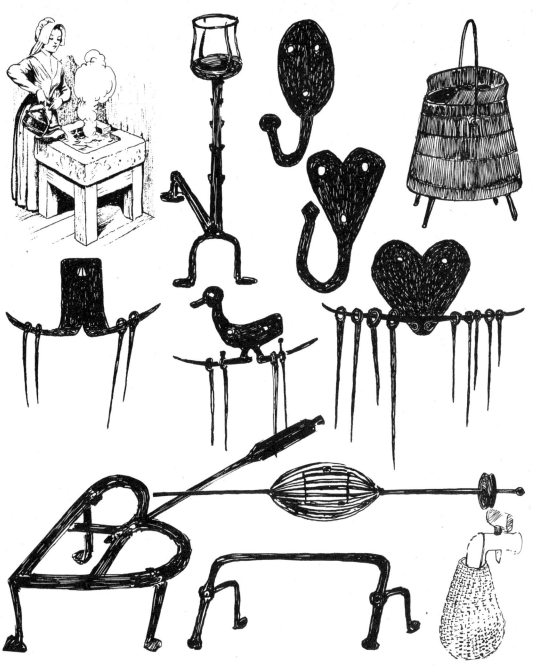

TOP ROW: Stone sink of 1750 in the Cloisters at Ephrata, Pa.; cresset-top andiron, 1660. The cresset was filled with fuel to provide light, or heat for small saucepans. Protuberances on shaft are to hold spit; pair of jamb hooks, of iron and brass, used from 1660s to 1860s; iron cooking pot owned by Miles Standish, c. 1620.   SECOND ROW: Three skewer racks of diverse types, made from wrought iron, and racked with skewers of various sizes for use in cooking meats.   BOTTOM: Heart-shaped trivet, c. 1750; basket spit of iron, c. 1750. Meat and trussed birds were placed in basket to roast; roller on end was connected to clockwork to keep spit turning; cob iron, a type of fireplace fixture used from 1620 to 1700; Pushkin, a wickerwork strainer hung on barrel faucets to keep drawn vinegar, cider, et cetera, clear.

29

TOP ROW: Cob iron with serrated edge, from New England, *c.* 1650, and plain cob iron from Virginia, *c.* 1750. Cob irons were generally placed "front to back" and not crosswise in a fireplace. Logs were piled on from both sides; figural andiron, *c.* 1770; bottle jack, a roasting oven with a spring to turn spit slowly as jack stood before fire. Sheet iron, *c.* 1785–1800. SECOND ROW: Fire fan, used instead of bellows to bring embers to a flame; iron trivet, *c.* 1750; barred grill, *c.* 1800; trivet with pierced brass top, *c.* 1760. BOTTOM ROW: Wooden grain mortars for pounding meal. These were used from 1610 to 1840; standing gridiron, adjustable, with nine spit hooks for impaling small birds, chops, and steaks; standing trivet—broiler with adjustable spit arm; box bellows, adapted by the Dutch from a Chinese pattern, *c.* 1720–1800.

TOP ROW: Cone of sugar hung from ceiling with insect stopper above the cone; early advertisement of Baker's cocoa, c. 1770; molds for making cone sugar, eighteenth century; advertisement of a meat smoker, Philadelphia, 1786; advertisement for mustard and chocolate, Philadelphia, 1765. CENTER ROW: Sausage meat cutter, 1850; pounding corn into meal, a pioneering activity of 1840; still-gallon measure, copper, eighteenth and nineteenth centuries. Term derives from use at the still where spirits were distilled. BOTTOM: Interior of a sugar refinery, c. 1840, and views of the pouring and wrapping of sugar cones. Small jars at the bottom of cones caught the drip from the sugar. This was molasses; pair of sugar cutters, or nips, used to cut pieces off sugar cones.

TOP ROW: A collection of iron pots and kettles of types used from 1620 to 1900. CENTER: Two iron meat choppers with wooden handles, and a rare copper skillet. The original skillet was a two-piece utensil. The top of skillet could be used as a porringer while the footed bottom could be placed over coals and used as a small saucepan; cresset fire lighter, eighteenth century. Hot coals were placed in the open receptacle. Also used to carry fire from one room to another; "infallible fire kindler," ancestor of the Cape Cod fire lighter, c. 1860. BOTTOM ROW: View of the Eagle Air Furnace, where thousands of iron pots were made. Albany, New York, 1845; high-legged trivet, c. 1750–1770.

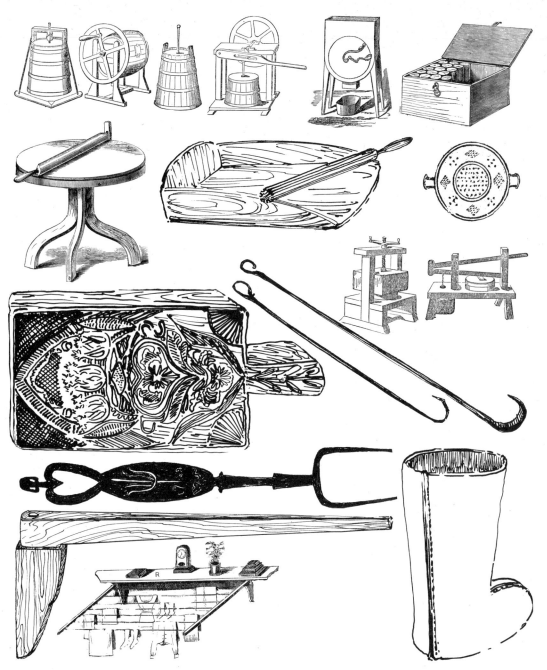

TOP ROW: Four butter churns 1660 to 1860; curd mill used in cheese making, *c*. 1850; butter box to hold rolls of butter, *c*. 1850.   SECOND ROW: Butter worker on table. Used to squeeze moisture out of churned butter. California type, *c*. 1850s; butter worker, *c*. 1750; colander of silver, *c*. 1750.   THIRD ROW: Butter mold, hand-carved from pine, *c*. 1750; meat hooks of wrought iron, *c*. 1750; cheese presses. The stone press was used from *c*. 1660. The screw was used to raise stone. The stone itself acted as a press when released.   BOTTOM ROW: Decorative iron meat fork, *c*. 1750; blanket crane, fixed to walls at side of fireplace. Clothes dryer of 1850; guttus, or leather boot jug, *c*. 1650. These vessels of unbreakable type were made by the cordwainers, or shoemakers.

TOP ROW: Kitchen of 1825 and kitchen of 1885. All cooking was done in the fireplace of the first kitchen, while in the kitchen of 1885 the cooking was done in a patented cast-iron range; dining room of the Hasbrouck House, Newburgh, N.Y., c. 1750. CENTER ROW and downward to the right: A series of home and kitchen utensils as follows: still for making whisky and tinctures; oval saucepan; wire food protectors; teakettle with self-heating elements; coffee grinders, apple parer; device for making soda water, milk skimmer, milk bowl; fish boiler; reversible chopping knives. All of these date from 1840 to 1880. BOTTOM LEFT: Kitchen in the Sister House of the Cloisters at Ephrata, Pa., c. 1750.

Millville No. 3 Fruit Jar.

This Jar is sealed on the same principle as our **Millville Atmospheric Fruit Jar**; but instead of having a Screw Clamp to hold the lid in place, it is furnished with a Steel Clamp as shown in cut. This is made in two pieces, hinged together, and so shaped that when extended in line upon the Jar the spring of the metal causes a strong pressure upon the lid. The under side of the pivot forms a button which fits into a socket in the middle of the lid. The clamp is applied by placing the two parts at an acute angle, pushing the button into the socket, and then drawing one end around until the two are in line.

Prices of Pints, Quarts and Half Gallons furnished upon application.

Fruit jars for home canning, displaying various methods of achieving hermetic sealing. The most unusual examples are the fifth jar in the top row, the second jar in the second row, the fourth jar in the third row, the first jar in the bottom row, and the Millville jar of blown glass first offered in 1858. Most of the jars pictured are either of pottery, stoneware, or glass.

The **Jack Frost** Freezer is constructed on an entirely *new principle*. Instead of having the ice and salt outside of the can containing the cream as in other freezers—the cream is on the outside and the ice and salt are *inside*.

TOP ROW: Pair of refrigerators of the 1850s; parlor refrigerator, 1850. Two ice-cream freezers of rotary type and the Hoxie automatic, patented, 1892, which made ice cream at the table. This type of freezer is now being introduced as a new idea! CENTER: Early ice wagon of type seen on the streets of American cities and towns from the 1840s. Below the ice wagon, an iceless refrigerator of 1850. Coolness was achieved by evaporation of water; Jack Frost ice-cream freezer, 1891. In this machine and the Hoxie a cylinder was packed with ice and salt, turning in a pool of cream mix. The cream froze to the cylinder and was scraped off with a sharp knife. BOTTOM: Harvesting ice on a grand scale from a New England pond, *c.* 1850.

CHAPTER IV

Guns, Traps, Snares, and Hooks

K EEPING alive by filling the pot," or "Self-protection and pres- ervation" could well be subtitles for this chapter. Our pioneers had to accomplish both objectives in order to remain above- ground and unscalped. In the environment and under the circum- stances that marked pursuit of their efforts, the pioneers also had an opportunity for some profit. They did not desire any kind of war- fare with the native American Indians yet they were encroaching on the natives' land, game preserves, and fishing waters. In some cases treaties were made to be broken and in others were maintained to the letter. Had the pioneers been left to themselves it is likely they would have lived at peace with the natives; but the politicians of the courts of England, France, and frustrated Spain had other ideas. They were playing with maps as a part of colonial power politics. Colonists were simply pawns in the game—fodder to be used when the war game was played.

No matter what other products the Spaniards took out of their conquered territory, they were primarily interested in capturing the gold, silver, and gems mined by the Indians. They were not greatly concerned with stuffs that had to be traded, manufactured, or proc- essed before they could be converted into hard money. They wanted most the metals from which money could be coined. The pattern would seem to have been simply this: Spanish interests forced the Indians to give up all hoarded gold and silver and to mine more. This the Spaniards loaded on treasure ships. English privateers waited until the treasure ships were on the high seas and then highjacked the silver and gold. This simple formula was in use before our North American colonization. It angered Spain to the point of attempting the invasion of England—with disastrous results to Spain. The Span- ish Armada was outmaneuvered, scattered, defeated in squadrons, destroyed in formations, and practically in toto. That victory did not end England's gentlemanly piracy but it did create a new idea in empire expansion. The victory over the Armada indubitably set the eyes of the common man on the western horizon.

What every colonist needed was tools—a gun, some powder, some fishhooks, lines and nets, some traps; an ax, a spade, and a hoe. With this equipment he could erect a cottage from available materials, gather furs for trade, shoot game, and catch fish for the pot. Corn, as all bread grain was designated, was carried as seed. But here was found a new kind of bread grain: the "corn" of the Indians—the native American maize. Today we designate this native grain exclusively as "corn" while naming the wheats, oats, rice, and so on by these, rather than "corn," the old generic name for all grains. But we are apt to err if, when reading old deeds of gift, we imagine the annual payment of ten grains of corn to mean what we call corn. Ten grains of any cereal sufficed.

Among the first gunsmiths in the colonial scene were Thomas Nash at New Haven, Connecticut, in 1638, and Eltweed Pomeroy, who set up shop in Massachusetts in the 1640s. These men are supposed to have made the first colonial firearms. There was a gunsmith at the Dutch trading post, now Hartford, in 1640, and it is believed a few gunsmiths were working in Virginia by 1650 and in New Sweden by 1660. Most likely the major work of these men was repairing firearms, sabers, pikes, and other weapons.

The firearms used in the colonies in the seventeenth century were largely imports from France, Switzerland, England, the Netherlands, Spain, and Sweden. These arms were individually made; parts were not interchangeable. The firing mechanisms are called matchlocks, wheel locks, firelocks, and flintlocks.

The first rifled guns or, more properly, rifle-barreled guns, made in the colonies were made by Swiss emigrants in the Conestoga Valley of Pennsylvania about 1719. Two rifle-boring mills were set up by Swiss in Lancaster County. Swiss, English, Swedish, and Dutch gunsmiths came to this country and began using rifled barrels in their completed rifles. Two cities, Philadelphia and Lancaster, became centers of rifle production.

Actually, what is now called the Kentucky rifle should be called the Conestoga rifle, for practically every rifle that earned the name "Kentucky" was made in the Conestoga Valley. It happened in this way: Andrew Jackson's Kentucky riflemen were the star performers at the battle of New Orleans and winners of that great victory over the crack troops of General Pakenham. They carried Conestoga rifles. In 1816 a song, or ballad broadside, memorialized the activities of these troops. The title of the song was "The Hunters of Kentucky, or The Battle of New Orleans."

Strangely enough the Mennonites, a non-aggressive sect founded by the Dutch priest Menno Simonus, introduced the snailed or rifled gun barrel to America. This secret of gunfire accuracy was known in Helvetia before 1500. It seems to have been an idea that sprang from the mind of Leonardo da Vinci. The first man in Conestoga to snail a gun barrel was Martin Meylen, a Swiss Mennonite. A colony of Swiss gunmakers were at work by 1721. The rifle-barreled gun achieved immediate popularity because it made every shot count; and powder and ball were precious commodities. A pioneer did not eat meat unless he could shoot straight; that is, unless he stooped to trapping his meat or killing porcupines with a club.

The great gunsmith of the Conestoga Valley was William Henry of Lancaster, who was apprenticed to M. Roessière, a Flemish rifle-maker. In 1750 Henry engaged in rifle manufacture with a partner named Joseph Simon, a well-to-do Jewish merchant and trader. The partnership was dissolved in 1759. During the Revolution Henry was in charge of all gunmaking in the Conestoga Valley and in eastern Pennsylvania.

In the little-known but valuable source book *To All Sportsmen* by Colonel George Hanger, London, 1814, is this comment: "I never in my life saw better rifles than those made in America: they are chiefly made at Lancaster . . . in Pennsylvania. The barrels weigh about six pounds, two or three ounces, and carry a ball no larger than thirty-six to the pound." Colonel Hanger then cites an example of shooting as follows: "Colonel, now General, Tarleton and myself [during the Revolutionary War] were standing a few yards out of the wood observing the situation of the enemy we intended to attack. There was a rivulet in the enemy's front, and a mill on it, to which we stood directly with our horses' heads fronting, observing their motions. It was an absolute plain field between us and the mill; not so much as a single bush on it. Our orderly-bugle stood behind us about three yards, but with his horse's side to our horses' tails. A rifleman passed over the mill dam, evidently observing two officers, and laid himself down on his belly; for in such positions they always lie to take a good shot at a long distance. He took a deliberate and cool shot at my friend, at me and the bugle-horn man. It was in the month of August and not a breath of wind was stirring. We were in close consultation. A rifle ball passed between him [Tarleton] and me. I have passed several times over this ground and can assert that the distance he fired from was a full 400 yards."

The original Swiss rifle was a heavy firearm with a short barrel. In Conestoga shops the barrel was lengthened and the entire piece made lighter. Instead of forging the barrels in the solid and boring them, Conestoga gunsmiths wrapped a plate of iron around a cold rod and thus forged the barrel with the basic bore in it. The rod was removed and the barrel was then reamed and snailed with mathematical precision of twist that seems impossible with the now crude-looking machinery they used.

In the stock of these early rifles there is a cavity covered by a decorated metal lid. This is the patch box. It contained patches of oiled cloth in which the bullet was wrapped and rammed down through the muzzle of the gun onto the powder charge. Ignition of powder was from the sparking of flint on steel, directed to a little priming pan on the outside of the gun barrel, connected to the charge in the gun barrel through a tiny touchhole. Aim had to be steady and prolonged because ignition was slow. When the charge exploded in the gun barrel, a little miracle happened. The ball, actually smaller than the bore of the gun and made tight in its oiled patch, offered resistance to the exploding powder, which partially consumed the patch and forced the ball into the grooves of the snailing or rifling. The ball began to spin on an axis that was the line of flight established by the aim of the gunner.

Captain Dillin, one of today's historians of American firearms, calls the Conestoga Valley the birthplace of the American rifle. As early as 1803 the gun manufacturers of Lancaster petitioned the Federal Government for a higher tariff on rifles and the end of free trade in this item. From this Conestoga section of Pennsylvania went gunsmiths who established shops in Maryland, Virginia, Carolina, Tennessee, Kentucky, Ohio, Michigan, Indiana, Illinois, and Missouri.

Examples of typical colonial and federal firearms are pictured in this chapter. The collecting of guns is so specialized a pursuit that this book cannot attempt to cover any part of the field. At the end of the chapter certain gun books are recommended. Most of these are in print, or exist in sufficient numbers to make loan or procurement possible, either in libraries or from new and secondhand bookshops.

The making of traps and the use of traps to take furred and feathered game connote a form of cruelty so base that most of us do not care to contemplate the scene. To imagine a beaver, fox, bear, or other animal clawed by a staked trap which held the beast in place to starve, die in agony, or be devoured by another beast, is not a pleasant thought. Yet it was done on a wholesale scale. Wholesale killings of pigeons, buffalo, and other beasts are covered pictorially in this chapter.

The mass curing and smoking of fish and game developed certain of the foods today prized by gourmets—smoked turkey, duck, quail, whitefish, and shad. Smoking, pickling, and drying meats of all sorts were necessities with the pioneers. There was no other way of preserving it except by freezing, and that method could be practiced with assurance only in the cold country north of latitude 54. Fresh meat was obtained only from freshly killed game or cattle. Otherwise the meat or fish was pickled, corned, smoked, or dried. The vast array of utensils for the preservation and preparation of all kinds of food is pictured partially in another chapter.

The antiques having to do with the subjects of this chapter exist mainly as firearms from the days of Nash and Pomeroy down to the mass-produced inventions of Whitney, Colt, and Remington. We are fortunate in being able to picture not only the objects but also some advertisements of early and late gunsmiths.

Below is a list of gun books, together with a book on American sports which will be helpful to every student interested in these subjects:

The Kentucky Rifle, by Captain J. G. W. Dillin, revised edition.
American Gun Makers, by LeRoy D. Satterlee and Arcadi Gluckman.
American Arms and Arms Makers, by Robert E. Gardner.
Firearms of the Confederacy, by C. E. Fuller & R. D. Steuart.
Remarks on Rifle Guns, by Ezekiel Baker.
The Muzzle-loading Rifle—Then and Now, by Walter M. Cline.
The Cabinet of Natural History & American Rural Sports, by J. & T. Doughty.

TOP ROW: Advertisement of Gilbert Forbes, gunsmith of New York, eighteenth century; trade card of powder flask maker, 1855; flintlock pistol by James Haslet of Baltimore, 1772. Courtesy James F. Graham & Sons. CENTER: Original bill from Tryon & Company, Philadelphia, dated 1832. Well over a century ago this firm advertised as a gun, fishing tackle, and military store; label from gunpowder can, *c.* 1840. BOTTOM: Advertisement by Frank Wesson of Worcester, 1866. This preceded the firm of Smith & Wesson; advertising poster of John Krider, gunsmith of Philadelphia, established 1826.

COLT'S REPEATING PISTOLS,
With the latest Improvements of 1844 & 1845.

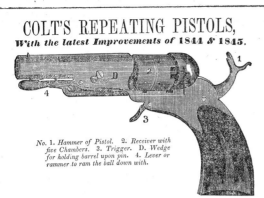

No. 1. *Hammer of Pistol.* 2. *Receiver with
five Chambers.* 3. *Trigger.* D. *Wedge
for holding barrel upon pin.* 4. *Lever or
rammer to ram the ball down with.*

The Pistols have 5, Carbine and Shot Guns 6, and Rifles 8 chambers. Pocket Pistols with 2 inch to 3½ inch barrel, Belt pistol 2½ inch to 6 inches, and holster or Ship pistol 5 to 12 inch barrel. The pocket pistol will carry from 40 to 50 yards, belt pistol 50 to 60, and the holster or ship pistol 80 to 100, with a very small quantity of powder; and the pocket pistol with ball and cap only, without any powder, from 12 to 15 yards point blank; pistols in Mahogany cases, from $16, $20, $30, to $100.

The above is a true representation of the COLT'S PATENT REPEATING PISTOL; which is acknowledged to be superior in every respect to any other Pistol manufactured in this country or Europe. The Emperor of Russia, the Emperor of Austria, the King of Prussia, the Prince de Joinville of France, the Imaum of Muscat, all have them, and speak in the highest terms of them. The Texan Army and Navy are supplied with them, and the U S Navy has been supplied with them to some extent, and the officers have given a most favorable report of Colt's repeating fire-arms. *Great impositions have lately been practised upon the Public by representing and selling the Six Barrel or Self Cocking Pistol as Colt's Patent Pistol.* The Colt's Repeating Pistols, Carbines, and Shot Guns are sold for Cash reduced prices, at

No. 2 Barclay-street, Astor-house, New-York, by
JOHN EHLERS, *Proprietor*
W. H. HORSTMANN & Co., *Maiden-lane.*
HYDE & GOODRICHE, *Chartres-street, New-Orleans.*
H. E. BALDWIN & Co., " "
B. DAFFIN, *Baltimore.*
MULFORD & WENDELL, *Broadway, Albany.*

ABIJAH CUTTER,
No. 15 MIDDLE STREET, Lowell,
MANUFACTURER OF
FIRE ARMS,

Improved Gain Twist Target and Sporting Rifles

ALLEN'S
PATENT
SEVEN SHOOTER,

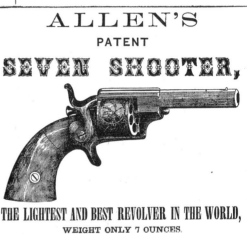

THE LIGHTEST AND BEST REVOLVER IN THE WORLD,
WEIGHT ONLY 7 OUNCES.

VOLCANIC REPEATING FIRE-ARMS.
[PATENTED 1854.]
RIFLES, CARBINES AND PISTOLS LOADING WITH FROM 7 TO 24 BALLS!
Can be discharged with Greater RAPIDITY and Certainty than any other Pistol or Rifle.
Thirty Balls can be loaded and discharged in 50 seconds.

REPEATING FIRE-ARMS,
AND PATENT LOADED BALL.

This Arm and Ammunition, lately introduced by the manufacturers into public notice, has deservedly met with great favor, its excellence is claimed to be far superior to all other Repeating Arms. It is simple in its construction, *compact and elegant* in its *proportions,* of great strength and durability, and NOT LIABLE to get out of order. The barrels are all RIFLED with great exactness. It can be loaded with seven to twenty-four balls in four to ten seconds, and can be discharged (in any weather) *twenty-five times* in *fifty seconds.* No cap—no priming—no recoil—no lateral discharge. The Ball is a *Patent Loaded Ball,* on the Minie principle, and is perfectly water-proof, and yet always SURE and SAFE, and of unequalled range and accuracy.

No. 3.

ELLIOT'S NEW REPEATERS

Are now ready. The most safe, compact, durable, effective, sure and reliable Revolvers made. Carry large balls (No. 32 cartridge), are rapidly loaded and fired—conveniently carried in the vest—whole length five inches—four barrels—each rifled gain twist. Wholesale and retail.
ELLIOT ARMS CO.,
494 Broadway, N. Y.

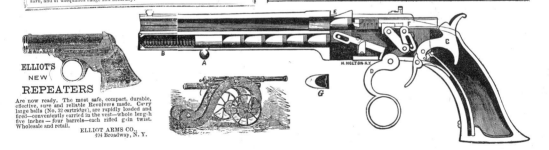

TOP LEFT: Colt's repeating pistols, as advertised in 1845.   TOP RIGHT: Advertisement of Eli Whitney's rifle works, 1850s, and of Abijah Cutter, Lowell, Mass., 1856.   CENTER: Advertisement of the Volcanic repeating pistol, made by the New Haven Arms Company, New Haven, 1854; Allen's seven-shooter revolver, as advertised, 1860.   BOTTOM: Elliot's repeating pistol of 1863; cannon operated by compressed air, invented by A. Stewart of Boston, 1828; working view of the Volcanic repeating pistol showing how the store of cartridges was kept in a magazine, the firing principle, and cartridge construction. This automatic arm was offered in models including four-inch pocket pistols at $12 to twenty-four-inch carbines at $40. Ammunition was offered at $10 and $12 per thousand.

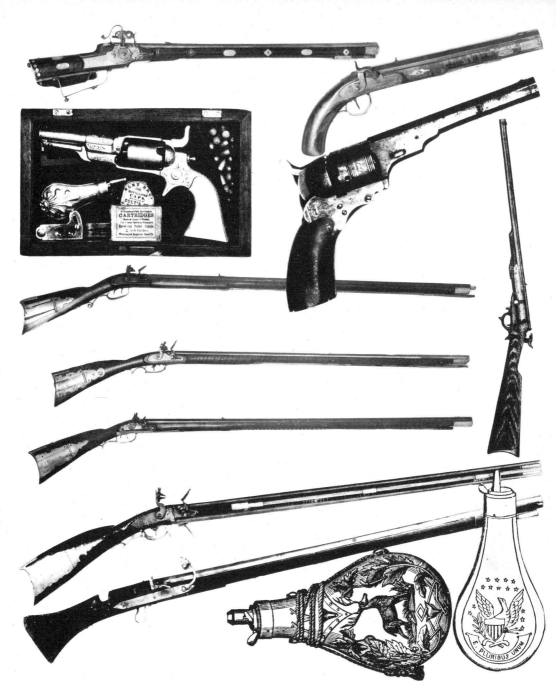

Rare arms and accouterments. TOP TO BOTTOM: Seventeenth-century wheelock of the sort used by early settlers; pistol by John Drepperd of Lancaster, c. 1830. Both from Herman P. Dean Collection; presentation Colt pistol with accouterments, from James F. Graham & Sons; Colt pistol made at Paterson, N.J. This is numbered 182. From James F. Graham & Sons. Gun with muzzle up is a Colt repeating rifle of 1857. Guns across page, from top to bottom: (1) Pennsylvania rifle with long barrel, c. 1770; (2) Pennsylvania rifle, c. 1790; (3) Pennsylvania long-barreled rifle, c. 1770. (All from Collection of Herman P. Dean); (4) double-barreled rifle, commonly called "under and over," Pennsylvania, c. 1800. From James F. Graham & Sons; (5) New England matchlock, c. 1650. Powder flasks, 1860s.

TOP: Buffalo trap, *c.* 1710; pigeon shooting in Iowa, 1860. CENTER: Cattle roundup, Colorado, 1870. BOTTOM: Netting an entire flock of wild pigeons with the aid of decoys, New England, *c.* 1850.

Pioneers combining sport with food procurement. TOP: Shooting wild turkeys; winter fishing for pike. CENTER: Indians hunting the bison on the prairies, shooting prairie chickens. BOTTOM: Hunting the moose on snowshoes. The Kentucky rifle gunpowder can by the Hazard Powder Company of Connecticut, c. 1840, contained powder for the famed rifle-barreled gun that contributed much not only to the winning of the Revolution and the War of 1812 at the Battle of New Orleans, but was also, in many cases, the weapon that spelled the difference between starvation and plenty. Wild game was abundant in the United States to the 1870s.

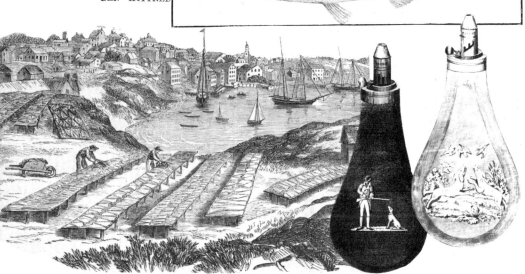

BEN KITTREDGE & CO.,

NO. 55 ST. CHARLES ST., NEW ORLEANS,

AND 134 MAIN STREET, CINCINNATI,

SPORTSMANS' Depot.   FILIBUSTERS Warehouse.

IMPORTERS OF

Guns and Sporting Apparatus,

IN ALL ITS BRANCHES,

WHOLESALE AND RETAIL

DEALERS IN

FIRE ARMS,

OF EVERY DESCRIPTION,

Powder Flasks, Shot Belts, Pere,

AND EVERYTHING CONNECTED

THE GUN TR

☞ We are happy in being able to announce
completed arrangements, by which we hope to be c
FINE GUNS, from the most celebrated manufact
of ENGLISH and SCOTCH POWDER, WI
and every variety of SPORTING AMMUN
quality.

☞ We devote our entire business and attenti
to this line.

BEN KITTRED

FISHING TACKLE.

MARTIN L. BRADFORD,

142 Washington Street,

THREE DOORS NORTH OF THE OLD SOUTH CHURCH,

Offers, at Wholesale and Retail, the best assortment of FISH-
ING TACKLE for New England trade to be found in
the United States, comprising every variety of

Jointed Rods, Walking Cane Rods, Bam-
boos, Cane Poles, Bradford's improved
Reels; English Reels, multiplying
and plain; Silk Worm Gut. Gimp,
Lines, Hooks, Flies, Artificial
Minnows, Mice, Frogs,
Grubs, &c., Fly Books,
Bait Boxes & Ket-
tles, Baskets,
Covered Bot-
tles, Leath-
er Cups.

PATENT SPRING FISH HOOKS, that spear the fish
the head the moment he touches the bait NETS of all
kinds. Also, POWDER, SHOT, PERCUSSION CAPS.
FLASKS, SHOT BELTS, &c. &c.

JOHN J. BROWN,

ANGLERS' DEPOT,

And General Emporium for the sale of

FISHING TACKLE, FISHING SEINES, NETS, FYKES, SEINE TWINE, SPORTING ARTICLES, &C. &C.

No. 103 FULTON STREET NEW YORK.

TOP ROW: Kittredge, of New Orleans, filibusters' warehouse advertisement,
1857; advertisement of fishing tackle, 1847; pair of copper powder flasks
by James Dixon of Sheffield, England, made for the American market.
CENTER: Advertisement of fishing-tackle dealer, 1855. BOTTOM: Sun-
curing fish at Marblehead, Mass., 1854; powder flasks, c. 1835, made for
the American market.

CHAPTER V

Tools, Implements, and Machines
of Agriculture

M UCH of our social and economic history is embraced within the antiques of our pioneer farmers and the men who made tools, implements, and machines for them. This chapter would have to be expanded into a complete volume in order to do justice to the subject.

Surprisingly, there are a number of collectors of agricultural items of the sorts pictured. Of course these collectors need barns to house their finds. They emulate the magnificent Farmers Museum of the New York Historical Association at Cooperstown, New York, where, perhaps, the very finest collection of antique farm and rural manufacturing equipment in this country is housed under one roof. This delightful village, center of the "Leatherstocking" country, on Lake Otsego where the Susquehanna River begins, is a sort of Williamsburg of the North and boasts, among other things, the American baseball museum and shrine. Our number-one national sport started at Cooperstown.

Henry Ford's museum at Greenfield, Michigan, contains a great collection of farming equipment. The museum of the Bucks County Historical Society at Doylestown, Pennsylvania, has a sizable collection, and numerous private collections are being constantly enriched. It was my good fortune a few years ago to participate in one of the strangest collecting journeys imaginable. My host was the president of an electric light and power company. On that trip he purchased a few small tin utensils, a wooden shovel, a complete carpet weaver's loom with six huge bundles of sample carpet patterns, a complete up-and-down sawmill, a complete Conestoga wagon, and three stoves. His collection is housed in some sixteen structures, large and small. He, too, is planning to build a little pioneer village with every store, shop, schoolhouse, smithy, sawmill, church, and other structure complete with every tool, every appurtenance, and all equipment.

One of the great controversies which, probably, will never be laid to rest until all partisans have passed on is the question of who invented and constructed the first mechanical reaping machine. Obed Hussey and Cyrus McCormick are the outstanding candidates. There is much to be said for both claimants. The McCormick reaper, like the Singer sewing machine, was launched by interests having the best manufacturing sense coupled with the better quality of salesmanship. Nonetheless, there is a printed memorial to Obed Hussey, characterizing him as the "Man Who Made Bread Cheap." The chief memorial to the McCormicks, in the mind of the public, is the colossal fortune they made out of their reaper business. An original Hussey reaper would be a find of finds for any antiquarian. We may suspect a few examples still lurk somewhere in the top timbers of an abandoned barn. But where? You never can tell. In 1940, on an excursion in the Welsh Hills of Pennsylvania, we were taken to a fine old house standing in lonely splendor by the side of an almost abandoned road. The stable door was opened. There stood a Pierce-Arrow car of the year 1902. It had never been used: the buyer died before it was delivered. It was run into the stable, kept brightly polished by a hired man as long as the widow lived, and then forgotten. The estate, tied up in litigation, with in-laws and outlaws wrangling over who would get what, kept the old Pierce-Arrow, and everything else, right on the premises.

Everything from apple corers and cherry seeders to sawmills, reapers, and harrows is pictured in this chapter. There are corn planters, pruners, sugar mills, cane cutters, cotton gins, tobacco balers, dung forks, shovels, axes, and saws. Ax handles, post augers, and many other tools are found today here and there in antiques shops. Often they stand with a phantom question tag on them, asking "What is this?"

We should remember that our nation was chiefly agricultural until the 1890s and that the emphasis on our manufacturing economy has existed for only a little more than half a century. We are apt to overlook that we are still a great agricultural nation. Yet most of us are prone to go to the country when collecting antiques. Our cotton, corn, wheat, barley, tobacco, and other money crops are enormous. We raise more vegetables than did all of Europe in its heyday; our vineyards are larger than those of France. Only here did we first think in terms of raising cattle on tremendous ranges, of planting wheat in fields that could be harvested only by steam-driven reapers and combines that threshed the wheat as it was cut. Other nations, with land available on the same scale, saw what we had done and began doing the same thing, but the pioneering idea was nurtured here.

Today we are feeding millions of hungry peoples living in lands devastated and impoverished by war. We are again pioneering in that our farmers and cattlemen are trying every possible device in efforts to increase production. But out of the great mass of scientific promotion for chemical farming and the use of chemical fertilizers comes a stern warning from quiet researchers who are also pioneers. They claim the use of chemical fertilizers, while boosting food-crop production to new high levels, is causing the growth of foods with great vitamin lacks. Thus we have the very real but nonetheless complex situation of millions of seemingly well-fed people requiring diet aids in the form of vitamin concentrates that should be found in our daily diet. There is very real pioneering now under way in respect of this problem. Men of other arts and skills are turning to farming, experimenting with non-chemical fertilizers, with the elimination of the plow, with the prevention of soil erosion, and even with the development of bigger and better breeds of earthworms for soil conditioning.

In all likelihood an observer of one hundred years hence will be able to write a most interesting monograph on the pioneering in agriculture that marked the twentieth century in this country of ours. Some of our ablest economists are now convinced that our sewerage systems which have polluted so many of our once crystal-clear rivers and streams should be reconstructed to provide organic fertilizers for our soil. All of this is pioneering. Let us be glad we still have a great company of pioneer-minded men with their minds devoted to the problems of agriculture and food production.

TOP LEFT: Felling machine for cross-cutting and buck-sawing timber, invented by Colonel James Hamilton of New York, operated by two men. TOP RIGHT: One-man saw operated by riding it like a bicycle, made by W. W. Bostwick & Company, Cincinnati, Ohio, 1870s. CENTER LEFT: Another view of Colonel Hamilton's felling machine, showing it in a buck-sawing operation. CENTER RIGHT: Circular saw and other cutlery tools manufactured by A. M'Bride, Louisville, Ky., 1850s. BOTTOM LEFT: Frazee's patented up-and-down sawmill, advertised as the cheapest, most durable, simple, and efficient sawmill in the world. Operated with an eight-horsepower engine and sold complete for $1,250. The date is 1856. BOTTOM RIGHT: Two-man cross-cut saw of 1650s, used to 1890s; framed pit saw of the type used in 1640–1870s.

51

TOP ROW: Cahoon's broadcast sower, 1870; windmill scarecrow with tin-kling bells, 1850s; dead hawk tied to a pole to serve as scarecrow, 1830s. SECOND ROW: Field roller, 1850; horse rake, 1850; straw cutter, 1850. BOTTOM: Coal or cob barrow, 1810; seed broadcaster, operating by bolt and pulley from wheel of the barrow, 1850; cuttings patented "chest-of-drawers" beehive, promoted by Whitman of Baltimore, 1850.

TOP ROW: Chaffing and cleaning machine, 1850; corn sheller and husking machine, 1845; straw and hay cutter and "cornstalk lacerator," 1850. CENTER: Noyes centrifugal gristmill with upper and nether stones enclosed, 1850; Victor cane mill for pressing sap from sugar cane and sorghum. Made at Cincinnati, 1850s and 1860s; corn sheller that shot the grain to bags and extruded the bare cobs like bullets from a gun, 1850; apple parer, 1870s and a cherry seeder of same date. BOTTOM: Vegetable cutter, for producing animal feed, 1850; vertical cast-iron corn sheller, 1850; a horsepower machine; treadmill for one or two horses, 1850.

ONE HUNDRED and Twenty DOZEN of SICKLES, ready prepared for the Harvest, by JAMES HENDRICKS, Cutler, at the Sign of the Sickle, the 4th Door above the Prifon, in Market-ftreet; thefe Sickles are carefully made, will be fold at the loweft Rates, and enfured to be good.

TOP ROW: Sickles, as advertised and pictured in 1770; lye leach, c. 1760. Filled with wood ashes and covered with water, a strong alkaline fluid seeped out of trough. This was conveyed in sanded runlets and left to crystallize. The poor stuff was lye, the good stuff was baking soda.   CENTER: Ketchum's one-wheel mower, 1854; grain drill, 1856. It planted eight rows at a time; crude device for coring and quartering apples in one operation, c. 1800.   BOTTOM: Winnowing machine, 1850s; potato parer, 1870; metal plow with steel point, made at Boston, 1853.

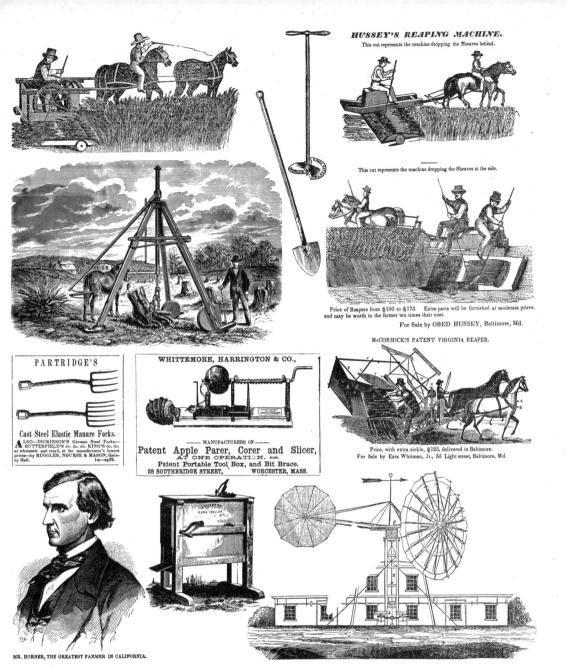

Machines of agriculture that made America boom. TOP: The original reaper as invented by Obed Hussey, 1842; a posthole borer and posthole spoon, 1850; Hussey's reaping machine of 1850. SECOND ROW: Screw power stump puller, 1867; Hussey's three-man reaper of 1850. THIRD ROW: Advertisements of manure forks, 1843, and of a patented apple parer of 1855; the reaper that made good in a big way, the McCormick machine of 1850. BOTTOM: California's greatest farmer who, in 1854, was making gold in the growing of vegetables, fruits, and flowers; corn sheller for the Southern market as advertised in 1850; the windmill powerhouse, invented by Page in 1849 and extensively advertised in the journals of that day. A folio-size lithographic poster for this machine was also issued, c. 1850.

55

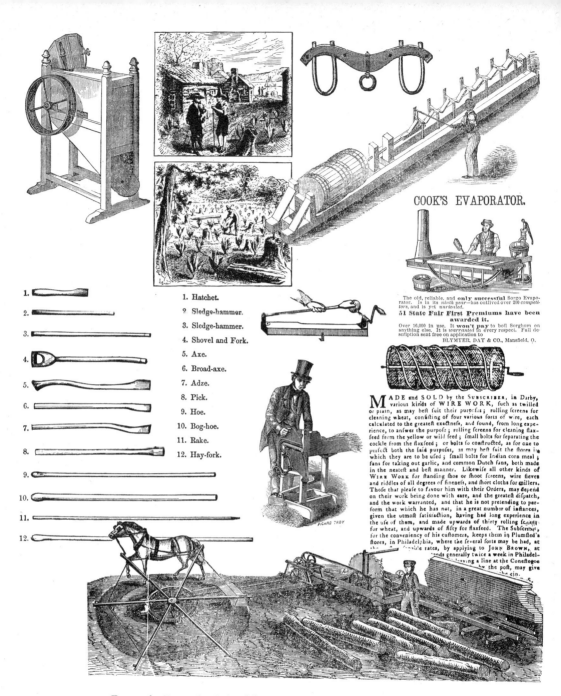

TOP ROW: Corn sheller of 1835. Note cabinetmaker quality of case; streets of Jamestown, c. 1620 (tobacco growing in the lanes) and a James River tobacco field, c. 1615; ox yoke, c. 1770; tobacco press. The lever in the hands of the slave leveled the kinks in the block chain and squeezed the cured tobacco tightly in the hogshead. CENTER: Farm-tool handles, 1840s. All identified by name: apple parer, 1840; hay cutter for a high-hatted farmer, 1850; cook's sorghum juice evaporator, 1867; wirework "riddle," or circular sieve, advertised at Philadelphia, 1770. BOTTOM: Circular path "horsepower" with shaft drive, attached to a sawmill. This machine was patented in the 1840s and sold generally in the 1850s.

CHAPTER VI

Ornaments and Elegancies

A CTUALLY, within the categories of ornaments and elegancies should fall any pioneering effort away from crudity and every addition to the basic necessities of food, clothing, and shelter. As has been observed, the pioneering state of mind does not seek crudity, lowliness, or other generally accepted badges of humble station. The entire movement is away from such conditions. Improvement and progress are continuous efforts. On many an occasion the pioneer in his efforts to effect progress has hit upon the cosmic foundation of all success: it is never by the selfish establishment of an end or goal to be gained that we make real progress, but by constantly practicing a *means whereby* we can use ourselves, and our environment, to reach constantly higher levels. As the present-day philosopher Aldous Huxley has said, "In all that concerns life it is only through the indirect approach that the most substantial goods are achieved. Thus religion is valueless when it seeks the immediate advantage of the devotee . . . the moralist perceives that happiness is not achieved by the direct pursuit of happiness. Happiness is a by-product, the result of pursuing other ends than happiness, by other than merely pleasurable means."

Had our pioneers followed the European pattern of personal maximum improvement, those who had been common soldiers might have been content to consider petty officership their goal; ditch tenders might have set chief gamekeeper as their highest dream; tenant farmers would have considered ownership of a few acres in fee simple as their achievement of success; millers might have considered owning or renting a mill as their final objective; artisans might have deemed keeping their own shops the last word in position improvement or end gaining.

But it wasn't like that at all. The pioneer could possess acreage larger than the holdings of barons and lords. Not a few fish, but a

wine tun of fish could be taken in a day; and hunting yielded unbelievable quantities of game. The land was fresh, unworked, and fer-
tilized by nature. In 1721 the commissioners of Penn's Grant, in
printing the report of an Indian treaty at Conestoga, were so impressed by the *land* whereon the treaty was held that they made a part
of their report read, ". . . the lands thereabouts being exceedingly
rich, it is now surrounded with diverse fine plantations, or farms,
where they raise quantities of wheat, barley, flax, and hemp without
the help of any dung."

So the pioneer went quietly on his way, using the means whereby
one picture might grace his house wall today, but whereby he might
build a new house next year and have new pictures on his new walls.
This year he, or his wife, might limn a crudity but next year, or the
next, they might pay, or feed and board a limner to paint pictures for
them. The first window curtain might have been a piece of drugget or
a pliable piece of animal skin, the next a ruffled piece of linen woven
from flax raised and spun on the premises. The next curtain might be
dyed indigo color, and following that a colorful print from the Injes.
Progress was the order of the times in the use of ornaments and elegancies of all types.

It is, of course, the different types of pioneer ornaments and elegancies that constitute a portion of the antiquities which can and
should be collected and preserved today. Included are certain of the
floor and wall coverings, boxes and containers, mantel decorations
and garnitures, personal adornments, and so on. Without false modesty
we can survey the progress from the traditional backhouse to night
chair, then to earth closet, and finally to the sanitary flush toilet as a
phase of elegancy achievement. From bathing in a staved wooden tub
once a season to having a real bathing tub in a specific room in the
home is a real record of progress. Few of us may want to collect
early staved tubs or early zinc-lined bathtubs, but some of us, if not
many of us, do collect sit baths and other elegancies even though we
might use them to hold tiers of potted and flowering plants.

There are many collectors of so-called chalkware who persist in
calling it chalk even though they know it is just plaster of Paris.
Unfortunately, in collecting quantities of this once very cheap ware
we have also collected a lot of misinformation about it. It is the most
inexpensive statuary ever produced. It is in imitation of (1) Staffordshire ornaments and elegancies, (2) continental European majolica
and porcelain figures, (3) cut marble, bronze, brass, and carved

wooden ornaments, and (4) genuine Chinese and other oriental figures
and figurines. Most of it was made by Italian and French workers in
plaster of Paris. It was cast in lead or pewter molds, in plaster molds,
wood molds, and even in glue molds somewhat like thick gelatine.
Any Staffordshire figure could be encased in hot gelatine, the cover-
ing cooled and peeled off. Then liquid plaster of Paris could be
poured in the mold and lo, a plaster replica of the figure was available
for a dabbing of color—and sale for a few cents to anyone.

Pictured as a part of the cavalcade of chalkware are some contemporaneous prints of the vendors of this cheap elegancy. The date of
most of the genuine ware is from about 1810 to 1890. In the 1850s
you could buy lead or zinc molds and make your own. Chalkware
should not be classified as a form of folk art; it was cheap commercial
ware, vended from barrows, carts, and trays; perhaps sold in cheap-
John shops and perhaps given away as premiums in other shops and
stores. Had there been a Woolworth chain in the 1830s we can be
quite sure that chalkware would have been included in their merchan-
dise, perhaps any three pieces for a dime. When the price and supply
of real Staffordshire figures became reasonable, the chalkware imitation was discarded. The last phase in the use of plaster-of-Paris
ornaments seems to have been the making of small figures for use as
Christmas decorations. These appeared as late as 1910. And Woolworth stores did sell them at that time.

Calligraphy, illuminated tracts and penwork, now generally—and
usually wrongly—designated as fractur, engaged the interest of a
large part of our pioneer population. For more than the past twenty
years special emphasis has been placed on the so-called fractur of
Pennsylvania. Pennsylvania fractur should not be considered the prototype of all pen pictures made elsewhere in the colonies and states.
The story of pioneer penwork, in terms of origins, practice, and practitioners is not a deep secret. Behind the biased, even if pleasantly
sugar-coated explanations of sources, these facts are at the disposal of
every interested collector. The first known effort at this form of artistry
is found in the *Book of Kells,* preserved at Trinity College, Dublin.
This work is believed to have been executed in the sixth or seventh
century, A.D. The Vatican Library has many as yet unpublished parch-
ments of a date prior to A.D. 1400 displaying fine handwriting and
illumination. One of these, by Saint John of Venice, displays the
famed and fabled tulip now claimed to be "Pennsylvania."

A recent and monumental treatise on this art as practiced in Pennsylvania mentions Boltzen's *Illumnirbuch,* printed at Rufach in 1566 as a shining example of instructor in this art. It is just that. Boltzen wrote and compiled this book, not in Germany but in Switzerland, where it was *first* published at Basel in 1548. The German edition is a copy—a reprint—and not the original. A *Kunstbuchlin* (little book on art) was published at Frankfort in 1560 and again in 1566. These books are pointed out as published *before* the first English book, *A Very Proper Treatise on the Art of Limning,* London, 1573.

Actually the first printed book on pen writing and letter formation, but without illustrations, was written by Fanti of Italy about 1496 and published in 1500. In 1514 the same book was published by Rubeus, of Venice, in a magnificently illustrated format. This, the first known illustrated book on pen writing, contains minute details of letter formation and deals with round writing, the execution of bastard Gothic lettering, and the making of perfect Roman letters. Damianus Moyllus (1480) and Pacioli (1509) had commented on the classic beauty of the Roman characters and spoke for their re-adaptation and use as the characters to use in the new art of printing.

At Ephrata, in Lancaster County, Pennsylvania, a great deal of magnificent penwork was done by the inmates of the Seventh Day Baptist community. There was an organized effort to keep the nuns employed at this painstaking and exacting craft. At this school of instruction and practice many hymnals, missals, et cetera were made, lettered entirely by hand, and illuminated in colors. Far more work was done at Ephrata than the few now famed surviving masterpieces would indicate. At one time there was hardly an antiques shop within ten miles of Ephrata that did not have at least one example of hymn-book or tract made by hand at this Seventh Day Baptist Protestant cloister.

Conrad Beissel, the Master Builder and High Priest of the Ephrata venture, had no training in art and design when he came to the colonies. He was a baker by trade. He did not immigrate from Germany directly to Pennsylvania but lingered at Boston. From there he drifted to Germantown, where he learned a new trade, that of weaving, under a Dutch master. Significantly, weavers' patterns and pen-illuminating patterns are almost interchangeable. And significantly, too, many of the Ephrata books are illuminated with textile patterns not found generally in German pattern books but in Swiss, French, and Italian pattern books made for weavers, 'broiderers, and lace-makers.

Popular art should not be imagined another term for folk art. Folk art, what there is of it, is an impressed tradition, usually in imitation, no matter how crude, of the finer arts of the ruling classes. Popular art is the art of a trade or calling; the patterns popular in weaving, lacemaking, potting, ironworking, pewtering, silversmithing, clock and watch making, cabinetmaking, wood turning, and so on.

The Dutch at New York, and in what became Pennsylvania, practiced pen picturing and writing. The same art was popular in New England, Virginia, and Maryland. The scriveners of England were once among the most accomplished of all practitioners of illuminated writing; the deeds issued by William Penn and his heirs are examples of pen writing so fine that any popular fractur, whether from Ephrata or anywhere else in the colonies, with but few exceptions, are crude in comparison. The Dutch masterpiece pictured is comparable in many ways to Penn's deeds.

Perhaps one of the most delightful forms of penmanship art is to be found in the true pen pictures created by the flowing, round, and shaded script so popular in the mid-nineteenth century. Every animal, bird, and beast, the human figure, flowers, landscapes, ships, and so on were pictured by many people in pen and ink, and within the technique of writing. Examples of this work are pictured in this chapter, along with the other types of work herein mentioned. Innumerable instructors in this art toured the land and some printed instruction books were published. These books represent a pioneer effort in publishing and, of course, are collectors' items. Finished examples of the work are also collected but, strangely, are seldom offered under the category of *fractur,* but rather as examples of pioneer art.

Conversely, much common stuff that is offered as fractur and much fine work offered as fractur are really pioneer art—essays at portrayal of the human figure, famed people, heroes, scenes, memorials of inventions, and so on. We have been all mixed up in nomenclatures, origins, derivations, and attributions in nearly all of our collecting but, like the pioneers themselves, we are beginning to unscramble. Most of the facts refuting current misconceptions are not new or recent discoveries. They have been stated and restated by researchers and commentators of twenty-five, fifty, and even one hundred years ago. But what the original commentators said has been buried in the mass of enthusiastic misinformation published by organized groups of historical promoters. For example, in recent years the decision has been made finally that what has been called Lowestoft china and Lowestoft porcelain are not Lowestoft at all but Chinese export porcelain. This final dictum now has the authority of gospel. Experts have agreed upon it. Of course it always was true. It was revealed in the book *The China Hunters Club,* published by Harper & Brothers in 1878. Similarly, Esther Singleton, in *Furniture of Our Forefathers,* first published by Doubleday in 1900, reveals many truths that are again being brought forth as new discoveries.

One of the most delightful by-products of collecting anything is digging into the social history of the era that produced it and into the entire history of the pursuit responsible for creating the object. It doesn't matter if the object is a shaving-soap container, a paper-collar box, a lamp, or an article of furniture; there is history in it, around it, behind it, and in respect of it. Most of the history is a record of pure pioneering effort.

In this chapter are also pictured some examples of the elegancies known as valentines. The rarest of these love tokens are the handmade ones, laboriously and cunningly wrought by designing spinsters and already hooked males to pave the way for a proposal of wedlock. But there was some pioneering in this love-making missive business, and by a young girl named Esther Howland of Worcester, Massachusetts. In 1848 Esther saw an English valentine, perhaps by the firm of Raphael Tuck, and decided to construct a few valentines herself. She did. Giving these to her brothers with instructions to take orders for them, she was amazed to get orders for five thousand pieces. What did this young girl do? She simply set up a production line of girl friends and neighbors, organized the work, and filled the orders. Finally, her business grew so large that she employed die cutters to make dies for paper lace, purchased motto cards and colored pictures from lithographers, and, up to 1876, produced millions of fancy valentines each year.

TOP: Carpet woven for Washington by the Philadelphia Carpet Manufactory in 1790s. Picture courtesy Mt. Vernon Ladies' Association. CENTER: Scenic wallpaper from Newburyport mansion, c. 1800. Courtesy Miss Kate Arnold; Pennsylvania-Swiss valentine, dated 1776. Courtesy New York Historical Society. BOTTOM: Excellent calligraphy on a deed by William Penn, 7th April, 1682.

TOP: Document issued by Van Courtlands, June 17, 1697. Courtesy Phillipse Manor Restoration; pair of paper silhouettes of Ten Broeck Bouwerie. Courtesy Miss Emman Ten Broeck Runk. SECOND ROW: Pennsylvania birth certificate of Sally Annis, 1799, from New York Historical Society; family tree in heart form, dated 1806. From Arthur Sussel. THIRD ROW: Penwork from Ephrata Cloisters, 1746. Library of Congress; Swiss fraktur, dated 1744. Courtesy Urs Graf, Basle, Switzerland. BOTTOM ROW: Penwork family register from Halifax, Vt., dated 1834; cutwork valentine, Pennsylvania, 1818. Both from New York Historical Society; circular pen drawing of 1850s. From Harry Shaw Newman Gallery.

TOP ROW: *Ecriteau de Gratulation,* Swiss, dated 1809; examination certificate, Swiss, dated 1805.   SECOND ROW: Swiss *Fraktur,* dated 1771; details from Swiss fraktur of seventeenth and eighteenth centuries. These examples demonstrate the source of most so-called Pennsylvania Fraktur, which is almost wholly Swiss in tradition and pattern. All Swiss examples shown courtesy Urs Graf, Basle, Switzerland.   BOTTOM: Examples of penwork of the Spencerian era, made in the 1860s and 1880s.

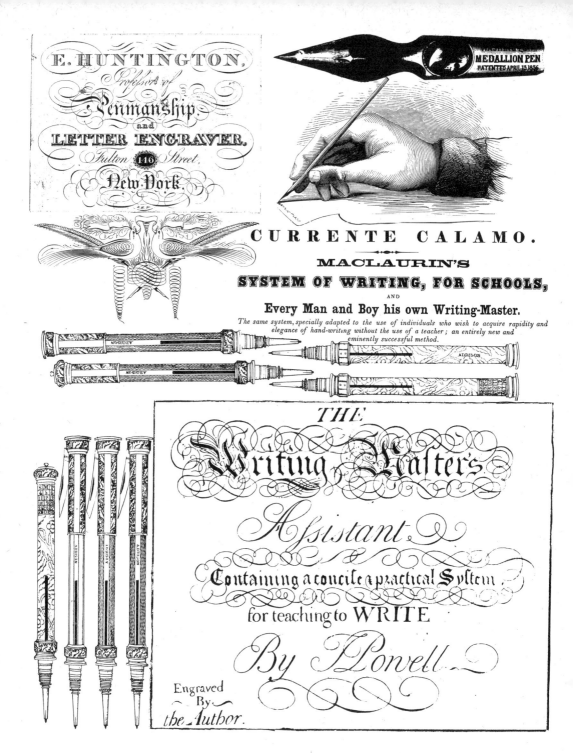

TOP: Trade card of E. Huntington, teacher of penmanship, 1817; the Washington medallion pen, 1856; Currente Calamo, a new system of writing, advertised 1855. LOWER RIGHT: Title page of the *Writing Master's Assistant,* by T. Powell, mid-eighteenth century. Shown courtesy Montgomery County Historical Society, Norristown, Pa. Eight everpointed pencils, produced by Addison Willmarth & Co., of N.Y. between 1836 and 1841; exquisite piece of freehand penwork of two birds, *c.* 1875.

Three centuries of effigy making and use. TOP: Grenadier and vrow fireside figures, made for Loderwyk Bamper, glass maker of New York. These date from c. 1750. Owned by and shown through courtesy of H. Armour Smith, Yonkers, N.Y.; King William and Queen Mary, embroidered and stretched on wooden frames to make a pair of fireside figures, c. 1690. From Parke-Bernet Galleries. BOTTOM: The English potter, Champion, produced this memorial to his daughter Eliza, "a tribute to the memory of an amiable girl," 1779. It became the property of Mr. Desaussure of South Carolina; "lady" bird cage, seventeenth century, Netherland Dutch. From Parke-Bernet Galleries; Moody and Sanky memorialized in Staffordshire pottery.

This is chalkware, so-called. But it isn't. It's plaster-of-Paris ware cast in molds, hand-colored, sometimes waxed, and sold as the cheapest cottage ornament ever offered to the American people. Shown are contemporaneous views of the vendors from American publications and from an advertisement of a plaster image maker of 1850. Pictured are mantel ornaments in the form of pineapples, birds, squirrels, dogs, busts, deer, compotes of fruit, and barnyard roosters. Shown also are two pictorial plaques, one of Isaac Hull, the naval hero, the other an allegorical figure of spring. Courtesy of New York Historical Society and Metropolitan Museum of Art.

TOP: Pair of painted window shades of the 1870s, in transparent oil colors, size 6 × 6 feet. Courtesy C. R. Maurer.   CENTER: Three fancy painted window shades of the 1840s and 1850s, and an advertisement of W. O. Jenks, 1855; paper hanging advertisements of S. P. Hurlbert, Boston, 1829.   BOTTOM: Paper hanging store of Breed, New York, 1850s; upholsterer's shop, Philadelphia, 1831, featuring Venetian blinds.

TOP LEFT: Advertisement of the Philadelphia Carpet Manufactory, 1791, mentioning the rug made for George Washington, pictured in this chapter. TOP RIGHT: Margaret Gibbs's portrait, painted 1670, showing painted cloth on the floor. Courtesy Mrs. Alexander Quarrier Smith and Worcester Museum of Art. TOP CENTER: Two floor cloth patterns, 1660–1760. CENTER: woodcut, early, showing decorative floor cloth; Brussels rug of 1880s. BOTTOM: Carpet emporium advertising, Boston, 1856; floor cloth advertisement, New York, 1817.

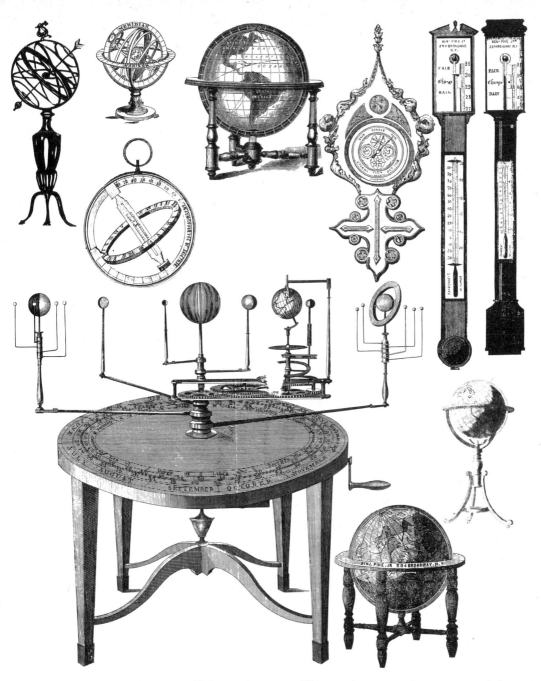

TOP ROW: Armillary sundial, *c.* 1800; armillary sphere, *c.* 1850; terrestrial globe, 1874; ornamental barometer, shown at Crystal Palace, 1853; barometers by Pike of New York, 1848. CENTER: Pocket ring sundial, 1848. BOTTOM: Orrery on a Hepplewhite-style table, 1788; celestial and terrestrial globes, 1840s.

Prices in New York, 1877.

Hide and Seek (Boy)	$50 00	Country Post Office	$15 00
" " (Girl)	50 00	Weighing the Baby	15 00
Pedestal for do. (Iron)	20 00	Checkers up at the Farm	15 00
Bubbles	35 00	Washington	15 00
Fairy's Whisper	25 00	School Examination	15 00
Fugitive's Story	25 00	Charity Patient	15 00
Council of War	25 00	Uncle Ned's School	15 00
The Mock Trial	20 00	Returned Volunteer	15 00
Challenging the Union Vote	20 00	Playing Doctor	15 00
Taking the Oath	20 00	The Shaugraun and "Tatters."	12 00
The Favored Scholar	18 00	Parting Promise	12 00
Tap on the Window	15 00	Rip Van Winkle at Home	12 00
The Foundling	15 00	Rip Van Winkle on the Mountain	12 00
Coming to the Parson	15 00	Rip Van Winkle Returned	12 00
Courtship in Sleepy Hollow	15 00	We Boys	12 00
One More Shot	15 00	Mail Day	10 00
Wounded Scout	15 00	Town Pump	10 00
Union Refugees	15 00	Picket Guard	10 00
Home Guard	15 00	Going for the Cows	10 00

NO CHARGE WILL BE MADE FOR PACKING.

Orders can be sent with the price of the Group, directed to

JOHN ROGERS, 1155 Broadway, New York.

NEIGHBORING PEWS. Price, $15.00.
Also other designs varying from $10.00 to $25.00.

ROGERS' GROUPS OF STATUARY.

JOHN ALDEN AND PRISCILLA.
"Why don't you speak for yourself, John?" Price,
Also other designs varying from $10.00 to $25.00.

"Checkers up at the Farm." Price, $15.00.
ALSO, OTHER DESIGNS, VARYING IN PRICE FROM $10 TO $25.
ROGERS, 860 Broadway, Corner 17th St., New York.
(Formerly 23 Union Square.)

TOP LEFT and ENTIRE CENTER: Advertisements of Rogers statuary groups, 1877. EXTREME RIGHT: Two figures by Copeland (Spode), the Water Carrier and the Fruit Girl, introduced in the 1850s. BOTTOM: Everybody had them—bisque figurines popular from 1850 to 1900. These sold for ten cents each in the 1890s.

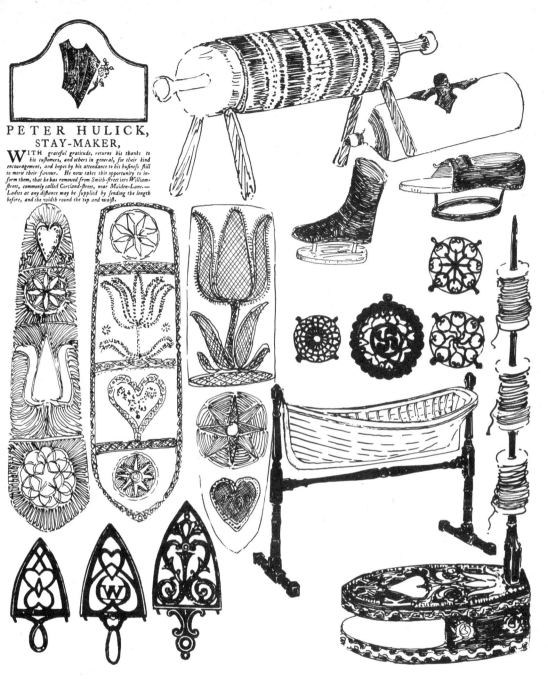

PETER HULICK,
STAY-MAKER,

WITH grateful gratitude, returns his thanks to his customers, and others in general, for their kind encouragement, and hopes by his attendance to his business still to merit their favour. He now takes this opportunity to inform them, that he has removed from Smith-street into William-street, commonly called Cortland-street, near Maiden-Lane.—Ladies at any distance may be supplied by sending the length before, and the width round the top and waist.

TOP ROW: Advertisement by a stay-maker, 1774; footrest covered with carpet, *c.* 1790; foot warmer of pottery, *c.* 1840.   CENTER: A trio of stays or busks, dating from 1733 to 1790; Go-Low shoes (from whence galoshes!), also called pattens, New England, 1690–1750; group of four cast-iron trivets, *c.* 1850.   BOTTOM: Three laundry iron stands of cast iron, 1850–1890; boat cradle, 50 inches long, *c.* 1790. Swank elegancy for a ship captain's baby. From Parke-Bernet Galleries; sewing tree holding three spools of thread on long spike, and clamping over the edge of a table, New York State, *c.* 1810.

TOP: Funeral invitation, 1835; memorial card, 1797; effigy of a departed child, under glass, 1850. CENTER: Shakers at worship by song and dance, 1830; the Kaplan satchel desk, shown open and closed. It was a brief case to end all brief cases, 1878; memorial to a Good Doggie, 1853; advertisement of G. Gatty, who had woven-wire screens for sale in 1835; coal scuttle or vase, of decorated japanned iron, with fire tools in rack, 1870. BOTTOM: Cemetery memorials as advertised by a maker of Philadelphia, 1831; a shocking and delightful style of 1890—the divided skirt.

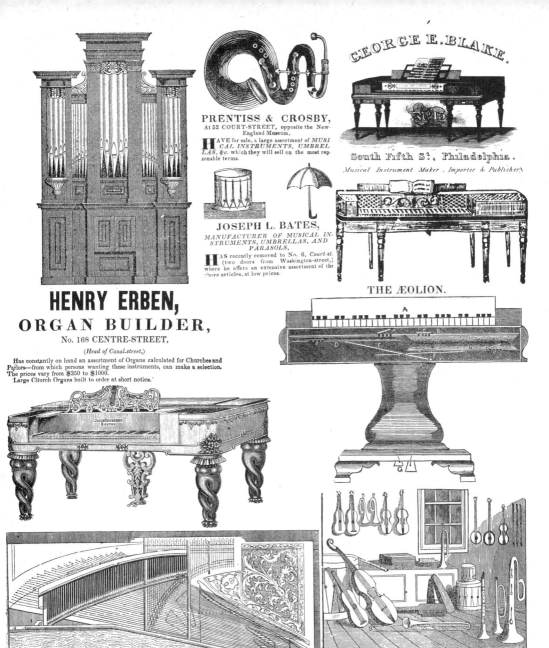

TOP: Pipe-organ builder advertisement, 1841; musical instrument advertisements of 1829 and piano advertisements of 1820. CENTER: An early Chickering piano, from an advertisement of 1856; the original aeolian, a combined harp and melodion, 1847. BOTTOM: Diagonally strung pianoforte—an improvement featured in 1853; advertisement of Edward Baack, musical instrument maker of New York, 1847.

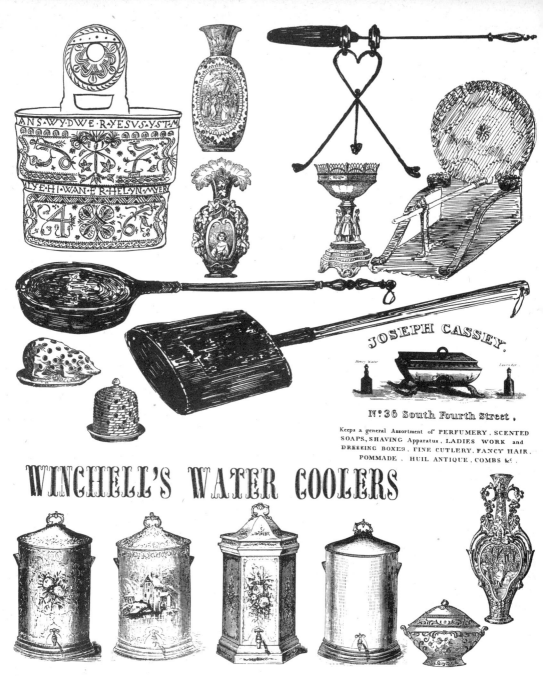

WINCHELL'S WATER COOLERS

TOP ROW: Swiss milk pail dated 1746, as used by Swiss immigrants, Pennsylvania. It is definitely an elegancy of the dairy; three porcelain elegancies by Haviland, as introduced at Crystal Palace, 1853; curling iron and stand, eighteenth century; parrot perch, eighteenth century. CENTER: Hedgehog and beehive crocus pots that were very smart in the 1850s. Brass bed warmer and iron sheet warmer of the eighteenth century. Advertisement of Joseph Cassey, Philadelphia, 1820; he featured cosmetics and elegancies. BOTTOM: Four water coolers by Winchell of New York, 1850. Two elegancies by Haviland of Limoges, France, introduced in the 1850s and purchased by thousands of our best families.

HAIR MANUFACTORY,
137 *CHESNUT STREET.*
C. FOULADOUX,

HENRY WOLFE,

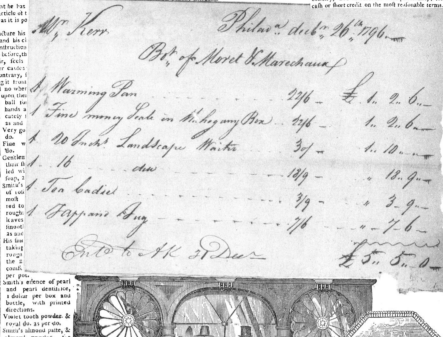

Nathaniel Smith,
Manufacturer of Perfumery, and Comb-Maker
from London,

At the New-York Hair Powder and Perfume
Manufactory, the ROSE, No. 137, Queen-Street.

TO the Ladies, Gentlemen, and Connoisseurs
of genuine and delicate perfumery, the goods
of the above manufactory are most respectfully
offered.

He assures the public that he has
persevere in selling every article of t...
though as low terms as it is po...
them.

He continues to manufacture his
glish white hair powder, and his ci...
soft pomatums, on a new constructions
introduced in this country before, th...
exceeding nutritive to hair, feels
sing to the head, and never causes...
agitation, but on the contrary, t...
nourishes the hair, keeping it from
or combing off, to be had no wher...
above, without his labels upon the...

His superfine English
white hair powder, 10s
per doz.
The very best common
do. 8s per doz.
Do. violet pink orris, &
marechall, double scent-
ed, 13s per doz.
The best of English and
French marechall, from
6 to 24s per lb.
His beautiful carnation
hair powder, for giv-
ing a natural shade to
the complexion, 18s
per lb.
Smith's nervous essence
for curing the tooth
ach, sold with printed
directions, 4s per bottle
His highly approved of
milk of roses, so well
known for clearing the
skin from scurf, pim-
ples, redness or sun-
burns, has not its e-
qual for whitening and
preserving the skin to
extreme old age, and
is very fine for gentle-
men to use after shav-
ing, 4 and 8s per bottle
or 3 dollars per quart,
with printed directions.
Highly improved sweet
scented hard and soft
pomatum, 1s per pot
or roll.
Smith's genuine pomaid
degraisse, for thickening
and strengthening the
hair, it keeps it from
falling off immediately,
4 and 8s per pot, with
printed directions.
Smith's liniment for de-
stroying nits and ver-
min in the hair, war-
ranted innocent, 1s per
box.
His white almond wash

All store-keepers supplied as usual, wholesale,
and retail, with the best articles in all the branches of perfumery, good and cheap.
Just imported, a large quantity of
LONG HAIR of all colors.
For braids, curls, &c. Where hair dresser
may be supplied on reasonable terms. Nov. 27.

Ladies' and Gentlemen's
Fashionable Hair Dresser,
from Paris, has the honor
to inform the public that
he continues to keep a
large assortment of Hair
Works, designed and fin-
ished in the newest fash-
ion; comprising Braids,
Plaited Braids, Greek
Curls, Ringlets, Frisettes,
Puffs, Bandeaux, Ladies'
Wigs, Gentlemen's Wigs,
Metalic Scalps, Scalps,
&c. Also, a store of the
finest French Perfumeries,
consisting in an unbounded variety of Pommades, Huiles
Antiques, Essences, Soaps, and many other articles belonging to the Toilette of either sex. The whole to be sold by
wholesale or retail.

Mr. Fouladoux also begs leave to mention, for the satisfaction of those disposed to honor him with a continuance
of their patronage, that he has prepared two rooms—one for
dressing and cutting the hair of Ladies and Children, the
other exclusively for Gentlemen. He commends his estab-

Smith's eïence of pearl
and pearl dentifrice,
1 dollar per box and
bottle, with printed
directions.
Violet tooth powder, &
royal do. 2s per do.
Smith's almond paste, &
almond powder, for
washing and clearing
the skin.
All kinds of sweet scent-
ed waters and essences,
with every article ne-
cessary for the toilet.
He still continues to
make the full dress and
half dress vergette tou-
pees, upon the same
principles that has giv-
en the greatest satis-
faction, particularly
made for ladies to
dress their own hair on.
To be had only as a-
bove.

RETURNS his fin-
cere thanks to his
former customers, for
the encouragement giv-
en him in the Comb ma-
nufactory, and begs leave
to inform them and the
public in general, that
he has removed from
No. 30 near the Fly mar-
ket, to No. 29 Old-slip,
corner of Little-Dock-
street, where he still carries on the Copper, Sheet
Iron, and tin plate working business, in an extensive manner. He has also just received from on
board the ship Union, from Liverpool, Captain
Whitlock, a large and general assortment of japanned ware, of every kind. Also, a large assortment of high polished block tin ware, a few
spades and frying pans all orders from town or
country, will be executed with punctuality, for
cash or short credit, on the most reasonable terms.

Nathaniel Smith, New York, whose advertisement is at the left, had many
elegancies for sale in 1788.   TOP: Hairdresser of Philadelphia, advertises
in 1830; semi-nude garden figure in cast iron, offered by the Mott Iron
Works, 1850; Henry Wolfe advertised combs and japanned wares, 1792.
BOTTOM: Fine furs and men's hats, on sale in the store of Cook & Aldrich,
Boston, 1861; japanned-top tea table, 1852.   CENTER: A bill for elegancies, rendered in 1796.

TOP: Shower bath of 1850, and pictures from advertisements of bathhouses and plumbing suppliers, including sitz baths, folding bathtubs, and sanitary toilets, all 1830s to 1880s.   CENTER: Sanitary toilets and bathtubs of 1840s and 1860s; advertisement of plumber and hydrant maker, Cincinnati, 1839. BOTTOM: The last word in bathtubs, as produced by Standard Sanitary Manufacturing Company, 1892; the first word in bathtubs, as advertised 1835. This bathroom was right over the kitchen. Tub and washstand were supplied with hot and cold running water. Note, also, there was a shower bath!

Clocks, in the American scene, began as elegancies. Eli Terry turned clocks into staples by his development of mass-production methods. TOP: Advertisement by Aaron Willard of Boston, *c.* 1810; the original Terry mantel clock of 1814; plush-framed, willow-patterned face clock of 1880s, and advertisement by Joseph Clark of Danbury, Conn., 1787. BOTTOM: Thirty-day clock by Joseph Ives, in a case attributed to Duncan Phyfe. Date is 1825. From the collection of Richard Newcomb; original pillar-and-scroll clock by Heman Clark of Plymouth, Conn., *c.* 1810–1813. From the collection of Mr. and Mrs. Frank Beaven, Allendale, N.J.; magnificent tall-case clock by Martin Schreiner, Lancaster, Pa., *c.* 1790, in a case by John Bachman. From Israel Sack.

CHAPTER VII

Jewelry

THE jewelry pictured in this chapter dates from the seventeenth century down to the 1890s. Most of it was made between 1840 and 1880, a period during which pioneering in jewelry manufacture on a mass-production basis marked our American scene. The pictures speak for themselves. The pioneering effort to produce this jewelry was matched by desire for it and concerted action in terms of public buying. We had very few jewelers keeping shop exclusively as jewelers in our colonial and federal periods. Those who, before the beginning of factory operation, made jewelry, also worked as clock-makers and watchmakers, sometimes as goldsmiths, and in many cases as painters of miniatures and makers of miniature frames and lockets. These men also made gold, silver, and brass buttons, sometimes cut gems and set them, and remade old stones into new jewelry.

In recent years in the antiques business there has been much said about old "rose-cut" diamonds. These precious stones of an earlier day have been considered rich, choice, and rare. The fact of the matter is that a rose-cut diamond, in almost every case, is a flat, shallow stone —and often worth one half or less than a modern cut stone of the same diameter. The moral should be obvious—don't buy antique rose-cut diamonds or old diamond jewelry in the fond belief that you are buying good diamonds cheap. By all means buy whatever antique jewelry intrigues you, but with your eyes wide open.

One of the most precious gems in the world is a cocoanut pearl. This rare type of pearl was mentioned by several clipper-ship captains in the Far Eastern trade, along with the man-eating clams of the Java Sea. The captains were laughed at as gullible believers of tall tales out of the East. The man-eating clam doesn't eat men, but it does trap divers in its huge shell and they never again reach the surface. Pearls of gorgeous quality do grow in cocoanuts. A cocoanut "sport" develops without the eyes, or sprouting spots, in the hard shell. This is the only cocoanut in which a pearl can be formed. Thwarted in its sprouting, this cocoanut *may* develop a pearl by the accretion of the chemical elements around the spot where the eyes should be to permit exit of the sprout. Perhaps one cocoanut in 100,000 develops without eyes. Perhaps 1 per cent of these develops a pearl. It is easier to seek pearls in oysters, but in spite of this, every eyeless cocoanut found by the natives in the tropical Far East must be delivered to the headman or the maharajah.

It is perhaps likely that the finest pearls owned by the fabled potentates of India are cocoanut, and not oyster, pearls. Some oyster pearls, and perhaps a very few cocoanut pearls, were brought to our shores by clipper ship-traders. In this work we offer no formula by which a cocoanut pearl can be told from an oyster pearl. We cannot even tell how to differentiate between a genuine, naturally formed pearl, produced by the accidental entrance of foreign matter into the shell of a mollusc, and the pearls formed by oysters into which a bit of foreign matter has been inserted by a wily Japanese. Precious-stone appraisal is a matter for precious-stone specialists. Even they may not agree unless they know that it is true appraisal that is desired and not a mere effort to discover the value of the stone in case the owner should decide to sell it. Some people conduct a sort of auction with a piece of jewelry of seeming value. They drift from one store to another saying, "What would you give for this?" and then, after getting six or eight offers, return to the highest bidder, saying, "It is yours."

The United States Government had some rather nice items, intended for use as jewelry, made for presentation to Indian chiefs. These were mainly silver medallions, gorgets, and medals. Various states made similar presentations. Indian traders purchased cheap beads and gewgaws from Europe and traded them to Indians for furs, skins, blankets, and land.

The parade of jewelry here pictured merely skims the surface of what remains of the jewelry of our pioneers within the definition of that term used in this work. What is needed is a definitive book on the subject of American jewelry. Meanwhile, if any reader desires to know how much interest there is in what is called antique, but which in many cases is just old, jewelry, pay a visit to the jewelry booths at any antiques show. Sometimes the crowd is three deep. People having no other antiquarian interest are buying this jewelry for personal adornment—buying it to wear as it is, or for conversion into earrings and clips, into brooches, pins, and many other objects.

The first jewelry, and by first is meant the jewelry of ancient Egypt, China, Assyria, Sumeria, and Chaldea, was either a form of amulet or charm against evil or a form of signature or identification card for the wearer. Sometimes it served as both. The scarab pierced from front end to rear was mounted on wire so that it could be turned on the ring or bracelet of which it formed the ornament. The frontal carved scarab form was an amulet or charm; the underside was inscribed with owner's mark and dating within the reign of the monarch. This was the "seal" of the wearer.

Most gold jewelry was first wrought from almost pure, and therefore easily worked, gold. It was readily formed into finger rings, or smaller rings and links which, in turn, could be made into chains— for adornment and for use as money. The ancient history of jewelry is not a subject for this present work. In ancient days, so the story goes, the male decked himself to the queen's taste while his queen was considered beautiful in terms of how little of anything she wore, or how cleverly she could wear only golden and jeweled ornaments to accentuate her naked beauty, displayed under the sheerest of fabrics or no fabrics at all. Of course climate had something to do with this display of the form divine, but most jewelry seems to have originated in tropical, semi-tropical, and sub-tropical countries. From time immemorial man seems to have been the human who used most jeweled adornment. It was Solomon in all his glory, and not his queen, who was compared to the lily of the field.

Leaving delving into the deep and dim past of jewelry production for another day, we can with some profit consider jewelry in America as made by and for our pioneers.

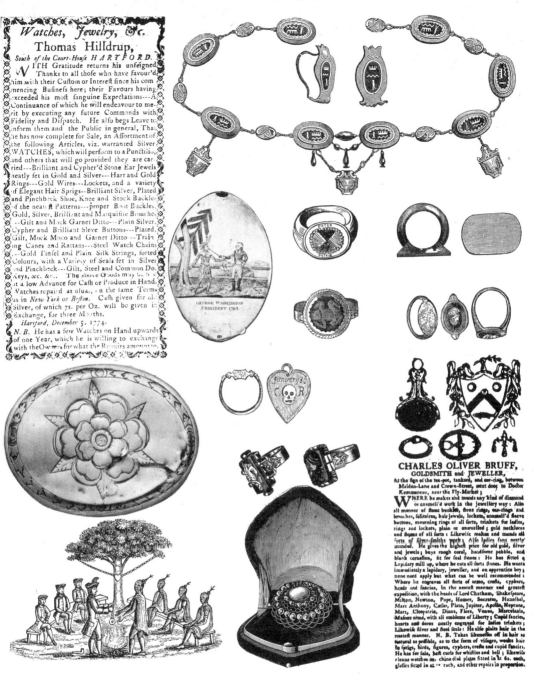

TOP ROW: Advertisement of Thomas Hilldrup of Hartford, Conn., 1774;
Egyptian jewelry at Crystal Palace Exposition, 1853. SECOND AND THIRD
ROWS: Indian medal of silver distributed by federal government at treaties,
made by Joseph Richardson, Philadelphia, 1793; ring containing lock of
George Washington's hair, c. 1800; gold signet ring ready for engraving,
c. 1770; toadstone ring of seventeenth century; three rings of Elizabethan
era. CENTER: Silver patchbox by Francis Richardson, Philadelphia, c.
1720. From Philadelphia Museum of Art; ring and locket of Charles I;
cheap rings of 1870s. BOTTOM: Presentation of medal to Indian chief, c.
1760; brooch belonging to Mrs. Abraham Lincoln, c. 1862; advertisement
by Charles Oliver Bruff, Maiden Lane, New York, 1770.

TOP TWO ROWS: Exquisite diamond and pearl jewelry by Tiffany, Young &
Ellis, 1850s. The bracelet with double tulip motif was considered the last
word in pearl jewelry designing; contemporaneous picture of the Tiffany
establishment on Broadway, 1853. NEXT THREE ROWS: Gold, diamond,
and emerald jewelry by Ball, Black & Company, 1850s. The brooch at right
with pendent pearl and emerald center was advertised as priceless! Included
is contemporaneous view of the Ball, Black establishment on Broadway,
1853. BOTTOM ROW: Red garnet jewelry of the 1880s, factory made at
Newark, N.J., and sold in several thousand jewelry stores throughout the
country.

CHAPTER VIII

Machines and Task-easing Devices
in the Domestic and Social Scene

OTHER than clocks and mechanical jacks to turn spits, the first generally used machine for the home was the spinning wheel. This device, supplanting the ancient distaff, speeded the spinning of thread and hence lessened the time, if not the labor, of preparing the household supply of warp and woof for the loom. American pioneers grew, retted, broke, and hatcheled their own flax, spun it, and often wove it into homespun linen cloth. They sheared sheep for wool, carded and dyed the wool, and spun and wove it. There are collectors of spinning equipment of all sorts, and even some lovers of the quaint and curious who, no matter how misguided, display lamps fashioned from spinning wheels and reels.

It was not until the pioneering genius Elias Howe invented the domestic sewing machine that a complicated mechanical device of epochal significance was offered to the pioneer housewife. Howe's machine took the nation by storm more than a century ago. Concerning it a commentator has said: "The people of the United States were conditioned to the use of machines in the home, and to the desire for and acceptance of more and more machines by that amazing thing, the sewing machine." In addition to making available an astonishing labor-saving device, the invention of the sewing machine and its rapid duplication on a mass production basis provided really gainful employment for thousands of mechanics and founded innumerable fortunes. The pioneer manufacturers of sewing machines were many in number. They competed with one another in mechanical design, style, decoration, price, sales policy, and terms. Master workmen, constantly using tools, dies, and jigs, pondered the application of mechanics to other household and housekeeping aids. A great deal of misinformation has been published, especially in advertising, about Elias Howe, the inventor of the sewing machine. He has been pictured as being bilked of fame and fortune, as too poor to pay for his wife's funeral, and as embittered by lack of recognition. The fact is that Howe reaped a magnificent fortune in royalties from all manufacturers of his basic machine. Those he licensed paid royalties at once; those who pirated his patent were sued, and eventually paid quite handsomely.

Collecting early sewing machines may, at first glance, seem a rather fatuous hobby. Certainly sewing machines are more useful than decorative, but many of them are quite fascinating in that they record not only the making of intricate machines for general use but also the making of that machine as an object for home placement. There is effort at styling and decoration displayed in cabinetwork, castiron frames, and the exterior metal parts of the machine proper.

For untold centuries the task of doing the home laundry was one of the long-drawn-out chores responsible for that line about man working from sun to sun but woman's work remaining never done. The pioneering effort in our country to lessen the labor of the laundry—washing, wringing, and ironing—resulted in many inventions which were produced, offered for sale, and purchased in quantities. Examples of these, together with spinning wheels, sewing machines, and other machines, are here displayed. In many cases the pictures are precisely the ones used originally to promote the sale of the devices.

Included are pictures of early portable typewriters and other machines which are far too often considered modern. It may come as something of a surprise to know that iceless refrigerators were advocated in the 1850s, and that, in the same decade, gas-making machines (actually miniature gas plants) were made for the American home. Today, in a certain New England home, bread is toasted in an automatic machine made by a Worcester clockmaker before the Revolution. A beautifully fashioned brass clockwork of huge size, with massive weights, is fastened to the side of the fireplace. This clockwork is geared to a basket turnspit in which eight to ten slices of bread are placed before the fire. The clockwork is started, the spit revolves, and lo! the bread is toasted golden brown all over—and as brown as one likes it. Of course this machine lacks one thing. It doesn't give a signal when the toast is done and then pop it out of the spit.

Elsewhere in this book will be found pictures of lamps with clockwork machinery driving a fan to promote forced draught, and others which use machinery to drench the wick with lighting fluid. Also there are pictured certain pioneer types of clocks which marked the beginning of factory production and of making good, low-priced timepieces that all people could afford to own.

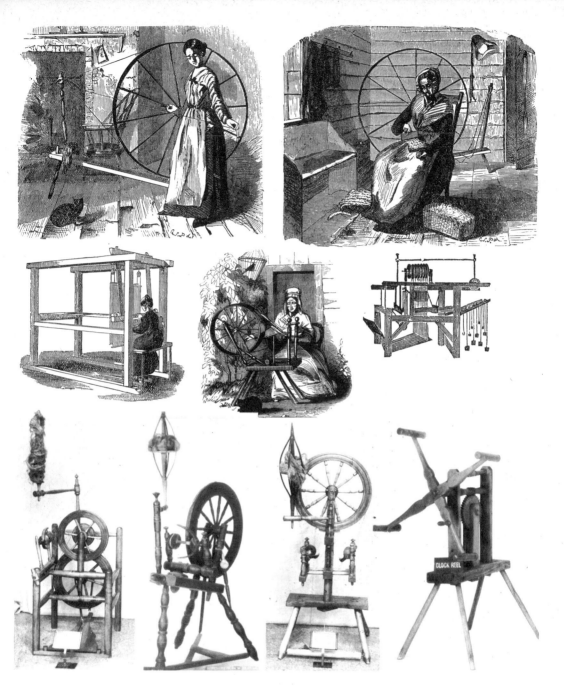

TOP LEFT: Wool spinning wheel, from 1660.   RIGHT: Wool carding by use
of cards, or stiff brushes, to prepare wool for initial working, before
spinning.   CENTER: Hand loom, early eighteenth century; flax spinning
wheel, type dating from 1650; lace loom, c. 1800. Lace-making centers were
Ipswich, Mass., and Newark, N.J.   BOTTOM: Flax wheel in chair frame,
c. 1750; flax wheel, c. 1750; two-spindle flax wheel of Irish type, c. 1800;
clock reel, c. 1800. Clock reel so-called because it registered yardage on a
dial. The Irish-type spinning wheel was used in the colonies from 1719,
when a number of north Irish Protestants emigrated to New Hampshire
and Pennsylvania. By 1850 there were more than 20,000 descendants of the
New Hampshire emigrants engaged in weaving.

COLBY'S PATENT
IMPROVED CLOTHES WRINGER.

1st. It will save time, which is money.

2d. It will save strength, which cannot be bought.

3d. It will save the clothes, which cost money.

4th. Any man, boy or girl, can use it, who could not wring clothes by hand.

5th. It helps to wash the clothes, and by running them a few times through the machine, out of hot suds, it will clean them as well as half the washing machines in use.

6th. It leaves the clothes in a better condition to dry.

7th. It helps to make washing day more pleasant.

HOWDEN, COLBY & CO.,
WATERBURY. VERMONT.

R. A. STRATTON,
MACHINIST,
CHERRY STREET. EAST OF BROAD, PHILADELPHIA,

Manufacturer of TURNING LATHES, PLANING MACHINES, SLIDE RESTS, and other varieties of Machinists' Tools. Also, Gas Fitters' Tools, Engravers' Ruling Machines, Patent Mangles, and Machine Work in general, executed in the best manner.

CATARACT
WASHING MACHINE.

DESCRIPTION.

It consists of a metal cylinder, with cleats on the inner surface, and an interior cylinder of wood, with cleats. There is a space of from six to eight inches between the two cylinders. One crank turns both cylinders at the same time in opposite directions, equally creating a suds, forcing the water through the clothes, and effectually removing the dirt.

ADVANTAGES.

This Machine dispenses entirely with the wash-board. The action of the suds cleans the clothes, consequently there is no wear or tear. The saving of clothing, and the saving of time and labor, are equally remarkable. The Machine is simple in construction and management; a child can use it. It is well made, of galvanized iron, and is very durable. It will wash the finest as well as the coarsest fabrics,—a single small piece, or a quantity of clothing. For Flannels (usually the most difficult things for the laundress to manage), its operation is astonishing, as it thoroughly cleans them, with no possibility of shrinkage.

Prices—No. 1, $12; No. 2, $14; No. 3, $16.

Machines can be seen in operation at No. 494 Broadway, east side, above Broome St. Ladies and gentlemen are invited to call and examine it, or about a letter.

Send your Dirty Clothes and test it.

SULLIVAN & HYATT, Proprietors,
IMPORTERS AND DEALERS IN
American & Foreign Hardware,
54 BEEKMAN STREET, NEW YORK.

FRENCH'S
CONICAL WASHING MACHINE.

Those who have seen this   *Machine acknowledge it to be*

The most Simple, Durable, Convenient, and Economical Article
EVER INVENTED FOR THE PURPOSE.

THE PATENT CLOTHES DRYER.
THE MOST SIMPLE, PRACTICAL AND CHEAPEST DRYER MADE.
WILL SAVE ITS PRICE EVERY YEAR.

A revolving, folding and portable dryer that can be placed on the post and open for use in one minute. Large size spreads 200 feet of line and occupies only 14 feet of space. In case of sudden showers, or at night, it can be folded and taken in without removing the clothes. No paths to make in Winter. Send for Circulars and Prices to

AVERILL & SHARP,
Successors to FISHER & LING,
PULASKI, N. Y.

TOP: Clothes wringer, 1850s. SECOND ROW: Cataract washer, 1850; laundry machine, 1857. BOTTOM: Conical washing machine, 1850; framework clothes dryer, 1887; pair of pressing irons, 1850s.

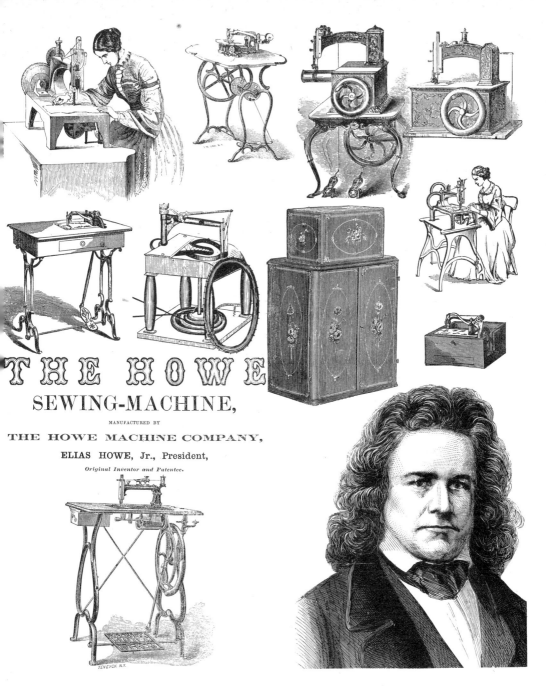

THE HOWE

SEWING-MACHINE,

MANUFACTURED BY

THE HOWE MACHINE COMPANY,

ELIAS HOWE, Jr., President,

Original Inventor and Patentee.

TEN EYCK, N.Y.

BOTTOM RIGHT: The man who made the sewing machine possible, Elias Howe, Jr., born at Spencer, Mass., 1819, died at Brooklyn, N.Y., 1867. His yearly revenue from his invention yielded him close to $2,000,000. TOP: Singer machine of 1855; Wheeler & Wilson machine, 1855; Howe's machine, 1854; and Howe's table model, 1855. SECOND ROW: Grover & Baker machine, 1856; Blodgett's rotary machine, 1852; Singer's "de luxe" in elegant cabinet, 1855; advertising picture of 1855 and small table model, or "portable," by Grover & Baker, 1856. BOTTOM LEFT: Advertisement of the Howe machine, 1866.

THE CALIGRAPH.

Life is too **SHORT** to **WRITE** the **OLD WAY.**

PINKERTON'S NATIONAL DETECTIVE AGENCY.
Chicago, Dec. 11th, 1884.

I am pleased to state that the **Caligraphs** recently purchased from you are giving excellent satisfaction. I have now four machines in my **Chicago** office, five in my **New York** office, and three in my **Philadelphia** office, and I think that the work done by these **Caligraphs** *is far superior to any writing machine I have ever used.* I remain, Yours very truly,
W. A. PINKERTON, Gen'l Supt. West. Div.

Address The American Writing Machine Co.,
HARTFORD, CONN.

HALL TYPE - WRITER.
Price, $40.00.

Awarded the Medal of Superiority over all its competitors at the Semi-Centennial Fair of the American Institute in New York. Also the John Scott Medal, by the Franklin Institute of Philadelphia.

(*It was not exhibited in the recent Fair at New Orleans.*)

Guaranteed to do better work, and a greater variety, than any other writing machine in the world.

It prints directly from the face of the type, requiring no ink-ribbon; uses interchangeable types, $1.00 per font, in all languages, French, Spanish, German, Italian, Greek, Armenian, Sanscrit, Japanese, and many others, besides a large variety of English types suitable for business correspondence, sermons, legal documents, &c.; weighs, in its neat walnut case, but 7 lbs.; equally admirable in the counting-room, parlor, or railroad train; accommodates paper of any size without adjustment, including a self-feeding roll of 500 sheets, with or without printed headings.

Remington

Standard

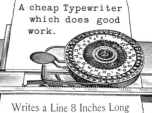

A cheap Typewriter which does good work.

Typewriter.

Writes a Line 8 Inches Long

TOP: Union carpet sweeper, 1865; one of the first typesetting machines, 1857; typewriter on sewing-machine stand with treadle-operated spacer. SECOND ROW: The calligraph typewriter, 1885; the Hall typewriter of 1885. Note the price was $40 and that it required no ribbon and had interchangeable type to write Sanskrit, Japanese, Armenian, Greek, and German. It would operate from a roll of 500 sheets of paper! BOTTOM: The Remington Standard of 1890; the National typewriter and the Yost typewriter of the 1890s; the Hammond, circular-keyboard typewriter of 1888; Child's typewriter of 1892, priced at $2.50.

CHAPTER IX

Philosophical, Mathematical, and Scientific Antiques

T HE antiquities of these three overlapping categories fall into two broad divisions: practical working devices or tools, and experimental or demonstrative apparatus. Since the first and only available transportation facility of the early colonists was by water, settlements were made on or near navigable water. Great rivers such as the Hudson, the Delaware, the Connecticut, and the Housatonic were, actually, water roads. The Chesapeake Bay made Tidewater Virginia a sort of Venice, on a grand scale. Inland and coastal navigation called for maps and charts, and for the use of a compass or "north indicator." On occasion, navigation called for instruments to determine noon, a good timepiece, and other localization aids.

When road building first began, the task was merely a widening of existing Indian trails or paths. Most of the traffic was on foot or horseback. Wagons and carts came into use only when the bridle path was widened to a cartpath. In Virginia, roads to tidewater were tobacco roads, wide enough to roll a huge round cask of tobacco. These were first pushed by man power and then hauled, or rolled, behind a team of horses or oxen. Road building involved some surveying. So did land allocation and the measuring of huge grants. This called for instruments many of which, if not in their seventeenth- and eighteenth-century forms, are pictured here in their early nineteenth-century forms. Clock, watch, and dial makers needed scientific, calibrated tools. In making clocks, watches, and dials they became makers of transits, compasses, and other mathematical and scientific instruments. Architects, housewrights, arkwrights, and other artisans who built big things needed more than the tools of construction and erection; they had to have rules, forms, calculators, and so on. They needed drawing instruments very much of the kind that similar employments require today. These, at first imported, were made in some quantities by local talent from about 1680.

After Benjamin Franklin became interested in the liberal arts and sciences he became an inventor and experimenter. His two-wick candle was a step toward the Argand principle; his Pennsylvania stove was a splendid engineering job in room heating. His experiments with lightning, proving that natural phenomenon was one with the electric fluid of the philosophers, gave great impetus to advances in electrical science and the production of what we must call either philosophical apparatus or scientific toys. The experiments of Mesmer, duplicated here in the practices of the Shakers, demonstrated that an unseen force could be transferred from mind to mind and body to body. Mesmer's electrical explanation of hypnosis gave rise to many devices for application of the electric fluid direct to patients. "Shock treatment" for nervous ills isn't a twentieth-century medical vagary—it was used more than a century ago.

So great was the popular interest in scientifics, philosophics, and mathematics after the War of 1812 that specialty shops for the making and sale of instruments and gadgets were opened in Philadelphia, Baltimore, New York, Albany, and Boston. Some of these shops issued trade cards. A few of them issued illustrated catalogues. Examples of most of the cards and the catalogues have survived the years. To them, rather than to photographs of surviving but unidentified examples, we can turn for pictures of actual things and for knowledge of who made them, when sold, for what purpose, and at what price.

Certain of these objects, actually deserving the designation of toys, will be found pictured in the chapter on toys. Others, of superior elegance, such as orreries, barometers, celestial and terrestrial orbs, sundials, and armillary spheres, are pictured in the chapter on elegancies. Here are pictured the early compasses, theodolites, astrolabes, and allied instruments; and certain of the electrical, chemical, physical, and natural science objects that our pioneers used and made a part of their amusement, education, wage earning, or pursuit. Many of the objects were designed for school use, but many, also, were made for home use.

Among the things pictured are some optical devices. There is an advertisement concerning "pebbles" that perhaps needs some explanation. When eyeglasses were made of glass they were designated as glasses. Benjamin Franklin invented bifocal vision glasses because he was nearsighted. His lower panes were almost flat glass; his distance lenses were set in the upper level of his frames. Both lenses were of glass. About 1835 we began importing natural rock crystal from

Brazil. This came in the form of "pebbles," which were sliced down and ground into lenses for eyeglasses. They were designated as "pebbles" in contradistinction to common, or even optical, glass lenses.

All students and observers of American social history are of course well aware of the fact that philosophy, science, and mathematics were parts of every art, trade, skill, and calling. Scales, balances, gauges, standards, measures, and instruments of all sorts were in use. Some of the instruments of our early artisans still pose problems to the collectors of such items. There are gadgets and "thingamajigs" reposing in many collections that still challenge definition in respect of original use and purpose. The very term "thingamajig," so commonly used by early mechanics, is the source of the present-day term "jig" for a template or working pattern.

One of the pictures on page 96 is an excellent representation of an electric machine or static generator. While this machine may prove a curiosity to some observers and laughable to others it is, nonetheless, the great-grandfather of the machine that made millions gasp at the New York World's Fair in 1939; the static electrical generator that loosed bolts of artificial lightning.

Everything we enjoy today as modern invention has its origin somewhere in the immediate or dim past. All of our artificial silks, spun and woven from viscose, begin with a very pretty philosophical story about a man who challenged the dictum "you cannot make a silk purse from a sow's ear." He took the ear of a pig, dissolved it in chemicals, reduced it to a viscous mass, spun it, dried it, and wove it into a fabric from which a purse was formed.

Very scientific aids to navigation, used in coastwise, Atlantic, and the Far
East trade. TOP: Compass, or north finder, in mahogany case, made at
Boston, c. 1790; Davis quadrant made by Benjamin Ring of Salem, Mass.,
1775; nocturnal, for night sighting, c. 1724. BOTTOM: Astrolabe, probably of Persian or Arabian production, c. sixteenth century. The Saracens
were our first great astronomers and produced many superior scientific
instruments which were used by our navigators even though the symbols
were in Arabic; ring dial for taking time by the sun. It could be suspended
from a cord to provide leveling. The date is c. 1680–1700. All pictures
shown by courtesy of the Peabody Museum, Salem, Mass.

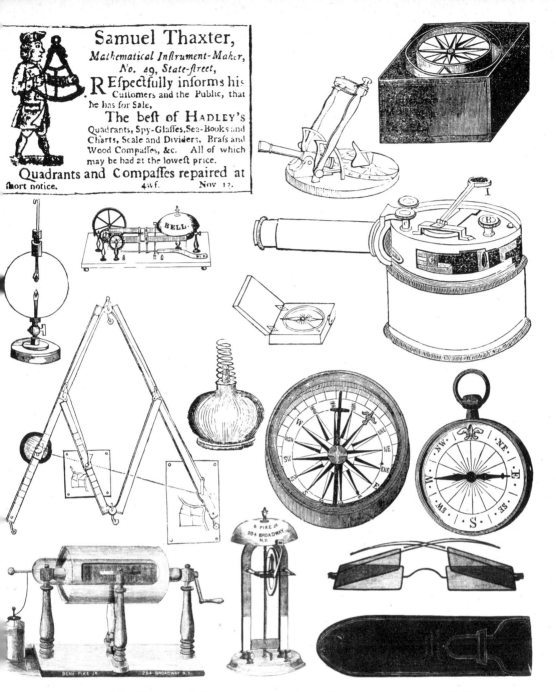

TOP ROW: Mathematical instrument maker, Boston, 1794; sundial gun, 1848; mariner's compass swung in gimbals, 1848. SECOND ROW: Carbon arc lamp, electric-battery operated, 1848; electric bell, 1845; pocket compass, 1848; sextant, 1848. THIRD ROW: Pantograph for enlarging and reducing drawings, 1848; flameless lamp, 1848—fumes of alcohol made platinum coil glow; pocket compasses, 1848. BOTTOM: Dynamo for generating static electricity, 1848; electric bell, 1848; side- and front-view glasses and case, 1848, for protection of eyes from glare and sunlight.

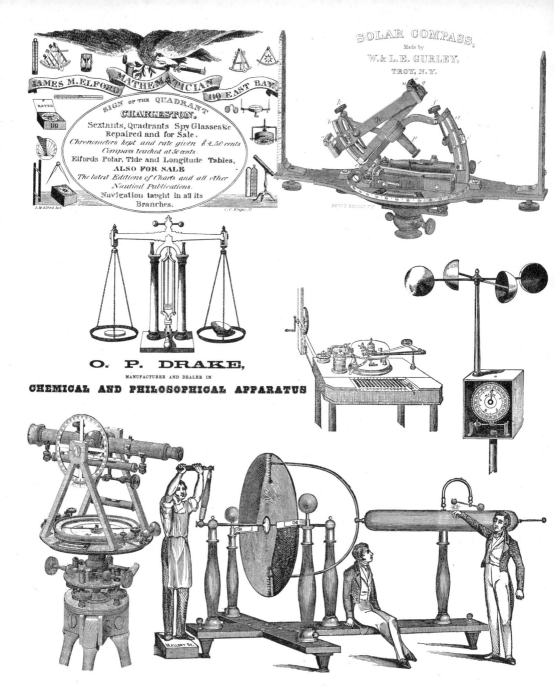

TOP: Advertisement of instrument maker, Charleston, S.C., *c.* 1800; advertisement of solar compass, Troy, N.Y., 1850. SECOND ROW: Advertisement of Drake, instrument maker of Boston, established 1839; printing telegraph machine with piano keyboard, 1851; anemometer or wind speed indicator, New York, *c.* 1870. BOTTOM: Surveyor's transit by Gurley of Troy, N.Y., 1850; mammoth dynamo for generating static electricity, Boston, *c.* 1840. America's first cyclotron.

CHAPTER X

Amusements, Diversions, Sports, and Pleasures

THE first sporting event of record in our early pioneer scene appears to have been a football game played on the strand north of Boston in the mid-seventeenth century between a team of native Indians and some residents of the new town of Boston. Spectators lined the shore to watch the match. The game was played barefoot; the ball was an inflated ox bladder.

During the first fifty years of colonization in New England there was little time for fun, as such. All the thrills of sport could be had in fishing and hunting to keep the pot boiling. The popular Sunday sport was going to meeting. Neither man's nor woman's work was ever done; there was little activity of any kind from the setting to the rising of the sun, and no leisure from sunrise to sunset.

New Amsterdam had a bowling green early in its history. The burghers of the New Netherlands also played their national game of "gowff." There is a record of the good fathers of Albany prohibiting the playing of "gowff" on the streets of the village because flying balls endangered bystanders and both house and shop windows. Governor Burnett, who died in 1729, owned a set of "gowff clubbes" and several dozen "gowff" balls. Fox hunting, of course, engaged the interest of the squires of Virginia. Since a good hunter—a horse that can take timber with the greatest of ease—is a necessary adjunct to this sport, we can understand why the blooded horse was first known in Virginia.

The pioneers had the healthy and wise habit of making all kinds of tasks a sort of sport or picnic. Apple-paring parties, husking bees, wood-sawing contests, barn raisings, reaping contests, flailing contests are all matters of record. Spinsters' conventions on Boston Common in which at least one hundred young ladies vied with one another in an open contest of thread spinning, must have been a lovely sight. Knitting bees, soap boilings, apple-sauce boilings, and perhaps a score of other tasks, including fish and meat smokings, were indulged in as seasonal events. Thus was pleasure made of work and a social affair made of a task. Wrasslin' matches were common, and it is fairly certain that Tabagos (Tobaccos) or men's smoking parties, after the Indian fashion, were indulged in.

There is good reason to believe that women and girls also indulged in smoking, chewing, and snuffing tobacco, even in the seventeenth century. We know women indulged in smoking and snuffing parties in the eighteenth century and we also know that so common was the chewing of snuff by women in the mid-nineteenth century that snobbish ladies were catered to with "Dental Snuff" which they could chew, not because they wanted to indulge in a low habit, but because "the doctor has advised it as good for my teeth."

Sea bathing, boating, May walking, moonlight excursioning from town to town by hay wagon, sleigh, or canal barge were both city and rural sports. Checkers, or draughts, backgammon, and cards were played. Simpler games, played on homemade boards, using pegs, buttons, or grains of wheat or corn as counters, are also a matter of record. By the middle of the eighteenth century horsemanship, horse racing, dicing, and shooting matches were the professed pleasurable sports of many men.

Mummeries, play-acting, stage singing, and musical entertainments seem to have begun by the 1750s. Wax works, automaton displays, peep shows, firework displays, riding exhibitions, balloon ascensions, bell ringings, trained bears—all of these were the forerunners of organized entertainment. Before theaters, as such, were built, taverns were centers of indoor entertainment. All important taverns had ballrooms, long rooms, dance rooms, or halls. These were fitted with a stage or dais to accommodate traveling troupes and itinerant players. Many French dancing masters toured the colonies in the eighteenth century, starting as early as 1710. Many more appeared after the French Revolution. Royalist *émigrés* taught dancing, fencing, and minor arts.

Richardson Wright, editor of *House & Garden,* began studying early American entertainment during the 1920s. In 1927 he incorporated much of his findings in his delightful book, *Hawkers and Walkers in Early America* (Lippincott). This book should be in the library of every collector of Americana. It is an ideal work in that the author's scholarly research is not paraded to produce fusty, fussy, and annotated text but to add sparkle to pleasant reading, often brilliantly pointed. According to Mr. Wright, this country enjoyed demonstrations of horseless carriages, lighter-than-air flying machines, and electrical phenomena as entertainment before George Washington retired as President. We had ventriloquists, magicians, and kaleidoscopic performances before 1825. Slack- and tight-rope performers were displaying their skill before 1725. Pierre Blanchard, the aeronaut who made the first balloon ascension at Philadelphia in 1793, also conducted a more or less permanent automaton theater at Lancaster, Pennsylvania, prior and subsequent to his aeronautical experiments.

Blanchard's Lancaster activities fired a young boy named John Wise with aeronautical ambitions. Wise became our outstanding aerial navigator and our first protagonist of air travel. In 1847 he advocated aerial warfare and the formation of an army and navy air force. By 1849 he advocated air mail and proved its feasibility by carrying United States mail in his balloon flights. He distributed leaflets by the thousands from his balloons. More will be found about Wise and aeronautica elsewhere in this volume. But it is pertinent here to consider the fact that early American aviation, even when the pursuit was conducted as an entertainment for spectators, provided mementos and souvenirs that are today rather rare antiques.

In the office of an airplane executive of some fame and fortune hangs a framed printed cotton handkerchief once sold by a hawker at an American balloon ascension. Folded for almost a century within the leaves of a family Bible, that relic was found in the 1920s. From a bookshop in Virginia it traveled to York, Pennsylvania, thence to New York, and then to a famed auction room. At the latter place, after spirited bidding, it found a new owner only after its bid-up price had reached a record—in four figures.

Among the relics of amusements, diversions, sports, games, and pleasures we have an enormous amount of collectible material including playing cards, silver race-meet cups, programs, tickets, playbills, invitations, dominoes, games, counters, gaming tables, toy theaters, peep-show machines, waxworks, silhouettes, clocks, sheet music, hand organs, carousel horses, and medicine-show bottles.

Actual stage plays seem to have been performed in New England by 1750. Charleston, South Carolina, had theatricals in a real theater in 1737. Lancaster, Pennsylvania, had performances by strolling players between 1730 and 1742. Cincinnati, apparently, had the first little-theater movement in the United States in 1821, when a group of local young people organized a players company and erected a playhouse. In 1853 P. T. Barnum commissioned H. J. Conway to dramatize

Harriet Beecher Stowe's tear jerker, *Uncle Tom's Cabin*. Barnum staged the spectacle as melodramatic entertainment, with jubilee music. An enterprising English paper stainer made a wallpaper design memorializing the affair and another near, and ephemeral, "antique" was added to our list: Uncle Tom's Cabin wallpaper, with the colored cast pictured in costumes of decided French flavor, and very, very stylish.

The two hundredth performance of *Pique* was celebrated in 1876 at New York by the issue of sterling silver theater tickets, designed and made by the Gorham Company. This item, together with an exemplary showing of the kinds and types of antiquities remaining from sports and amusements of pioneering nature, constitutes the pictorial display for this chapter. Many people who have never collected antiques of other kinds now collect mementos of the pursuits and pleasures here considered. Also, it would seem many girls in every age have treasured little souvenirs of pleasurable occasions, laid them away with lavender and lace, and passed them on to daughters and granddaughters.

Many balls were given to celebrate the visit of General Lafayette in 1824–25. These were affairs of high style and fashion. Every girl who attended was all atwitter. If she was asked to tread a few measures with the aged hero she was swooning with delight. Many of the girls were "touched" by the great French nobleman. Some had their hands kissed. It was all very wonderful. Perhaps half a million souvenirs of these balls were carefully preserved for years. Some of the souvenirs were dance cards; some were engraved invitations; some were menus; some were medals, buttons, cups, glasses, and napkins. Among the most delightful antiquities surviving from Lafayette's visit are marchpane molds used in making the ceremonial cakes that were the fashion of the day.

To collect antiquities of pioneering effort one need only drop a net into the stream of availables. To imagine that this present work even approaches definity, or covers most of the opportunities, would be an error. An entire volume, or two or three, would not hold the record of all that could be pictured in respect of almost every subject that is made a mere section of this book.

TOP ROW: A play printed by Elton of New York, 1838; posters for a fair and for that great melodrama, *After Dark;* sterling silver theater tickets produced by Gorham & Co., 1875, for the 200th performance of *Pique;* poster for Niblo's famed extravaganza, *The Forty Thieves;* advertisement of a carousal, *c.* 1825.   CENTER: George Christy, the great minstrel; Cordelia Howard, the first Little Eva of *Uncle Tom's Cabin.* Born at Providence, R.I., 1848, Cordelia played Eva the first time at Troy, N.Y., September 1852; advertisement of a slack-rope walker, Springfield, Mass., 1832; the immortal Jenny Lind, who inspired thousands of American girls with concert-stage ambitions.   BOTTOM: One of the earliest evidences of minstrelsy, London Mathews's comic songs based upon the folk songs of the Negroes. Published at Philadelphia, 1824.

TOP ROW: A feat at the New York Hippodrome, 1853; advertisement of an acrobatic act, Philadelphia, 1795; a New York circus as advertised in 1847. CENTER: Another thrilling act at the New York Hippodrome, 1853. The performer toed the ball from the top to the bottom of the incline; view of the great Chestnut Street Theater, Philadelphia, 1839. BOTTOM: Opening night, featuring a Roman chariot race, at the New York Hippodrome, 1853; Niblo's Garden, New York, 1854. Admission was fifty cents for any seat in the house except for the opera. In this woodcut there is evidence that the upper half of the figures were recut and inserted in the block.

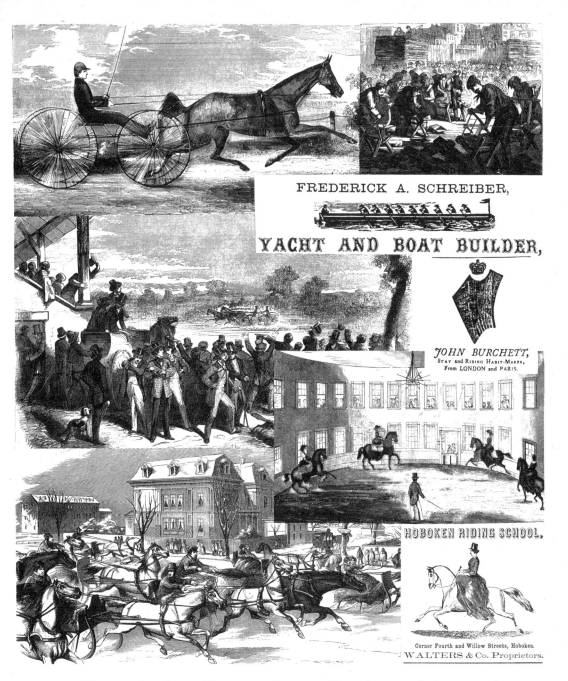

TOP: The trotting horse Taconey, 1853; wood-sawing match between the team of the Y.M.C.A. and the Hoosier Baseball Club at Lafayette, Ind., November 30, 1867. CENTER: Trotting race between Taconey and Mac, Philadelphia, 1853; advertisement of a yacht and boatbuilder, Jersey City, 1859; advertisement of a riding-habit maker, New York, c. 1785; interior of the Boston Riding Academy, 1849. BOTTOM: Sleigh racing on Boston Neck, 1854; advertisement of the Hoboken Riding School, 1859.

TOP: Playing the elegant game of croquet, 1866; view at Saratoga Springs, 1859. CENTER: Chowder party, 1849; American Indians playing a game of hockey, or "shinny." The team captains wore antlers. The audience is quite blasé. BOTTOM. Cornhusking party, 1857 finding a red kernel in an ear meant the girl could be kissed. This was better than the game of post office; sea bathing at Long Branch, 1866, showing the delightful costumes of the ladies and gentlemen.

D. D. WINANT.   71 GOLD ST.

COUNTRY WEDDING

TOP: Interstate regatta at Troy, N.Y., 1867, showing the singles shell race between Randall and Smith; theatrical poster, Lancaster, Pa., January 2, 1800. Governor McKean and his staff, together with local society, thus ushered in what they thought was the beginning of the nineteenth century. Instead, they were celebrating the last year of the eighteenth century. CENTER: Elegant steam yacht offered by William Osborn, boatbuilder, 1887; ladies playing billiards, 1856. BOTTOM: The Prohibition Girls enter a saloon for a knitting party and thus keep the trade away, 1850; country wedding, Pennsylvania, 1820, with Bishop White officiating. This picture is by Louis Krimmel. The interior shows the kind of furniture and furnishings which then graced the American pioneer home.

TOP: Scottish games at Randall's Island, 1867; fun in the hayfield, *c.* 1850.
CENTER: Sea bathing at Cape May, one of the most exclusive resorts then
on the Atlantic seaboard, 1849; playing fox and geese, 1857.   BOTTOM:
Much Ado About Nothing, as staged at Wallach's Lyceum, New York,
1853; just fishing, 1854. Note the gentlemen anglers in the foreground.
One of them sports a high silk hat.

CHAPTER XI

People, Personalities, Characters, and Queers

A SIGNIFICANT thing to be found in every commentary about America's pioneers, written by visitors, is the element of *fear* that is found buried in the words of ridicule, sarcasm, or praise the writers had for our people, our ways, and our land. Our ideas of freedom and liberty were unthinkable. Our ways were uncouth. We were shameless, fierce, boastful, gauche, awkward, immoral, amoral, deceitful, foolish—in a word, impossible. The ways in which we had fun were curious and inexplicable. The way we did things, the way we thought, fought, planned were just not in the pattern of civilized man. We had the courage to think of canals five hundred miles long. We had the temerity to laugh at kings and lords. We had corporals who were smarter soldiers than European generals. We had shopkeepers who, within a few short years, made fortunes.

If an aunt from Dubuque, visiting Coney Island for the first time, is literally flabbergasted, to us it is laughable. To the average European traveler of the eighteenth and early nineteenth centuries a visit to the land that is our part of America was just like the visit of the old lady from Dubuque to Coney Island. We were an unbelievable midway, a circus, something out of this world and out of the experience of the traveler. Some of them liked it. But at first almost every one of them was scared, and afraid.

In one of the many early exercise books that have survived the years, a young lad in 1788 wrote: "The cub does not fear the lion or lioness, nor does the calf fear the bull. Why, then, doth the lion and the bull attack man? Let us be brave. It is because they fear us, and so strive to destroy that which they fear." No matter what congratulatory and laudatory praises were showered upon us after the Revolution, we were *feared* as a people and a nation by all the ruling classes the whole world over. We were dangerous to all the ancient organized rackets, systems, techniques, and methods of keeping the mind of man in chains and his body within narrow limits of freedom. We were dangerous to organized churches; in fact, we had groups that would form a new church at the drop of a hat, and did just that. If there were just two or three who didn't like the way anything was done, one became a leader, ready to form a new group.

Men and women, and boys and girls of all ages, were touched with this devil-may-care, take-a-chance, try-and-do-it state of mind. No matter what the stimulus, it was conditioned to response by a mental set that was pioneering in quality. That most of the response during the Revolution resulted in what we term patriotic courage cannot be denied. But we should not dismiss the Tory or the traitor with a sneer. They had the courage to stand fast, and to act as their consciences dictated. They were just as fearful to contemplate as were the patriots.

Great men, great women, great deeds, and great events and circumstances within our scene are collectibles today generally as prints and pictures. But characters, queer customers, originals, and minor events also had their little audiences who, in many cases, wanted memorials printed. There are scarce little pamphlets and prints, some quite rare prints, and some even unique ones which, while never having had national significance, now have significance to those who delve deeply into local history.

Were it not, for example, that the late Vachel Lindsay wrote a delightful poem about Johnny Appleseed, it is doubtful whether popular knowledge concerning this character would now exist. There was a cheap penny lithograph of Johnny Appleseed from a drawing made from memory, issued as a memorial to the man for the folks in Ohio who remembered him. Try to find one today. You'll hunt high and low, and perhaps always have a gap in your portfolio where you hope to put the print when you find it. Yet this print of Johnny Appleseed should be the capstone of every collection of Arboriana Americana. Johnny Appleseed's chosen task in life was the planting of nurseries of apple trees. Ragged, tattered, and forlorn, he is one of the great men of our country and a great man of Ohio. His name was John Chapman. He had but two missions—to plant apple seeds and to preach the religion of Swedenborg. That our great novelist Herman Melville also preached Swedenborg in his *Moby Dick* is more or less proved to the satisfaction of many scholars in William S. Gleim's *Theory of Moby Dick*. This work, too, is ephemera of the sort which, a century hence, may be rare Americana.

Among American personalities deserving special mention are Tobias Hirte, a Moravian who traded drugs to cure rheumatism to the Indians in exchange for rattlesnake oil, which he sold to accredited physicians who used *it* as a better cure for rheumatism! By the time of the Revolution, Hirte was well known in eastern Pennsylvania. His last act as a Moravian was to stage a party for wounded American soldiers hospitalized at Lititz. He invited girls of the sect to the party to dance with the soldiers. Shortly thereafter Hirte was read out of meeting. He appears as a character in two of Rudyard Kipling's stories in *Rewards and Fairies*.

Lord Timothy Dexter of Newbury was an ignoramus with a sense of humor and the faculty for making money. He shipped coals to Newcastle at a profit; warming pans to Jamaica; made a killing on whalebone. Also, he had so much faith in Continental currency that he bought it for hard money when everybody was getting rid of it at any discount. After the Revolution he cashed in at par. Dexter's fortune was the envy of his Newbury neighbors. Because all and sundry were curious about it, he published a book titled *A Pickle for the Knowing Ones*. Tongue in cheek, he had it printed without punctuation from beginning to end. His neighbors knew less than they did before. Dexter had a dog, a palace with outdoor statuary, and a poet laureate. He was quite a card.

Benjamin Ley was a gnomelike crippled Quaker only four and a half feet tall, who died in 1759. He published an anti-slavery pamphlet and would enter meetinghouses and speak against slavery. Once he broke all his chinaware in public as a protest against tea drinking. His portrait, engraved by Henry Dawkins, a colonial engraver who turned counterfeiter, is now a collector's item.

Dr. Johnson, the great English man of letters, once said that it is the biographical part of literature that people love best. Our American literary record is proof of the soundness of Johnson's observation. Each year we have more proof that the biographical resources provided by the lives and deeds of our greats, near-greats, obscures, and unknowns are far from exhausted. In further proof of the depth of the well of biographical material at our command, either as inspiration for writing or as inspiration to seek antiques of a provenance with the people, this chapter will display a sample—and only a sample—drawn almost at random from that well. No special comment is required here in respect of any of the types of characters and personalities. Each picture is captioned as briefly as possible, but, with that caption as a starting point, any courageous researcher can proceed with assurance.

Libraries will yield more data. You may find fifty or a hundred books recommended by some librarians for further study. On some of the characters you might find only a line or two, buried in an obscure journal.

The term "hunyak" for almost any foreigner was once as commonly used in Pennsylvania as the term "Portygee" is still used in the same sense by the natives of Cape Cod. The late William Frederick Woerner of the Keystone Commonwealth was very much interested in the characters, queers, and original odd ones of his region. He traced the term hunyak to the first Chinese laundryman in eastern Pennsylvania, an amiable celestial whose name was—you guessed it—Hun-Yak.

Very frequently we discover that local mathematical wizards were also quite queer in the head—that is, on all other subjects. Also, we can find many records having to do with Jacks-of-all-trades who, in their own way, dabbled with such ridiculous things as fireproof glass, malleable glass, glass-coated wire screens, light without heat, cheaper foods, paints that would work equally well with either oil or water, or wallpaper that would stick to walls without the use of pot paste or glue. They were all considered queer in their day. But the things they pottered around with in their efforts to unscrew the inscrutable are commonplaces in stores, shops, and in industry today.

As we study the history of our so-called originals we at times feel it is a great pity they were so far ahead of their time. Most of them would not be considered screwballs at all if they could tell their stories to the directors of modern research laboratories.

TOP ROW: The cat inspector of Little Rest, R.I. Courtesy Richardson Wright; Benjamin Ley, eccentric Philadelphia Quaker, c. 1760. Courtesy Historical Society of Pennsylvania; Timothy Dexter, Newburyport, Mass., "character." Courtesy Richardson Wright. MIDDLE ROW: Wooden statue from the Dexter mansion, Newburyport. Courtesy Essex Institute; Peter Deshong of Lancaster, Pa., a mental mathematical wizard of the 1840s; Amos Dean of Albany, N.Y., founded the Young Men's Association, 1840s; Frederick Moon, fortuneteller, puppet theater proprietor, and confirmed jailbreaker, 1810–1820. BOTTOM: Mrs. Anna Ritchie, famous actress of the 1840s; Harriet Beecher Stowe, author of *Uncle Tom's Cabin;* Phyllis Wheatley, remarkable Negro girl; Lydia Sigourney, poet and writer.

TOP ROW: Johnny Appleseed. From rare print owned by Allen County-Fort Wayne Historical Society, Fort Wayne, Ind.; Governor Burnett. He died early in eighteenth century, possessed of a set of "gowff clubbes and 4 doz. gowff balles"; silhouette of John Randolph of Roanoke "silver-fluted voice of the halls of Congress." BOTTOM: Harriet Farley, a girl from the mills of Lowell, Mass., who started a literary career by writing for the first employee house organ; the *Lowell Offering*; Brigham Young, the greatest Mormon of them all; Sarah J. Hale, editor of the *Ladies' Magazine* and *Godey's Lady's Book*; Charlotte Cushman, queen of the U.S. stage 1830s to 1850s; Laura Bridgman, born at Hanover, N.H., 1829, lost her sight and hearing at the age of two.

TOP RIGHT: Elizabeth Greenfield, the Black Swan. A slave girl from Mississippi, born, 1826. She made her debut March 31, 1853, at the Metropolitan Opera House in New York and took Europe by storm, creating a sensation with her voice wherever she journeyed. BOTTOM RIGHT: The marriage reception of General Tom Thumb and his wife (Mr. and Mrs. C. S. Stratton). Greeting guests from the top of a grand piano at the Metropolitan Hotel, New York City, February 10, 1863. LEFT, from top to bottom: Street criers of New York: peanut girl; mudlark or street sweeper; window-glass man; bootblack; chiffonier or ragpicker. From Ballou's *Pictorial*, 1857. Every city and town had similar street characters.

TOP ROW: William Penn, born, 1644, became a Quaker, was imprisoned, but fell heir to his father's claim on the British Crown and was granted the Swedish colony on Delaware, which he named Pennsylvania; Nathaniel Bowditch, mathematical genius, born Salem, Mass., 1773; Count Zinzendorf, born in Poland, purchased land as a refuge for Moravians. He came to America in 1741 and founded the city of Bethlehem, Pa.   SECOND ROW: Major General Sam Houston, born in Virginia, 1793. Emigrated to Texas and aided that state to achieve independence from Mexico. First president of Texas; Colonel David Crockett, born in Tennessee, 1786, died fighting for the freedom of Texas; John James Audubon, born New Orleans, 1780. BOTTOM: Simon Kenton saving the life of Daniel Boone, July 1777; drawing of a backwoodsman, 1820, by Captain Basil Hall.

TOP ROW: Outacite, King of the Cherokees, 1723; Henry Hudson; Gurdon Saltonstall, born at Haverhill, Mass., 1666, governor of Connecticut, 1707–1724; Ferdinand De Soto, who discovered the Mississippi. SECOND ROW: Increase, the father of Cotton Mather, born Dorchester, Mass., 1639; General James Oglethorpe, born c. 1688, founder of Georgia; Peter Stuyvesant, governor of New Amsterdam, 1646–1666; Black Hawk, Chief of the Sacs, 1767. THIRD ROW: Charles Carroll of Carrollton, born Annapolis, Md., 1737; Stephen Van Rensselaer, patroon of Albany, born, 1764; Daniel Webster of New Hampshire, born, 1782; Samuel Morse, artist and inventor of the telegraph, born, 1791. BOTTOM: Henry Wadsworth Longfellow; Ralph Waldo Emerson; Dolly Madison, the lady who made a president famous; Horace Greeley, born at Amherst, N.H., 1811.

CHAPTER XII

Toys

THERE is an admonition, generally misunderstood, to do with the necessity of having the faith of a child if one desires to enter the kingdom of heaven that is happiness. Toys and the faith in a Santa Claus to provide the desired toys are contributing factors to the happiness of every child.

If there be any skeptics as to the number of child-minded adults we have had in this country, a study of the files of the United States Patent Office is recommended for a complete cure. The number of, patents issued on toys alone, in any decade after 1850, compares favorably with the totality of patents issued in any decade of years in England, France, or Germany. Every toy ever made for children originated in the mind of an adult. This is not to say that the making of the toy was not born of an understanding between the mind of a child and the mind of an adult. It may well be that the making of dolls began because an adult just knew what a girl child was doing when she wrapped a stick of wood in a leaf and cradled it in her tiny arms.

Perhaps the most important fact revealed by study of American toy history is this: the world toy industry was born right here in the United States. The tin toy industry, the mechanical toy industry, the iron toy industry, the indestructible doll industry, and the scientific toy industry were either born here or else converted from a luxury custom business into staple production for all children. Many people still imagine that the cheap tin mechanical toy industry originated in Europe. It did not; that industry began here. When our ever-rising living standards made the cost of production too high for our toy jobbers, they sought other sources of supply. They submitted samples of American toys to German agents and arranged for production at fantastically low prices.

The toy business was not an all-year or year-'round sale industry. Consequently the history of toymaking reveals many firms which, if they made toys primarily, had side lines of other products and, conversely, many firms having a more or less standard line of production had a side line of toys.

One factory studied is revealed as having as its main business the production of malleable castings for harness making and carriage and wagon building. Its side line was making cast-iron toys and mechanical banks. The final phase of side-line production included painted metal art novelties—toys for grownups and cheap elegancies for everybody—bronze- and silver-plated cast-iron lamp bases and frames. To this day this firm continues to produce two mechanical toy banks, cast-iron wheel toys, and a line of cast-iron cap pistols. The production of these was begun a half century ago.

Thus far our scientific researcher in American toy history has been Louis H. Hertz. The psychology of the toy can be compressed into a few non-technical words. Any toy should be an effort to aid the child in becoming a well-integrated adult. Being a well-integrated adult means that every experience, every situation, event, and circumstance brought by life is met with courage, without fear, and with the quality of faith that characterizes childhood. Thus a toy should be instructive, educational, fun, point to cause and effect in a mechanical and scientific sense, and inculcate certain moral and ethical principles. Briefly, it should be a painless lesson imparted on the beam of pleasure, consolidated more and more with each use of the toy.

The parade of American toys begins with toys laboriously fashioned by fond mothers and fathers in the days when toy shops and toymakers were non-existent. It is fairly certain, however, that all artisans and craftsmen, once they set up shop, were called upon to make miniatures of everything as toys for children. There are small, and even tiny, pewter, silver, and iron utensils, candlesticks, pots, pans, mugs, dishes, and so on that are to be classified only as doll size. Some of these are of seventeenth-century make. Ever since we have had arkwrights and cabinetmakers they have produced miniature furniture. Milliners, hatters, and mercers made toys in the form of dolls, mirrors, combs, and costumes. Miniature drums, fifes, and horns; miniature harps, cradles, and such were made in the first half of the eighteenth century. With the dawn of the year 1750 there were toymakers in Boston, New York, Philadelphia, Baltimore, Charleston, and Lancaster.

The *New England Primer* was a "toy" book designed to teach the dreary and bitter thing that was life under the aegis of John Calvin. That children had to cut their teeth, so to speak, on pictures of the burning to death of a dissenter while his wife and seven children stood by and gave him courage is a fearful thing to contemplate. Early New England primers are among the scarcest and most valuable of toy books. These little pamphlets have been studied by bibliographers and scholars with as much eagerness as the works of Shakespeare. There is a little library of literature about them. Yet they were just moral toys.

In this volume we cannot even scratch the surface of toy books—of that delightful phase of printing and publishing known as the world of children's books. More is known about them, and more has been written and published about them, than any other toys of childhood. That great book collector and merchant, Dr. A. S. W. Rosenbach, is more famed for his catalogue of children's books than for his *Books and Bidders*. The catalogue, *Les Livres de L'Enfance,* issued by Gumuchian, an American who developed a rare-book business in Paris, was issued at a few francs and now sells for more than fifty dollars a copy. In picturing but a few children's books in this chapter, obeisance to the subject is hereby made, with the full knowledge that he who would pursue the matter further has a great amount of definitive information at his command.

The major interest of most toy collectors is not much out of line with the interests of children. They collect toys that run, toys with wheels, toys that do things or with which things can be done, toys that make a noise, toys that make music, or toys that reflect, as manikins, the age of their making. They collect mechanical toys with clockwork motive power, steam toys, electrical toys (some of which date from 1760), dolls, dressable paper dolls, toy stages and circuses, moving dioramas, mechanical banks and cap pistols, pull toys of wood and iron, and lead and tin soldiers. Not all of these toys are old. The term "antique" becomes just a little humorous when applied to them. But many men and women of means, with the spirit of childhood in their hearts, collect them and gloat over them no end. Fame of a sort is theirs, wherever they live. On occasion, fame on a national scale seeks them out and makes them the subject of an article in the *Saturday Evening Post, The New Yorker, Life, House & Garden,* or *American* magazine. Sometimes they appear in the movies. Often they are guests on radio programs. All because they have retained that precious "be as little children" spark and have collected toys.

"There goes a man with whom I would trust my life and fortune," said a hard-headed banker. "Why?" asked a colleague. "He spends all his leisure hours fixing toys, free, for the children of this town. He fixes toys as a mechanic. But he wipes away tears. He resurrects laughter. He puts new sparkle in the eyes of children. They trust him with a trust that I wish I had, as a banker, from every customer."

Not until the great significance of any kind of collecting is appreciated does the collector really begin to realize where his hobby can lead him. Like the toys of childhood it is painless education; a delightful drawing out of things long forgotten, to be long remembered. Collecting, at its peak of joy, is a means whereby the collector is forever reaching new and higher levels of understanding. "Seek not an end, for an end is a limit; seek to make progress, little by little, and soon progress is at a delightfully dizzy pace, but as safe as a church" is an observation that all toy collectors can know is a truth, extendable to infinity.

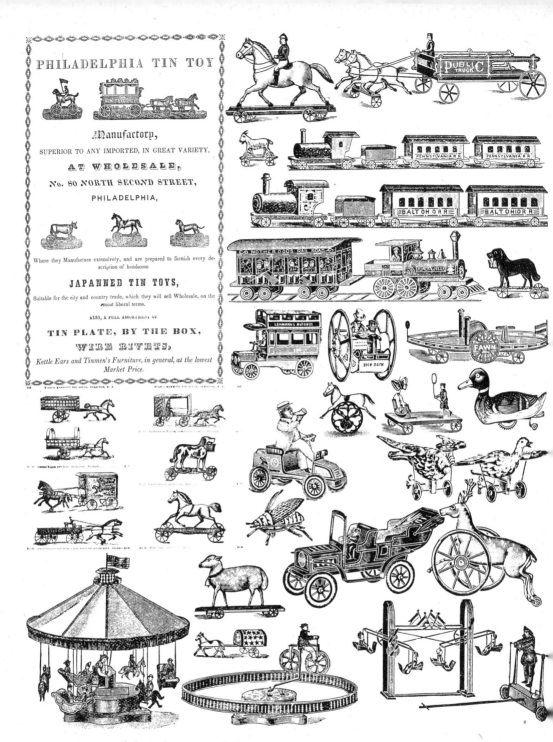

TOP LEFT: Advertisement of the Philadelphia Tin Toy Manufactory, 1848. CENTER LEFT: Pages from the catalogue of Ruben Wood, Syracuse, established 1850. BALANCE OF PAGE: Mechanical and pull-type tin toys of the sort sold from 1850 to 1900. The world tin toy industry started in the United States and moved to Europe in the 1870s because production costs increased to the point where jobbers could not sell American toys. They took samples to Europe and had replicas made at low prices. This actually started the tin toy industry in Germany.

120

Examples of the most avidly collected toys in the American scene—mechanical cast-iron banks. TOP ROW: Advertisement of the race-course bank, 1884; Santa Claus bank; lost dog bank; barrel bank. CENTER: Registering clock bank; balky-mule bank; frog bank; bucking-goat bank; mad-dog bank. BOTTOM: Hat-tipping Negro bank, imported; bulldog bank; squirrel bank; football bank; Uncle Sam bank; William Tell bank. The most definitive history of mechanical banks has been written by Louis Hertz, *Mechanical Toy Banks*, published by Mark Haber & Co., Wethersfield, Conn., 1947.

Another group of mechanical cast-iron banks, all illustrations from the catalogues of the manufacturer, except as noted. TOP ROW: Santa Claus, speaking dog, stump speaker, and Uncle Sam banks. SECOND ROW: Registering trunk, trick Pony, trick Dog, and owl banks. THIRD ROW: Banker's bank, balky-mule bank, and motor bank, which would run across the floor when coin was deposited. This picture from the patent papers dated 1889. BOTTOM ROW: Teddy and the bear bank, scarce bank-teller bank, high-hat bank, and minister-in-pulpit bank. The bank teller and minister-in-pulpit examples from the collection of William F. Ferguson.

TOP ROW: The most publicized mechanical bank and the most valuable. Manufacturer's illustration of the Harlequin and Columbine bank which has an auction record of more than $500; eagle's nest bank; kaleidoscope on stand; fountain top.   SECOND ROW: Photographic outfit, 1891; steam train of 1891 and steam train of 1889, on circular track; roller organ, 100 tunes available, 1892.   THIRD ROW: Toy sidewheel steamboat, 1891. It actually ran by steam power; Weeden upright steam engine, 1890; toy typewriter, 1891.   FOURTH ROW: Steam launch, 1891; magic lantern, 1890; historiscope panorama of thirty-two scenes, 1891.   BOTTOM: Nodding-head figures of papier-mâché, fifteen to eighteen inches high, operated by spring and clockwork, running for five hours at one winding; steam engine with walking beam, 1889.

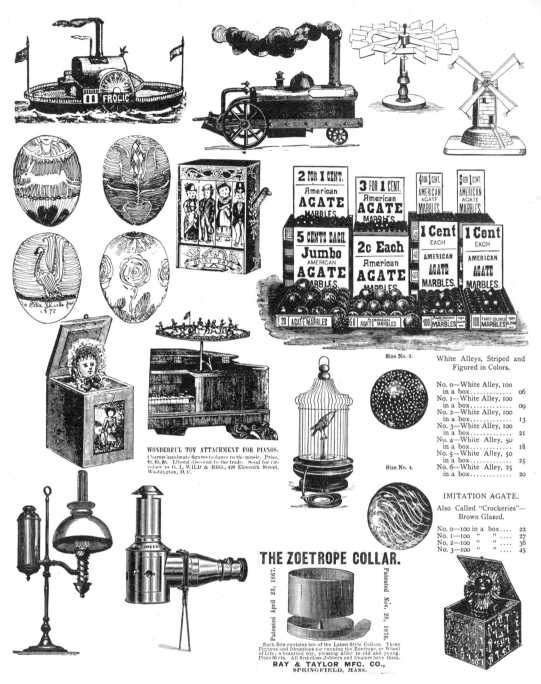

TOP ROW: Buckman's steam-driven boat, *The Frolic,* 1880s; working model of steam locomotive, 1845; electrically operated windmills, 1848. SECOND ROW: Four decorated Easter eggs, 1840s–1880s; metamorphosis box by Ruben Wood, Syracuse, 1850; glass agates and American pottery marbles of the 1880s. Note they are advertised as American-made. THIRD ROW: Jill-in-box, 1880s; automatons that danced from vibration of piano music, 1872; bird in cage. Blowing through tube caused bird to sing and flap wings, 1885; advertisements of marbles, with prices, 1885. BOTTOM ROW: Student lamp with magic-lantern attachment, 1889; Zoetrope collar box, 1877; Jack-in-box, 1870.

Full-page advertisement of the J. & E. Stevens Company, 1876. This firm of iron founders made all of the toys pictured. They seem to have entered the toy-manufacturing business about 1870 or 1871. They offered seven mechanical banks, one non-mechanical bank, two steam engines, and a cap pistol, together with doll furniture, gluepots, and mirrors.

In 1868 the Mills Company of Philadelphia offered these molds for the making of "clear toys," a transparent candy, examples of which are still offered for sale at Christmastime. While no one collects the original candies, there are many collectors of candy molds. It is refreshing to note that some American candy manufacturers are now collecting the antiques of their industry and are among the most avid searchers for items of this kind.

TOP ROW: Mechanical toys of cardboard, articulated and operated by fly-wheels that turned in a draft of warm air. Many toys of this type were homemade. Popular from the 1840s to the 1890s. SECOND ROW LEFT: Monkey organ-grinder hot-air toy, c. 1870. BALANCE OF PAGE: Papier-mâché figural toys, known as squeak toys, now collected by many enthusiasts. Pressure on the bellows yielded a squeaking imitation of a bird whistle, a dog's bark, or a cat's meow. Early squeak toys have hollow wax figures, middle period toys are of papier-mâché, and late ones are of plaster-of-Paris or similar composition.

127

CHRISTMAS TREE ORNAMENTS.

To Retail at "5 and 10" Cents Each.

FLYING WAX ANGELS.

2 F 3780—4½ in., painted features, mohair wigs, glass wings, lace trimmed skirt, trumpet. 1 doz. doz. box. ...Doz. **40c**
2 F 3781—6 in., ribbon sash, as 2F3780. 1 doz. in box. Doz. **79c**
2 F 3782—6¾ in., fine model, painted features, mohair wig, ribbon bow, white fur skirt, sash, hinged glass wings, gilt ornaments, spray and trumpet, elastic hanger, ⅓ doz. in box............ .... Doz. **$2.25**
2 F 3783—9 in., as 2F3782. 1 in box...Each, **35c**
2 F 3784—12½ in., as 2F3782. 1 in box.
                                                   Each, **75c**

Advertisement of Christmas balls, 1871, and a collection of glass Christmas-tree ornaments (including one flying wax angel), dating from the 1870s, 1880s, and 1890s.

TOP ROW: Cast-iron mirror, *c.* 1880; Noah's arks with complete equipment of animals in pairs, dating from 1825; log cabins, 1890; and pewter soldiers, 1865. CENTER GROUP: Doll furniture, most of it in cast iron, made by J. & E. Stevens, 1880s. The toy piano was imported. BOTTOM: Shell furniture, upholstered to serve as pincushions, an elegancy in the way of toys for the ladies, 1885.

THE SCHOOL IN SESSION.

Crandall's wooden toys of the 1870s, as illustrated by the Orange-Judd Company in the *American Agriculturist*. A tremendous quantity of these wooden toys was produced. They were popular because they were all adjustable and could be rearranged in various forms. They were made with interlocking parts. It is almost impossible to find complete sets of them that have survived the years.

KINDERGARTEN ALPHABET AND BUILDING BLOCKS.

THE ZOETROPE.

CHECKERED GAME OF LIFE

MODEL DIORAMA OR KRISS KRINGLES CHRISTMAS TABLEAUX.

Crandall's HEAVY ARTILLERY.

No Powder.]   FIRING THE "BIG GUN" AT HOME.   [No Smoke.

TOP ROW: Kindergarten alphabet blocks, 1880s; the Zoetrope, early motion-picture machine, sometimes called the "Wheel of Life," 1880; wooden soldiers, 1865. SECOND ROW: Toy theater with changeable scenery and motion, 1876; alphabet blocks, 1860; checker game, 1880; the Capitol at Washington, from wooden building blocks, 1890. BOTTOM: Rubber-band cannon of huge size firing rubber balls at wooden block fort and wooden soldiers. Offered as part of the Crandall collection of wooden toys, 1880.

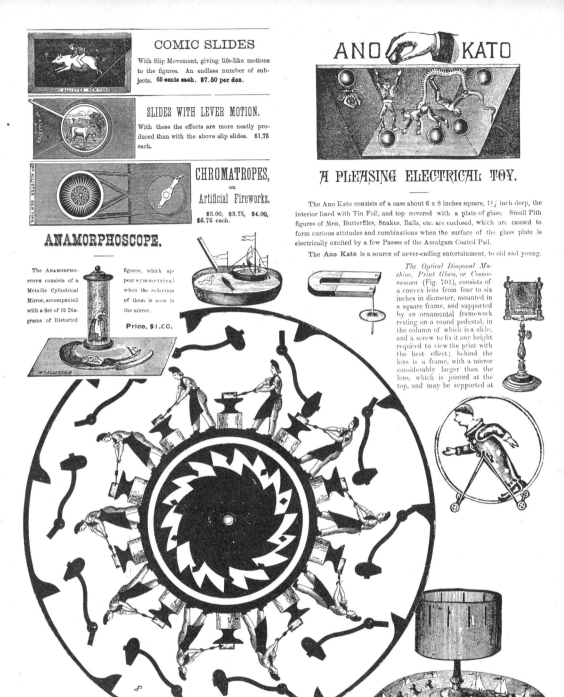

COMIC SLIDES

With Slip Movement, giving life-like motions to the figures. An endless number of subjects. 65 cents each. $7.50 per doz.

SLIDES WITH LEVER MOTION.

With these the effects are more neatly produced than with the above slip slides. $1.75 each.

CHROMATROPES,

OR

Artificial Fireworks.

$3.00, $3.75, $4.00, $5.75 each.

ANAMORPHOSCOPE.

The ANAMORPHOSCOPE consists of a Metallic Cylindrical Mirror, accompanied with a Set of 12 Diagrams of Distorted figures, which appear symmetrical when the reflection of them is seen in the mirror.

Price, $1.00.

ANO KATO

A PLEASING ELECTRICAL TOY.

The Ano Kato consists of a case about 6 x 8 inches square, 1½ inch deep, the interior lined with Tin Foil, and top covered with a plate of glass. Small Pith figures of Men, Butterflies, Snakes, Balls, etc. are enclosed, which are caused to form curious attitudes and combinations when the surface of the glass plate is electrically excited by a few Passes of the Amalgam Coated Pad.

The Ano Kato is a source of never-ending entertainment, to old and young.

The Optical Diagonal Machine, Print Glass, or Cosmoramma (Fig. 701), consists of a convex lens from four to six inches in diameter, mounted in a square frame, and supported by an ornamental framework resting on a round pedestal, in the column of which is a slide, and a screw to fix it any height required to view the print with the best effect; behind the lens is a frame, with a mirror considerably larger than the lens, which is jointed at the top, and may be supported at

TOP LEFT: Lantern slides with motion, made from 1830s to 1880s. TOP RIGHT: Electrical toy, 1870. SECOND ROW: Anamorphoscope, a cylindrical mirror which reflected a grotesque drawing and brought it into complete focus; electrical water toys; top spinning on magnet; optical viewer as described in text beside it. All dating from 1848. BOTTOM: Phenakistoscope slide. When spun in a special device and viewed in a mirror, one saw the triphammer in action; tumbling toy, 1890; Zoetrope with examples of "films," 1876.

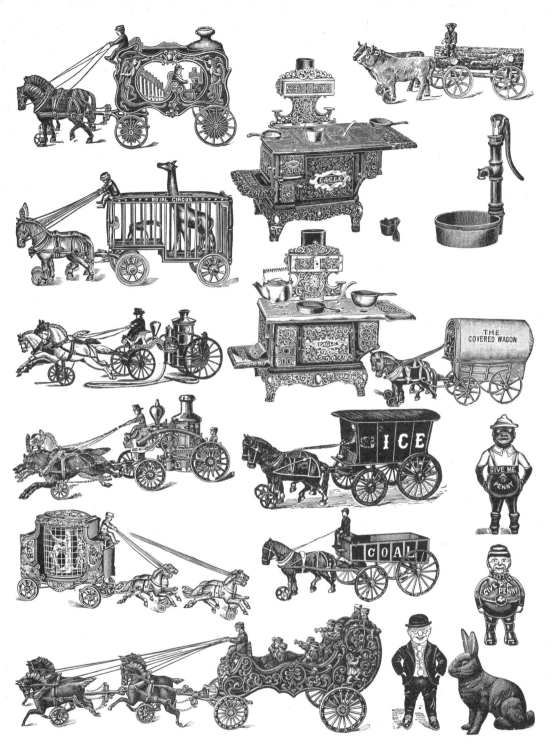

Magnificently made cast-iron pull toys by the Hubley Manufacturing Company, who offered a complete circus parade, a complete line of toy kitchen ranges, and every conceivable type of delivery wagon and wheeled vehicle, 1896–1910. Two small penny banks, Foxy Grandpa and a great big rabbit of the 1890s.

A LITTLE PRETTY
POCKET-BOOK,
INTENDED FOR THE
INSTRUCTION and AMUSEMENT
·OF·
LITTLE MASTER TOMMY,
AND
PRETTY MISS POLLY.
With Two LETTERS from
JACK the GIANT-KILLER;
AS ALSO
A BALL and PINCUSHION;
The Ufe of which will infallibly make TOMMY
a good Boy, and POLLY a good Girl.
To which is added,
A LITTLE SONG-BOOK,
BEING
A NEW ATTEMPT to teach CHILDREN
the Ufe of the Englifh Alphabet, by Way
of Diverfion.

THE FIRST WORCESTER EDITION.

PRINTED at WORCESTER, Maffachufetts,
By ISAIAH THOMAS,
And fold, Wholefale and Retail, at his Book-
Store. MDCCLXXXVII.

THE
NEW-ENGLAND
PRIMER
ENLARGED;
O, an eafy and pleafant
Guide to the Art of Reading.
Adorn'd with Cuts,

To which are added,
The Affembly of Divines,
and Mr. COTTON'S
CATECHISM, &c.

BOSTON:
Printed by E DRAPER, for B.
LARKIN, in Cornhill

THE
NEW YORK PRECEPTOR;
OR,
THIRD BOOK.

"'Tis education forms the youthful mind;
Just as the twig is bent, the tree's inclin'd."

NEW YORK:

PUBLISHED BY S. WOOD & SONS,
No. 261 Pearl-Street.

R. & G. S. WOOD, PRINTERS.

A
COLLECTION
OF
PRETTY POEMS
For the Amufement of
CHILDREN fix Feet High.
With a Series of LETTERS
FROM
Coufin SAM to Coufin SUE,

LONDON:

JANE AND ELIZA.

THE
HISTORY
OF THE
Children in the Wood.

EMBELLISHED WITH NUMEROUS COLORED
ENGRAVINGS

HARRISBURG, PA.
PRINTED AND PUBLISHED BY G B PETERS.
1840.

THE
ADVENTURES
OF A
PINCUSHION.
DESIGNED CHIEFLY
FOR THE
USE OF YOUNG LADIES.

The FIRST WORCESTER EDITION.

PRINTED at WORCESTER, Maffachufetts,
By ISAIAH THOMAS,
And fold, Wholefale and Retail, at his Book-ftore.
MDCCLXXXVIII.

A
TOY-SHOP
FOR
CHILDREN.
IN WHICH
LITTLE GIRLS AND BOYS
L FIND AMUSEMENT AND
INSTRUCTION.

PHILADELPHIA:
SHED BY JACOB JOHNSON,
o. 147. Market-street
1805.

A Milkwoman

THE
HISTORY
OF LITTLE
GOODY TWOSHOES;
OTHERWISE CALLED
Mrs. Margery Twofhoes.
WITH
The Means by which fhe acquired her Learn-
ing and Wifdom, and in Confequence
thereof her Eftate.

Set forth at large for the Benefit of thofe,
Who from a State of Rags and Care,
And having Shoes but half a Pair,
Their Fortune and their Fame would fix,
And gallop in their Coach and Six.

See the original Manufcript in the VATICAN
at ROME, and the Cuts by MICHAEL
ANGELO; illuftrated with the Comments
of our great modern Criticks.

THE FIRST WORCESTER EDITION.

PRINTED at WORCESTER, Maffachufetts,
By ISAIAH THOMAS,
And fold, Wholefale and Retail, at his Book
Store. MDCCLXXXVII.

Exemplary title pages and frontispieces from one of the most engaging items in all American literature—children's books. Every one of the items here pictured is today Americana of considerable value. There are hundreds of collectors of children's books who would be delighted to find examples such as these within a week of searching for such treasures. Several volumes, including Dr. A. S. W. Rosenbach's *Children's Books,* are in print, devoted exclusively to books for the amusement and education of children.

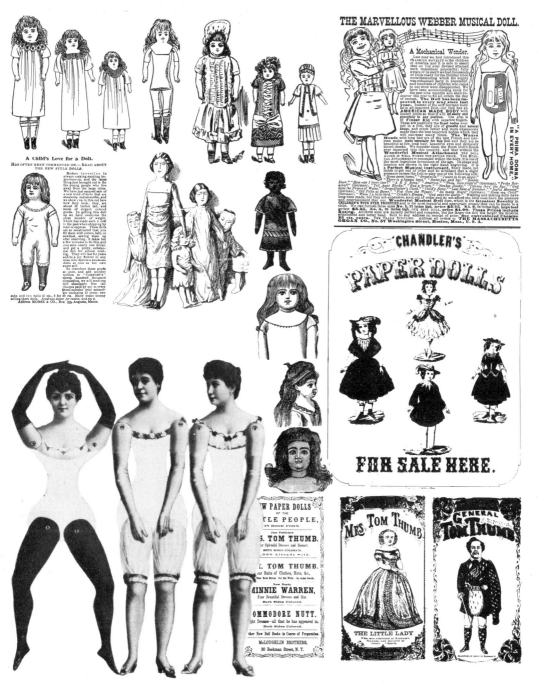

Dolls by mass production from 1850 to 1890. TOP: Advertisements and illustrations of unique, common, indestructible, and washable dolls. The Webber Musical Doll was all American, with kid body, made by the Massachusetts Organ Company, and played twenty different tunes. Pictured also are doll heads of the 1880s and 1890s. BOTTOM: Character paper dolls of famed actresses of the 1880s: Ada Rehan, Rose Coughlin, and Fanny Davenport; advertising poster of Chandler's Paper Dolls, 1850s; envelopes of paper dolls featuring Tom Thumb and his tiny wife, 1860s.

CHAPTER XIII

Masterpieces by Nobodies

D URING the two centuries embraced within the years 1660 and 1859 the fate, and the face, of the world changed considerably. The pioneers of our colonial and federal eras had more than a little to do with making world history because they were primarily concerned with bettering their own circumstances and conditions. In this pursuit it is quite logical, and in character, that they turned their minds to a consideration of what, for want of better words, we call the art of drawing and painting. In early days our pioneers called these things graphice, limning, and counterfeiting. In later days they just called them art.

A great deal of the history of American art, in its real and imaginary facets, has already been told from both biased and unbiased viewpoints. Apparently both have their place in that fantastic world of words that is art appreciation. One suspects that professional art appreciation is merely a form of sales promotion. A painting requiring 35,000 laudatory words of explanation must be worth $35,000, and so on. American art and artists, as a subject, engaged the interest of William Dunlap in the 1820s and 1830s. His *History of the Rise and Progress of the Art of Design in the United States* is the foundation stone upon which many present-day writers on art base their essays. They may agree or disagree with Dunlap, but they begin with him. Many others have written about American art since Dunlap's day. Most of the writing is about portraits and landscapes which are already famous and perhaps enshrined either in museum collections or held privately, without a chance of their being offered for sale. Except to those who are not concerned with art ownership, this is a bit frustrating. Any historic study dealing with objects is more fun if one is able to own certain of the objects. That is why, in this chapter, we shall not deal with or picture art by known painters.

Down through the years since 1660 our country enjoyed a noble company of very good painters, some of whom were trained, or self-taught, right here on our own soil. Others came as pioneers from Sweden, Switzerland, France, the Netherlands, England, Italy, and Spain. Also, we enjoyed a vast company of fair painters and a horde of amateur practitioners, some of whom were atrociously crude workmen. Occasionally a good painter painted a poor piece and, even more rarely, a poor workman produced a good picture. But we have only a few poor pictures painted by professionals because there were not many professionals of name fame. Inversely, we have fallen heir to a quantity of good work which is the result of a flash of genius or inspiration from the brush of a poor painter, simply because we had so many poor to fair amateur and professional artists.

About half of the really good paintings done before 1750 are unsigned. The painting of Madame Freak and her baby, done in 1674, is considered by many to be the finest portrait painted in the seventeenth century. The limner's name is unknown. Many artists at work up to 1750 are not known by name but as "painters of" this or that portrait. This is not very satisfactory as artists' history but we have the paintings and *they* are the one thing really important as history.

Therefore the group of pictures—portrait, landscape, and genre—selected for this exposition of masterpieces by nobodies is precisely what the title implies—paintings by unknowns. We need not attempt to construct imaginary lives for these unknown painters. They were either commissioned to paint what they painted, or they painted for the fun, or the hell, of it. When a pioneer had enough money in his sock to make manifestation of his progress a concrete thing, he turned, among other things, to having his own and his family's portraits painted. That he also had a better house built, wanted a better coach, cloths on his floors, real silver and china instead of redware, stoneware, and pewter, is nothing but the history of a pioneer making progress. We can well imagine an arkwright fashioning a sailing ship for himself and putting that ship in trade or in fishing. The arkwrights, a company of plain artisans, started our shipbuilding industry. They were pioneers not only in their own creative efforts but in buying the creative efforts of other pioneers.

Progress does things to people. Progress is a stimulant. Any stimulant causes a response of some kind. The response is always conditioned by the state of mind, or mental quality, of the individual experiencing the stimulation. We can be quite sure that progress affected some pioneers to the point of their becoming snobs or, if you prefer, beggars on horseback. We need only go to critics such as Basil Hall or Mrs. Anthony Trollope to know that some of our best people had atrocious personal habits. At least they were atrocious to those born and bred within the genteel, snobbish, and conforming upper middle class on the fringe of the noble circle of England. Unfortunately, most of our severest critics didn't know that what they thought was atrocious taste among our pioneers who had made good was a form of devil-may-care and do-as-you-please similar to that practiced by the sporting barons and other nobles of England. The nobleman had license by inheritance. Over here the pioneers could display everything with the simple crest of their own head and arms, and say, "By These I Got All I Have." In fact, one blacksmith in Philadelphia who waxed wealthy had an artist paint a pair of strong arms with just such a motto on his coach panels. This almost shocked the monocle off the eye of an English actor when he first saw it. It was preposterous to him; but it should be understandable to us, even today.

After our Revolution, as one of the thousand-and-one facets of liberty and freedom made fact, as a people we began to emulate, imitate, and compete on a great scale. In spite of this absolute proof that we knew all men were not created equal (for among equals, who can emulate whom?), we had the good sense to make all men equal under the law. The vagabond who broke a window and the senator who broke a window were equals under law; it was up to them to make good the damage. Also, if the vagabond applied himself diligently to study and practice, he, too, might become a senator. We had lives that were masterpieces by somebodies starting as nobodies.

At New Brunswick, New Jersey, in 1787, William Lawson and Jacob Dunham printed *The School of Wisdom or Repository of the Most Valuable Curiosities of the Arts*. This was an instructor in many crafts and in drawing and painting. That it was a pioneering effort is quite obvious. It started the publication of a chain of art, painting, and drawing instruction books that motivated children, grownups, and grandparents to drawing and painting in every village, on every farm and in every town.

In 1812 Paul Svinin, a Russian diplomat, looked at what art and painting instruction was doing to the people of the United States. He predicted that we would become a nation of artists. With perhaps a quarter of the nation's people dabbling in oil, crayon, and water-color expression; with clockmakers, snuff makers, silversmiths, harness makers, coach painters, and coppersmiths becoming professional artists, it is no wonder that we adapted art as a part of industry and concerned ourselves with art in everything. Not by accident did we become the world's leading exponents of art in advertising. We pioneered in it. Instead of reducing art to a "folk" status we raised our people to a new level of art appreciation.

The only so-called "folk art" we had in this country was the expression of continental Europeans who just couldn't escape its influence until they caught the pioneering spirit. Some of these, immigrants from the Palatine, were so close to serfdom that even the great Republican, Franklin, called them "boors." Most of them made an X mark as their signature on the entry rolls, and thus the poor devils did not even enjoy their own European names when settling here. They were named by an official when they made their marks; the name was what their foreign tongues uttered, set down phonetically in English. These people usually became laborers, but among them, as leaders, were some educated ministers, doctors, clerks, teachers, and artisans. One clerk, Henry William Stiegel, was fired with laudable ambition. He became a pioneer in glassmaking.

Apparently there is a fine line, drawn by some cosmic power, beyond which even the pioneering spirit may not go if it wants to avoid failure. Stiegel did not observe the line. It would seem that unselfish selfishness, or self-love that includes a similar love of one's neighbors, is the simple key to pioneering and all other kinds of progress. When selfishness ceases to be unselfish and when self-love no longer includes one's fellow man, then comes failure—failure that may be cataclysmic if enough people are actors in the scene and are influenced by the other actors.

Painting is an unselfishly selfish art. No matter how selfish the painter may be, he cannot express himself without leaving pictures as the result of his efforts. The only complete failures in this category of creative expression are the mad men who paint pictures only to destroy them. Thus they achieve self-destruction, and their self-centered love turns to ashes. They have left nothing to remind us of them.

But here we have Masterpieces by Nobodies—all American, at least as far as we know. Nearly every picture here reproduced is unsigned. The few that are signed, or attributed, involve names which mean nothing and therefore earn for the painter the honest attribution of "nobody." Some of these pictures cannot be bought for love or money; some are insured for tremendous sums. Others are in galleries and shops waiting for new owners. Most of them are recent finds which have come to light since the second decade of this twentieth century which marked the resurgence of interest in such paintings. Most of them came from garrets, attics, dark closets, cellars, and outhouses where they had been stored. But some had been cherished by a family, or a succession of owners, since the day of their painting. There are examples of portraits in oil, in crayon, and in tinted pencil drawing. Some of the small portraits were painted by itinerants for as little as fifty cents each.

The story of pioneering in cheap portrait painting is another of the amazing yet quaint manifestations of the pioneering spirit at work. Itinerants with some little talent, wanting to see the country and having a fancy to make progress in art, set out on tours that were literally peddling expeditions. They would visit a village or town, stopping at farmhouses and crossroad settlements en route, often on foot, sometimes on horseback or in little carts, selling the one thing they had—ability to paint a likeness. Sometimes they sold that service for cash, sometimes for a good meal, a night's lodging, or a bushel of apples, wheat, or potatoes. If they took produce, they peddled it as they went along. If they painted a tinsmith or clockmaker, a hatter or a saddler at his work, they probably had a clock, some belt leather, a string of tinware, or a hat for their pay. This was salable stuff somewhere, and sell it they did.

Portraits in oil were sold in this way—portraits of all types and conditions. Some of the masterpieces are pictured in these pages. Hundreds of thousands of them were painted—by nobodies. These itinerants are, of course, to be classed as professionals. No matter how many of them were at work, they were a small company indeed compared to the amateurs who also painted and painted and painted. These amateurs painted anything; they were unafraid to tackle a portrait, a battle scene, or the blacksmith's shop. They painted cemeteries, churches, schoolhouses, canal scenes, river scenes, ponds, farmhouses, barns, and animals. Some of their imaginary landscapes are wilder than the work of present-day screwballs in the world of fine art. They painted on discarded coach panels, on baking boards, on tin and sheet iron, on window shades, bed ticking, cardboard, and paper. They painted floor carpets, lodge aprons, fire engines, banners, and pictures.

If only half of what they painted can be discovered we shall have an enormous lot of painting from which to select our own choice of Masterpieces by Nobodies. One thing is quite sure. The vast volume of work enjoyed by the restorers of paintings during the past twenty years has included the restoration of thousands of examples of pioneer art which, half a century ago, would have caused a pitying smile to play over the face of an art expert. Now the experts are buying the paintings!

There are several notable collections of what with propriety could be called American pioneer art. One of these collections is already the property of a noted museum; the other is privately owned but scheduled for extension in a book illustrating every example. Pending publication of that work it is not out of order to state that the collection embraces paintings from almost every state in the Union, thus proving that pioneer art was not peculiar to the colonies, or to the thirteen original states. In fact, pioneer art marched westward with the pioneers who settled every new state and territory; it resided in all established settlements, whether two hundrd years old or two years old. We have Spanish, French, Norwegian, Swedish, Italian, and other pioneer expressions in art because pioneers from these several countries attempted to paint and did paint the American scene.

Many descendants of original owners of the simple art we can call pioneer have fallen heir to some paintings. These may be portraits, landscapes, or storytelling genre subjects, allegories, or just conversation pieces. It should be good news to all owners of these once little-considered pictures that all of them have some value today and that some of them might have considerable value. The time has passed when, to be of value, an American painting had to depict a hero, a battle, or display the flag or the screaming eagle. Now any subject is deemed worthy of consideration and, if it displays good painting, or rich and rare quaintness, the consideration can best be expressed by the sum a collector is willing to pay for it.

TOP LEFT: Connecticut landscape, artist unknown. Date is *c.* 1825–1840. This pioneering effort at art has certain of the qualities of a landscape by Breughel. TOP RIGHT: American portrait, unsigned, painted *c.* 1750. Shown courtesy Miss Elizabeth Howard, Boston. BOTTOM: New Jersey White House, the residence of Dr. Ward at East Orange. Painted about 1850. This is one of the most delightful efforts at pioneer art discovered in the past ten years. From Albert Duveen.

TOP LEFT: Virginia fox hunt. Oil painting by an unknown artist of the pre-Revolutionary era. Courtesy of Dr. Wyndham B. Blanton and Mr. and Mrs. E. W. Garbisch. TOP RIGHT: Portrait of Henry Gibbs of Boston, 1670, artist unknown. Courtesy Mrs. Alexander Quarrier Smith and Worcester Art Museum. CENTER: Swedish wall hangings, *c.* 1640, from an early Swedish church in what is now Pennsylvania. Collection of the late George Horace Lorimer. BOTTOM LEFT: The swan pool at Lititz, Lancaster County, Pa., *c.* 1770. A very similar painting is displayed at Williamsburg but labeled "View on the Schuylkill." From Joe Kindig, Jr. BOTTOM RIGHT: Portrait of Johan Kelpius, the mystic of Germantown, Pa. Artist unknown. Early eighteenth century. The clock on the wall appears to be signed by Dr. Christopher Witt.

A QUILTING PARTY IN WESTERN VIRGINIA.

Shining example of how unknown artists got inspiration for pictures. TOP: Woodcut titled "A Quilting Party in Western Virginia," which appeared in Gleason's *Pictorial Drawing Room Companion*, October 21, 1854. BOTTOM: An oil painting of precisely the same scene, but more crudely done. This picture is now one of the prized possessions of the Museum of Modern Art, N.Y., the gift of John D. Rockefeller, Jr. It is described as an oil painting on wood panel, 13¼ × 25¼ inches. The artist, whoever he may have been, made a most engaging copy of a delightful scene pictured in a weekly magazine. Thousands of other American genre or storytelling pictures were painted by the same technique of copying from woodcuts.

American pioneer art of unusual character. TOP LEFT: Hudson River portrait, late seventeenth or early eighteenth century. The lady is attired in a crewelwork gown. From Albert Duveen. TOP RIGHT: Lady at piano, *c.* 1810, from Albert Duveen. BOTTOM LEFT: "Connecticut Landscape," dated April 1853. This is one of the few nudes painted by an American artist prior to the advent of the "high academic tradition" in the 1870s. From Rockwell Gardiner. BOTTOM RIGHT: Pen painting of Lady Washington and His Excellency, the General. Crude, naïve, and perfectly delightful. The date is *c.* 1790. From Arthur Sussel. All of these examples are unsigned as to artist. The first three mentioned are done in oil on canvas. The pen picture is on paper in water colors.

TOP LEFT: The Domino girl, an American painting in the Dutch style. In 1948, a portrait in similar technique of a young boy was discovered by a Boston art dealer. Both are 18th century. TOP RIGHT: Gamaliel Painter (1742–1819), one of the founders of Middlebury College. Oil portrait, unsigned. Shown courtesy Middlebury College, Middlebury, Vt. CENTER RIGHT: Margaret Gibbs at the age of seven, painted, 1670. Shown courtesy Mrs. Alexander Quarrier Smith. BOTTOM LEFT: Silhouette portrait of George Washington, by Folwell. BOTTOM RIGHT: Oil painting of the bombardment of Charles Town and of the attack on Bunker Hill, June 17, 1775. This painting is a copy of the engraving by Lodge, appearing in Barnard's *Authentic History of England*.

TOP RIGHT: Decorative painting attributed to Sylvester Genin. TOP LEFT: Sebastian Algaier of Reading, Pa.—an amateur water color of excellent quality. The date is *c.* 1810. Shown courtesy Mrs. William Albright. BOTTOM LEFT: Salt Lake City railroad station with Mormon symbol of eagle carrying off lamb. The date is uncertain, the artist unknown. Probably a copy of an engraving which appeared in 1876, with additions by whim of the artist. The date 1876 appears on the tender of the locomotive. From Harry Stone Gallery. BOTTOM RIGHT: Sylvester Genin, a neurotic unfortunate who had art ambitions greater than his capacity, but who painted, and painted, and painted, at St. Clairsville, Ohio, in the first half of the nineteenth century.

CHAPTER XIV

Relics of Fire Protection

A T FIRST GLANCE it would seem that relics of fire fighting and fire protection would offer but few opportunities and therefore little encouragement to the average collector of antiques. It is necessary to study the history of fire fighting only a short while to discover that the subject has intrigued the interest of scores of historians, and that prints and pictures of fires are among the most energetically and enthusiastically collected items of specialized Americana interest. Currier & Ives issued a series of prints titled "Life of a Fireman." A Philadelphia lithographer issued prints of firemen, as did practically all of the other lithographers of note mentioned in Harry T. Peters's *America on Stone*. Those who did not memorialize fire fighters issued prints of fires. Our ancestors' thrill in building great buildings was perhaps equaled only by their interest, morbid or otherwise, in great destructions. The burning of steamboats, the destroying holocausts that wiped out regions and districts of towns and cities or destroyed great buildings, was not confined as an event of interest to the areas of destruction. Pictures of the event were salable everywhere.

Of course the biggest blaze we ever had was the Chicago fire. However, books about great American fires were published long before Mrs. O'Leary's cow upset a kerosene lantern and started the blaze that put Chicago on the front page of every newspaper in America. From these books we learn that Boston, Philadelphia, Baltimore, Charleston, and many other cities could boast of having fires that were fires. Books, prints, pictures, paintings, and pamphlets about fires, songs about fires—all these are to be found in some profusion, some of them priced as high as a Queen Anne lowboy. But these are merely the iconography of fires and fire fighting. There are other relics. Of course if one has huge space available and a well-filled purse, it is still possible to buy old hose carts, hand pumpers, and even steam pumper fire engines. One enthusiastic collector is seeking one hundred feet of old fire hose—leather hose—of the sort used in the eighteenth century.

The most exclusive fire-fighting relic is a fire company captain's ceremonial trumpet of silver, suitably engraved, and with the touch-mark of an American silversmith. Regularly used trumpets—and every fire company chief had one of these through which he shouted orders and directions—are now scarce, if not rare, items. Leather fire buckets are in many antique collections. Perhaps at one time there were a quarter of a million or more of them in use. Where are they today? Some that survived the years are now doing duty as wine buckets, scrap baskets, and lamp bases. Many are closely held in private collections and museums. Fire buckets were usually painted with the name and insignia of the company, sometimes with the name of the town or city, and with the date of organization of the company. Certain of the dates seem surprising. The Sun, 1711; the Globe, 1723; the Friendship, 1735; the Royal Mary, 1697; the Washington, 1788, and so on. Many people fondly believe that firemen formed lines to pass these buckets, filled with water, to a final expert who tossed the water at a blaze. Others imagine that a phalanx of firemen approached a blaze, full buckets in hand, and in unison tossed gallons of water at the fire.

Actually, these buckets were used to pass water from hand to hand, not in just one but in as many as twenty lines, from a source of supply such as a cistern or pond, to the fire engine. The fire engine had wells from which the hand-operated pump sucked the bucket-fetched water and forced it at the maximum possible pressure through a hose, the nozzle of which was directed at the fire. Earliest fire engines did not have a hose line. On top of the pump was mounted a gunlike nozzle that could be swiveled around and elevated or depressed. This was aimed at the fire. It is no wonder we had thousands upon thousands of fire buckets in use. The leather ones are the most desirable and, it must be admitted, often the fine leather buckets were only ceremonial pieces, the actual buckets in use being collapsible canvas or sailcloth containers stenciled or painted only with name and number of the fire company.

Firemen's helmets, badges, and other insignia are collectors' items within the fire-fighting scene. One of the most intriguing items that derived from the fireman's great pride in his company and equipment seems never to have been mentioned as an antique of note. Reference is made to the painted panels of fire engines and hose carts. Often these were painted by artists who later became famous as portrait or scenic painters.

The gallery of fire-engine art includes scenes, portraits, symbolic and allegoric, genre and historic subjects. For example, the man who did much to start the Revolution on its successful way was memorialized in a pair of portraits painted for a fire engine. This man, Captain Mugford, did more to help Washington's progress in the first six months of his generalship than all of Washington's staff, plus the Continental Congress, Paul Revere, and all the rest. Washington, in New England, was in sore need of powder. He had perhaps five musket charges per man in store. Powder, powder, powder—that was his need. Captain Mugford said he would get some. It didn't matter how; he'd get it. All he wanted was a bit of paper authorizing him to get powder by any means. With that paper Mugford put to sea from New Bedford. Lying in wait for the supply ship destined for the British Army in Boston, Mugford simply hijacked the King's vessel and its rich store of powder. He sailed home with powder, shot, cannon, fuses, leather stockings, and other war matériel. Just to prove that his first venture was not a fluke, he did the same thing over again. Sheer piracy, of course. But didn't he have a paper saying it was right to get the powder? That was his insurance against hanging for piracy if he and his crew lost their battle and were taken prisoners. There is, as one would expect, a fine print memorializing Captain Mugford and his exploits. But that print is not a fire-fighting relic. A fire-engine panel of Mugford Company ⚶1 of New Bedford *is* a fire-fighting relic.

Pictures for fire engines were either painted on wood panels or on panels of cast metal. It may well be that certain of the genre paintings on wood panels, now magnificently framed in collections of pioneer art, were once fire-engine panels. There may be some portraits from the same sources. The Mugford engine panels were purchased almost at once by a famed fire-insurance company collection and a collector of American pioneer art. They are twins in size, shape, color, and subject; replicas of the physiognomy of Captain Mugford, of whom it has been said: "His face and his name coincide."

Models of fire engines dating from *c.* 1750 and models of hose carts and other fire-fighting apparatus from about the same period and made as late as the 1890s were often produced by day-and-night shifts of firemen on duty at a firehouse. These toys were often made to exact scale and were a means whereby the firemen relieved the tedium of stand-by duty. As far as collectors are concerned, such activity produced engagingly delightful relics which might not have been made had the firemen played fip-loo or poker instead of indulging in model building.

The city of Philadelphia has contributed several thousand delightful relics of fire fighting in the form of cast-iron firemarks. These plaques of cast iron were issued by insurance companies who maintained their own fire-fighting equipment. All the insurance companies answered every fire alarm. Only those who found the fire in a structure bearing their mark fought the fire. So firmly planted is the tradition of preserving things as they were in Philadelphia that many old houses still carry their original firemarks.

With just so much of the fire-fighting story to launch our display of pictures it should be obvious that the subject itself has not been included in this volume as a space filler. It should also be interesting to students of automobile history that while Latta's steam fire engine of 1856 was considered one of the wonders of the age, only two years elapsed before another steam fire engine, self-propelled, was built by Lee & Larned for the city of New York. This machine was an automobile and is credited with being the first self-propelled fire engine ever produced in our country.

TOP ROW: Merrick & Agnew's fire-engine manufactory, Philadelphia, 1828; hand-pumper fire engine, 1740; using hand pumper in putting out a fire, 1840. SECOND ROW: Fire extinguishers in cart, 1836; Columbia hand pumper, 1853; Baltimore hand pumper, 1853. THIRD ROW: Steel cylinder extinguishers, 1836; the Button Manufacturing Co.'s steam fire engine of 1865; "piano-style" fire engine, 1881. BOTTOM: Print by Currier & Ives "The Life of a Fireman"; (above it) a hand pumper designed for use on Southern plantations, 1850; Lee & Larned's self-propelled steam fire engine, 1858. This motorized machine was in active service in New York City and is believed to be the first self-propelled fire engine built in the United States.

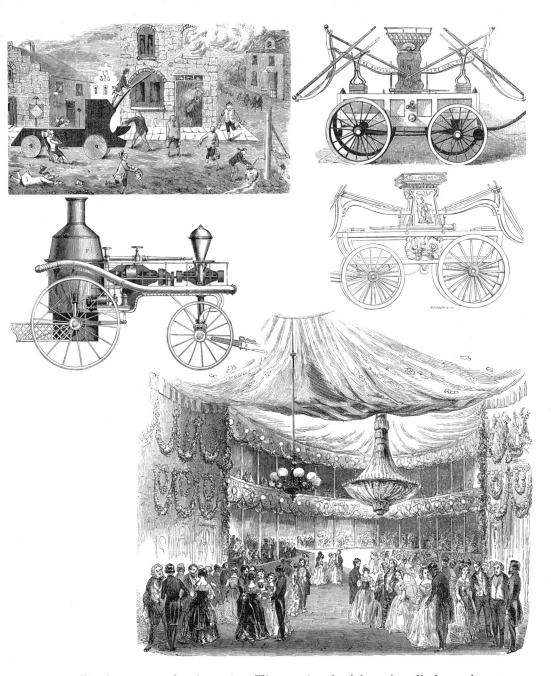

TOP: Putting out a fire in 1730. The engine had long-handled cranks at sides to work the pump. Water was poured from buckets into the trough at front end; hand-pumper engine of 1850. CENTER: Steam fire engine of 1850; the "Columbia" hand pumper, 1850. BOTTOM: New York Firemen's Ball of 1853. These balls were patronized by the wealthy society people, the merchants, and the manufacturers. Firemen sold the tickets. Who could refuse a fireman? They continue to sell tickets to balls, baseball games, and outings in the same old way, but the balls are no longer the fashionable affairs they were almost a century ago.

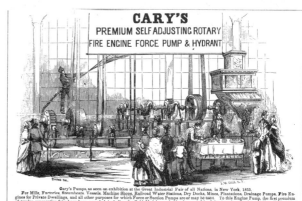

TOP: Button & Blake, fire-engine manufacturers, advertised like this in 1859; J. C. Carey demonstrating his rotary fire pump at the Crystal Palace, New York, 1853.   CENTER: Trade card of Jucket, of New Haven, advertising a hand pumper engine in 1856; ceremonial hose cart of 1854. Such equipment was generally reserved for parade use.   BOTTOM: Advertisement of Pittsburgh fire hose manufactory, 1837. They made hand-stitched leather hose; Latta's steam fire engine of 1856. The long tube hung on hooks at side could be put in a well and water sucked out for pressure pumping. This engine would throw a stream of water 100 feet.

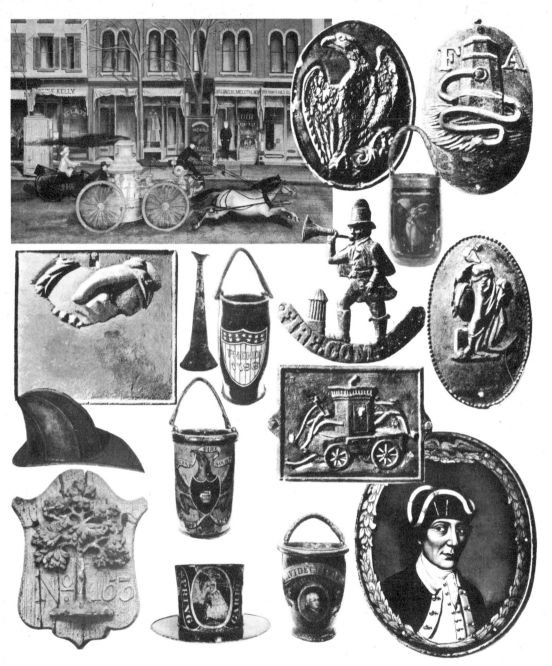

TOP: "Going to the Fire," an American pioneer painting of 1880, from Harry Stone Gallery; eagle fire marker of the Insurance Company of North America, 1796; Friendship Association fire marker, 1818; ceremonial leather fire bucket, c. 1790. CENTER: Clasped hands fire marker, Baltimore, 1794; fire trumpet, c. 1810; Phoenix Company fire bucket, 1796; fireman fire mark, Pittsburgh, 1850; oval fire mark with figure of "Hope," 1854; fireman's helmet, c. 1850; fire bucket, c. 1820; fire engine fire marker, Pittsburgh, 1834. BOTTOM: Green-tree fire marker, ceremonial hat, bucket of the Franklin Company, and a painted fire-engine panel with portrait of Captain Mugford. From the Mugford Company engine, Marblehead, Mass., c. 1840. Fire markers, buckets, helmets, and trumpet shown courtesy the H. V. Smith Museum of The Home Insurance Company, New York.

CHAPTER XV

Signs of the Times

BEN JONSON, in writing about the Sign of the Angel, an inn at Basingstoke, England, noted that it was kept by a woman named Hope who had a daughter named Prudence. Under these ladies the inn was of good repute. On a subsequent journey, Jonson stopped at the inn again only to discover that the house had changed both sign and mistresses. He composed a couplet which runs:

> When Hope and Prudence kept this house,
>   the Angel kept the door,
> Now Hope is dead, the Angel fled,
>   and Prudence turned a w———.

This choice bit of bawdy history is from a book the like of which could well be written, and should be, about the signs used by our pioneers in innkeeping, shopkeeping, road building, and manufacturing. The book is *The History of Signboards* by Larwood & Hotten, dealing entirely with the signboards of Old England. Our own history of signboards could be just as juicy, as bawdy, as hilarious, fearful, and significant as that of England. Here, too, plots of all sorts were hatched, editorials written, pieces composed, and scandals perpetrated in inns and shops. We, too, had our quota of holdups, piracies, and crimes hatched in taverns and coffee houses.

Since the first known newspapers in the colonies appeared in Boston in 1690, New York in 1725, Philadelphia in 1719, we cannot find any printed advertising or intelligence of earlier date. Instead, we must turn to commentaries, published or in manuscript, to letters, deeds, and other documents of record. We know, however, that seventeenth-century advertising of tradesmen and artisans, innkeepers, and professions was a matter of signs and signboards placed before the house. This was the traditional way of advertising one's business and service. Also, it provided the first means of locating other houses. "Catty-cornered from the Sign of the Glove" or "Opposite the Sign of the Mortar and Pestle" were quite common forms of direction. Practically every artisan advertised with a sign, but not always was it a painted signboard. Often—and this remained true up to at least 1860 —the sign was an effigy or symbol affixed or hung at or by the door. A large glove, goblet, garter, spinning wheel, chair, pan, pot, or other suggestive object was used to designate that makers of such things kept shop at that place.

As we progressed in trade, more and more signs appeared. Of record there were candlesticks, coffeepots, chocolate pots, ships, mechanical men, hammers and anvils, jugs, dishes, cups and saucers, clocks, watches, reels, chairs, bureaus, guns and pistols, statues of various kinds, animals, sieves, bedsteads, crockery, bottles, boxes and barrels used as tradesmen's and artisans' signs. Of signboards we had so many and so varied a lot that one could reconstruct a menagerie, a historical portrait gallery, a roster of crafts, and a collection of strange and mythical things from flying angels to loping geese on gridirons.

Almost every pioneer artist of record once painted signboards. John Singleton Copley, if he did not paint signboards, had the happy faculty of painting artisans at work. Benjamin West, when just a lad, was encouraged by the famed gunsmith and philosopher, William Henry. Henry gave West the use of a painting room and secured for him commissions to paint signboards and portraits. West's first painting job was the execution of the portrait of a hat for the Hat Tavern. The history of American art and artists is filled with episodes of this kind. Gustavus Hesselius, the Swedish portrait painter, painted signboards and crests on carriages. Making signs was in many cases as profitable as painting portraits. Furthermore, it was good advertising for the artist. "So-and-so painted that grand new sign for Host Willing at the Spotted Cat, or the William Pitt" was more effective than confidential whispers that the artist had painted a portrait. And far more people got to see the subject. It was publicly displayed, swung to the four winds.

We should, as a practical device, include weather vanes in the category of signs. Weather vanes, or weathercocks, were signs for churches, meetinghouses, and public buildings. This was generally true in the seventeenth century and through the eighteenth century to perhaps 1750. Then ale brewers, cider makers, and important artisans, tradesmen, and craftsmen began using weather vanes of symbolic design as additional advertising. By 1825 there were weather-vane makers whose business was assuming factory-like proportions. By 1850 several of these were full-fledged factories. By that time private residences and stables, firehouses, factories, churches, courthouses, and even barns sported weather vanes.

These are the high lights of our sign parade. Every old signboard, three-dimensional effigy, replica of object, and weather vane is now a collector's item. Items exemplary of what is being collected in the category of signs are in the exhibition which follows. Among them are wooden Indians, effigies, vanes, cocks, signs by famous artists, and signs painted by unknowns. Most of the examples are pioneering advertising efforts. There is another pioneering advertising effort far too voluminous, as a chapter, to include in this book—early printed advertising. Already there is literature on this subject which, making no attempt to reflect the breadth and scope of the subject, nonetheless points unerringly to its importance and its unbelievable mass in terms of surviving examples. A few typical advertisements appear throughout this volume as a part of the pictorial parade. These, together with early illustrated catalogues of goods, are now recognized as collectors' items of as much importance as the actual subjects. They are the documents that reveal who made what, where, when, and for how much.

TOP: Two signboards painted by the famed American artist, Benjamin West, 1755–1760; the "Hat" and the "Three Crowns." Now owned by the Stevens House, Lancaster, Pennsylvania. BOTTOM: Gambrinus, patron saint of brewers, Chinese mandarin, and Indian queen effigies, made for shop signs, 1855.

TOP CENTER: Sign Factory, New York, 1848. LEFT: Cigar-store Indian, 1800; Scotchman offering mull of snuff, 1785. RIGHT: Sign of Oliver Vanderbilt, bootmaker, New York, 1788; comb sign of A. Willard, Boston, 1820. BOTTOM LEFT: Tobacconist's sign, 1865. RIGHT: Indian queen, 1865. From Kennedy & Co. CENTER: Spectacles and watch sign of William Wise, Brooklyn, N.Y., 1840; the "Grape," a huge carved wood sign dating from 1750. Collection of William Lebzelter; mortar-and-pestle sign in hollow copper, made at Waltham, Mass., 1879.

TOP ROW: Gamecock, advertising cigars, 1876; candlestick sign of Whitwell, silversmith, of Boston, 1794; fish sign, 1860; breeches maker's sign, 1788; shoemaker's sign, the "Golden Slipper," 1765; sign of the Golden Californian, Boston, 1854.   CENTER: Fur-store sign, 1771; camera sign, Cincinnati, 1854; bath-house sign, 1810; copper still sign, 1834.   BOTTOM: Signs on a Philadelphia shop, 1831; Russian Guard, tobacco sign, 1865; exterior of a sign-painting establishment, Brooklyn, N.Y., 1850.

TOP: Umbrella manufacturer's trade card, Cincinnati, 1850. Courtesy Rhea Mansfield Knittle; signs on two shops, Boston, 1849. CENTER: The Boston tea party, planned under a tavern sign; gunsmith's sign, 1770. BOTTOM: Baseball player effigy, 1880s, from photograph by Wurts Brothers. Courtesy N.Y. State Historical Association, Cooperstown, N.Y.; carved effigy gateposts, c. 1786 to 1840s; Indian queen sign by Hamilton of Philadelphia, from Kennedy & Co.; milliner's sign, from Helena Penrose. Date is c. 1870s.

How does the wind blow? Wind direction spelled weather to our ancestors. They used weather vanes wherever there was a point of vantage. Pictures, across page, from top to bottom: Eagle vane, racehorse, sulky, Peter's crowing cock, racehorse, fire engine, William Penn, Samuel Carpenter, and Caleb Pusey's vane, 1699, running horse, fire engine, angel Gabriel, steam locomotive, dog, streetcar, and grasshopper. All vanes, excepting the 1699 example, produced by fancy metalworkers of first half of nineteenth century. Some of these weather vanes were priced as high as $500. They were made of copper, covered with gold leaf.

163

CHAPTER XVI

Pottery, China, and Porcelain

IT IS no longer necessary to begin an essay on pottery, china, and
porcelain with a discourse on when it was first made, how it was
made, and to touch upon the chemistry involved. There are
enough technical and explanatory books on the subject to fill several
five-foot shelves. The making of earthenware started in the colonies
almost contemporaneously with settlement. The brick kiln at Jamestown, small though it must have been, is credited with being a center
of glassmaking, brick and tile making, and pot making. The Dutch
West India Company sent Jan van Arsdale, a potter, to New Amsterdam in 1656. There were potworks in the New England colony before
there were cabinetmakers. The Swedes on the Delaware not only
made pottery but also used the pot stone of the Indians to turn and
carve wares from soft natural rock that could be worked to shape
almost as easily as clay.

The first fruit of pioneer kilns was what is commonly called mud
pottery—redware requiring little attention in the firing. Perhaps most
of these wares were unglazed and underdone. We have nothing but
shards and fragments as relics and even these are merely assumed to
be exemplary of the very first pottery made. There is plenty of evidence, however, that pottery made in Staffordshire, in the Netherlands, and in Sweden was imported, not only by the first colonists but
in successive supply ships bringing goods, wares, and tools.

As pioneers made progress in the consolidation of their position
two kinds of pottery, redware, and stoneware were produced. Redware is bricklike in quality and made from the same kinds of clay used
in making common brick. Stoneware is hard earthenware of a quality
approximating Chinese porcelain, although it was made with thick
walls and had none of the delicacy and refinement that mark even the
ancient porcelains of the Celestial Kingdom.

When we had both stoneware and redware potteries in production, the stoneware was preferred to red clay pottery. It was less breakable, far less porous, and cost little, if any, more than redware. Importations of Dutch and English wares did not end when we had potteries of our own. Actually importing increased. We had more customers with every immigrant ship. Also, there was considerable material and social progress among the colonists. More and more of them were advancing so sturdily in estate that desire and ability to buy imported wares of all sorts were fairly general. That is why many merchants, pioneering in importing, also made progress. They became men of substance and importance because they were willing to pioneer in merchandising.

There are historical records of many attempts—some failures and some successes—in the mass production of earthenware from early in the eighteenth century down to the late decades of the nineteenth century. The wares made by the unsuccessful companies are among the most precious objects we now collect. Tucker porcelain, for example, is one of our finest antiques. Greenpoint porcelain, made by the American Porcelain Manufacturing Company, is now considered exceptionally good. It won the highest awards, over all foreign competition, at the World's Fair of 1854. Silver, copper, and Sunderland luster-wares, all imports and originally imported in huge quantities to sell at low prices, are now avidly collected by thousands of people. The same thing is true of transfer-printed Liverpool wares, especially historic pitchers and jugs. When we come to historic blue Staffordshire, we must view a kind and quality of ware that is history, that made history, and that records history.

It happened this way and in this order: first, almost every artistically talented visitor to America was impressed with our scenery and culture, our towns and cities. All of them made drawings or paintings which were carried back to England to be engraved and published. Down through the years this practice resulted in a portfolio of American views that covered most of our important places, buildings, and scenes. Next, we had a second war with England. After that war our people were in a mood to boycott all things British, in spite of the fact that our Navy had mastered the British ships and that Andrew Jackson had beaten Pakenham and his superior forces at New Orleans. We didn't like them because the British had burned our federal buildings during the war. Out of that war we achieved our national anthem.

The potters of Staffordshire looked at the market they had lost and pondered ways and means of recapturing it. They started by swallowing their national pride. This was not a hard job for them since most

British manufacturers had been opposed to the war. Staffordshire potters began picturing American scenes, American victories, American everything, on china, in sets. When this new product arrived it was accepted with open arms. In the days when this china, in all historic patterns was generally available, it was purchased by more people than the roster of those who collect it today. That we have so much of it remaining after a century and more of use is evidence of the quantity owned by many, many original purchasers.

Perhaps the ware most exalted beyond its station is the redware of Pennsylvania, the slip and sgraffito decorated ware that was first commented upon by the late Edwin Atlee Barber late in the nineteenth century. This ware, in its most ornate forms, bears tulip and heart, distelfink, fuchsia, lovebird, figural, and lily type of decoration.

Actually the first tulip pottery used in Pennsylvania was imported English Staffordshire redware. Any English potter in Pennsylvania knew the simple secret of making this ware. The traditional tulip and heart patterns had been used on it in Staffordshire from the beginning of the seventeenth century. The second tulip-decorated red pottery in Penn's colony was introduced by the Swiss. That they, as potters, chose to decorate it with Germanic script should not lead to the assumption that they could not also have decorated it in French text. The earliest continental European tulipware thus far discovered—that is, ware of common type, tulip decorated—was produced in France. Because of selfish leadership that refused to give up its hold on the people, many Pennsylvania German immigrants actually resisted absorption. They were urged to cling to their ignorance of American customs and to learn German writing and reading rather than English. In this way they were always subject to leadership that could write and speak their tongue. It is a matter of record that political candidates wanting to capture the German vote had to learn German and talk to them in that language.

Potters, iron founders, mirror makers, cabinetmakers, and other artisans in Pennsylvania were quick to sense this state of affairs and to grasp its commercial significance. The potter who lettered some script in German on a pie dish had certain sale for that pie dish among the Germans. To put a label with some Germanic text on any object made acceptance and sale almost a sure thing. Not all the Germans who came to Pennsylvania resisted absorption. Many of them became outstanding citizens, contributing much to their new land. It was largely the religious groups, the sectarians of Seventh Day

Baptist persuasion and the mystics, who resisted. These people were not important as farmers, nor did they become true colonists. To call them pioneers is a trifle ridiculous. They lived in a new land but retained their old ideas and habits.

The Mennonites and Amish, from Switzerland, also resisted absorption. But they resisted worldliness, as did the Quakers. In remaining contemporaneous with their ancestors, the Mennonites and Amish peoples have held to their old religions and have clung to the soil as a means of livelihood. In spite of their severely plain garb, they have been good customers for all kinds of colorful pottery and china, for painted furniture, and decorated tin and woodenware. They were among the first to buy the ware now called "Gaudy Dutch," claimed by some to have been made especially for the German trade in Pennsylvania. Gaudy Dutch ware isn't Dutch, it is Staffordshire. The design isn't Dutch or German, Swiss or French, but Chinese. The pattern, in its original forms, was popular in England from 1750 to about 1800. It was used by the best English potters at Chelsea, Derby, Bow, and Worcester. Then, about 1810, a revival was attempted, using the design on soft paste wares. It did not sell well in England and was "remaindered" at bargain prices to America. Here it sold very well, not only in Pennsylvania but also in New England. Another version of it was made for the Welsh trade. This also sold well in the United States and is now termed "Gaudy Welsh." Another phase of the ware is "Gaudy Ironstone." This term designates the so-called gaudy pattern applied to the somewhat heavy, tough bone china called ironstone, made in great quantities after 1830.

Our pictures for this chapter include examples of most of the wares made, imported, purchased, and used by our pioneers. Some of the pictures are of majolica made at Phoenixville, Pennsylvania, as late as 1888. Others are of elegancies made by Copeland, Spode, and Wedgwood. Still others are from potteries of various locales in the colonial and federal scene. We should remember that the pottery pictured, in almost every instance, was purchased by a pioneer in relatively the same manner in which any of us would purchase new wares. Customers went to potteries, fairs, shops, and stores and bought it as something needful, something desirable, useful, or ornamental for their homes. They didn't buy it as antique, or as a substitute for oriental porcelain, Canton, majolica, Chelsea, Tucker, or Bennington. They bought the ware because they liked it and could afford it.

TOP: Ironstone china imported from England, 1850s. Decoration is in imitation of Chinese Imari. Sometimes called "gaudy," but only by present-day antiques collectors; seventeenth-century French pottery; squirrel bottle, North Carolina pottery, c. 1830. CENTER: Three stoneware crocks with blue decoration, made 1830s–1840s; double bottle in form of two Tobeys, back to back, probably by a potter of Lambeth, England, 1830s; pottery dog from West Virginia, in imitation of Staffordshire; Staffordshire tulip pottery of seventeenth century. Courtesy Virtue & Co., London. BOTTOM: Stoneware crock dated 1838; example of so-called gaudy ware made at Hagerstown, Md., c. 1810, by Peter Bell; pottery dish with white slip decoration, c. 1750.

TOP: Tulip-ware jar from Sweden, *c.* 1750; tulip-ware plate from Switzerland, 1786; tulip-ware plate from Romania, 1790; tulip-ware pitcher from England, 1799.   SECOND ROW: Shallow Staffordshire butter boat; slipware plate from the Netherlands, 1740; reflecting oven with tulip decoration from Staffordshire, 1692.   THIRD ROW: Tulip-ware pitcher from Winterthur, Switzerland, 1686; bird and tulip jar from France, 1750; leaping stag and tulip plate, Staffordshire, 1680; tulip-decorated water jug, Switzerland, 1760; tulip dish from France, eighteenth century.   BOTTOM: Tulips, hearts, and distelfinks, all on a plate from Beauvais, France, *c.* 1660; tulip plate made at Staffordshire and dated 1704. Courtesy British Museum; tulip plate from Savoy, eighteenth century. Musée Trocadero.

169

TOP: Slipware cradle with tulip decoration. Courtesy William Rockhill Nelson Gallery, Kansas City, Mo.; Pennsylvania tulip-decorated plate, *c.* 1810. Courtesy New York Historical Society. SECOND ROW: Earthenware plate and two jars, supposed to be Pennsylvania pottery of early to mid-nineteenth century. Courtesy New York Historical Society. BOTTOM: Another leaping stag and tulip dish from Staffordshire. Courtesy William Rockhill Nelson Gallery; Pennsylvania bird dish, *c.* 1800. Courtesy Pennsylvania Museum.

TOP: Sgraffito- or scratch-decorated plate of Pennsylvania pottery, from Arthur Sussel; slip-decorated plate with tulips and three rising suns. Courtesy William Rockhill Nelson Gallery. CENTER: Sgraffito-decorated plate by Samuel Troxel, Montgomery County, Pa., 1828; red earthenware plate, decoration scratched through yellow slip, c. 1800; sgraffito-decorated plate, Pennsylvania, c. 1810. All courtesy New York Historical Society. BOTTOM: Slip-decorated plate depicting pelican feeding her young, seventeenth century. Courtesy William Rockhill Nelson Gallery; Pennsylvania slipware of Swiss type, dated 1835. Courtesy Parke-Bernet Galleries.

While not the first porcelain maker in America, Tucker of Philadelphia, in the 1830s, began the production of a semiporcelain ware that is now avidly collected. These four examples are original designs from Tucker's own pattern book, owned by the Philadelphia Museum of Art.

Historic blue Staffordshire. After the War of 1812 all America was opposed
to buying British-made goods. The potters of Staffordshire recaptured the
market by issuing dinner services bearing American historic views. Today
these are among our most energetically collected antiques.   TOP ROW: Dam
and waterworks at Philadelphia; Hadleys Falls, N.Y.; Hudson River.
SECOND ROW: Steamship *Chief Justice Marshall;* Ship *Cadmus* at anchor.
THIRD ROW: The Exchange, Baltimore; Washington and Lafayette; Baltimore Courthouse.   BOTTOM: City view and entrance of Erie Canal into
Hudson at Albany with portraits of Jefferson, Washington, Lafayette,
and Clinton; Jefferson and Lafayette; Washington and Lafayette.

Fine pottery of the seventeenth and eighteenth centuries, of the type imported by the colonists who had achieved place and position in the New World. All of this ware is from the potteries of Staffordshire, dating from 1660 to 1760. Pictured by courtesy of Virtue & Company, London, from *The Ceramic Art of Great Britain*.

TOP ROW: Pottery jug from Boscawen, N.H., 1806; stoneware water cooler from Perth Amboy Potteries, 1853. Courtesy Arthur Sussel; Staffordshire cup marked with names of owners and place, 1771; Toby jug, c. 1820. CENTER: Bloor Derby porcelain in Imari pattern; Staffordshire combed ware; porcelain swan from Cincinnati Pottery, 1840; octagon-shaped dish from Pennsylvania, dated 1794; Caughley mug, dated 1776; ale pot, eighteenth century. Imported by the thousands and used by almost every American tavern in the reigns of George I, George II, and George III. BOTTOM: Staffordshire slipware with portrait of King Charles I; Chinese porcelain rice bowl with cover, c. 1600; Staffordshire bust of Washington, c. 1799–1800.

TOP: Fruit dish by Bonnin & Morris, Philadelphia, *c.* 1770. Courtesy Philadelphia Museum; earthenware ovens. Made in various sizes, ovens of this type were used all through the eighteenth century and most of the nineteenth century. A large one is shown at colonial Williamsburg.   CENTER: English tulip-decorated posset pot, dated 1697. Collection of Mrs. Nina Fletcher Little; early Wedgwood teapot; early willow-pattern plate; crudely potted butter jars, *c.* 1660–1700; oval open edge platter, *c.* 1770; Bellarmine jug, Dutch, *c.* 1660; Derby ware jug, *c.* 1720.   BOTTOM: Majolica fish pitcher, Ohio, *c.* 1870; stoneware jug, *c.* 1690; majolica "corn" teapot, Ohio, *c.* 1870.

Mass production ware from American potteries. TOP GROUP: View of Ott & Brewer's Etruria Pottery Company of Trenton, N.J., 1860s. This firm manufactured the whiteware shown. Bottom two rows are stoneware produced by the Ft. Edward, N.Y., Stoneware Association. The stoneware is all decorated with stamped or hand-applied blue pigment.

CHAPTER XVII

Tinware, Pewter, Britannia, Sheffield, and Silver

TO SAY "everybody knows what it is" is, on occasion, just another way of saying "everybody knows what it isn't." Most certainly this is true of the ware we designate as tin and which, in almost every case, is not tin but tin-plated sheet iron. Yet tinware has a noble history. The term tinware derives from wares made of pure, or block, tin, once a metal surpassed in preciousness only by silver and gold. Rome's expeditions to Albion were expeditions to get tin and to control the tin mines of the Anglicans. Carthage knew of the tin mines of England. Rome fell heir to that knowledge when it conquered Carthage.

No finer cooking utensil is known—not even excluding those made of silver—than that made of tin. This type of utensil was the original tinware. Naturally it was expensive. The early tinsmith took no sneers from the silversmith. He made more of his wares and had about the same profit per item as the silversmith had on his transactions. So much for what real tinware is, or was. What we call tinware today includes anything of sheet iron, even though not originally plated with melted tin, and everything made of sheet iron over which a coating of tin has been poured. Due to the ductility of tin, its brilliant silvery whiteness, and its medium melting point, it could almost be "painted" on iron by the simple process of melting and pouring on hot sheets of rolled iron. The plating bonded with the iron so firmly that the plated sheets could be worked into all sorts of shapes, soldered, planished, and fashioned into everything from a Turk's-head cake pan to a punched lantern.

Within the popular designation of tinwares, which we now know are actually tin-plated sheet-iron wares, we can turn to the price books of the Master Tin Plate Workers of Philadelphia for lists of things made, and at what prices. The 1835 list includes sugar boxes with hasps and hinges at $1.00 per dozen, square spice boxes of six canisters each at fifty cents, bathtubs at $2.00 each, flour boxes at thirty-eight cents, buckets for "liquor or oil, three gallons, made strong and straps on bottom" at fifty cents, beer mugs, "two quarts with covers on lips," at $1.25 per dozen, candlesticks from fifty cents to $1.00 per dozen, two-quart "coffee boilers" at $1.12 per dozen, shaving cups with soap boxes at sixty cents per dozen, one-pound round tea canisters at forty cents a dozen, punched lanterns, middle size, at $1.20 a dozen, and two-quart tea kettles at $2.00 per dozen. We can also turn to the lavishly illustrated advertisements of tinware manufacturers, most of whom made tin-plated ware but some of whom also produced block tinware—solid wares made of the pure tin metal.

It is wise also to remember that the finest pewter was an alloy containing at least seventy parts of tin; the other metal was copper. This made "right" or true pewter. The antimony, lead, bismuth, and scant-tin combinations used in lieu of tin pewter were quite common and were designated as pewter, but in all truth they were not true pewter alloys.

The story of pewter in America has been told by Ledlie I. Laughlin in *Pewter in America* and by the late J. B. Kerfoot in *American Pewter*. The Metropolitan Museum has issued pamphlets on this ware (*American Pewterers and Their Marks*) and numerous writers have dealt with pewter, chapterwise, in scores of books on antiques. There is no necessity here to repeat what they have said and what they reveal. Most American pewter is marked with some kind of stamp hammered in by the smith when he finished the piece. Almost all of the pewter now extant was made after 1750 down to as late as 1835. "What became of the pewterers?" is a question answered by survey of two other crafts —the making of that hard, near-pewter metal known as Britannia and the trade of plumbing.

Our pioneers used tinware and pewter in amazing quantities. Pewter utensils seem to have been confined to beakers, cans, basins, bowls, plates, platters, mugs, dishes, and porringers, but in tinware the ingenuity of the smith seems to have been the only limit. It will not be necessary to list other than the above-noted tinware items because the value of the pictures to come is far greater than further words. The captions at the bottom of each page give the rest of the story.

Tablewares of all sorts graced the boards and the sideboards of our pioneers. Ivory- and bone-handled knives, forks, and spoons, carving knives, skewers, plates and dishes of precious and semi-precious metals were not the utter luxuries we may sometimes think. Many pioneer families enjoyed ownership of pure silver drinking vessels, and enjoyed that ownership from as early as 1660.

It is not within the province of this present work to tell even a part of the colonial silversmithing story in words and pictures. But the briefest of outlines should be included if only to dramatize the size of the entire story by pointing out certain of its social and economic aspects. Silver tablewares and drinking vessels in New England, while apparently anti-puritanic in essence, were prized for their money value. They were, actually, a sound way of having the precious metal, as good as coinage, and using it too. Perhaps much, if not most, of the early silver of New England was fashioned directly from silver coins —the coins of the Netherlands, Spain, Portugal, France, and England. This hard money passed current, regardless of its place of coinage, all along the American colonial coast and in those rich possessions, the West Indies and the Mexican mainland.

A great deal of the silver in these coins was American silver, wrung from the American Indians by Spanish greed. The blood didn't show on the minted coins and the silver was good metal. Spain traded it in bars and in coin for what she wanted. New Englanders got it in exchange for fish and produce, and in trade. The Dutch colony of New York had its full quota of early silversmiths and the Quakers of Penn's colony were not averse to owning silver tablewares. Fine English silver was imported by the chief residents of Virginia and Maryland before 1700, and used by the almost royal planters as the natural exhibition of their high social and economic station.

By 1789 we were importing the near-silverware known as Sheffield plate. Some of this ware was imported before the Revolution, and it may have been imported as early as 1755. Bulsover, generally credited with inventing the sandwich of two layers of silver over a sheet of copper, made his first examples in 1743. He did not, however, invent the method; he merely changed the middle slab of metal from tin to copper. Silversmiths of low degree and great cunning used the very same method that Bulsover used, but in the seventeenth century. They used tin, which could not be distinguished from silver except by experts. Sheffield plate is a term used to designate the near silver of Bulsover's formula. Plate for untold years was the term used to designate gold and silver utensils made from solid metal. The term "Sheffield plate" was used to distinguish the cheaper ware from true, or solid silver plate, now called sterling.

No effort was made to produce Sheffield plate in quantities in the colonies or our federal states. Some few attempts at making it were tried. They did not end in failure because the makers could not produce the ware. It was not a secret process at all. Our makers could not compete with the factory production of Sheffield. The dies and tools required demanded broad-scale sale in a world market in order to keep the price down. We imported huge quantities of Sheffield, chiefly in the form of tea, coffee, and sugar pots, lamps, vegetable dishes, trays, candlesticks, chalices, mugs and tankards, boxes, and salt cellars. We did not stop general importation until the mid-1840s. By that time we had invented and perfected electroplating methods which, applied to a base metal form, made it look like Sheffield, or better. In addition, we developed a large manufacture of Britannia wares, as the improved hard pewter of the 1820s was generally named. Sometimes we silver-plated the Britannia wares. Most of the large silverware manufacturing firms of the United States started from one-man silversmithing businesses after 1835. These shops first turned to specializing in spoon and fork production, then in plating, and finally became factories making entire lines of solid silver and plated wares.

Up to this time apparently no effort has been made to list the makers of plated silver tablewares and Britannia wares in our country. Silversmiths, however, are well recorded. Stephen G. C. Ensko's latest volume is a dictionary of silversmiths and their marks from 1650 to 1850. There is a great opportunity waiting for a patient and interested researcher desirous of compiling a list of Britannia ware makers. All that is required is a careful check of all city and town directories published between 1835 and 1865, a scanning of the directory advertising, and a study of the local newspapers of the same period. This will yield an amazing number of names. A few advertisements of Britannia makers are included in our illustrations for this chapter. Some of these are handsome copperplate engravings. Most of the illustrations of Sheffield plate derive from the catalogues of Love, Silverside, Derby & Company and Dixon & Sons. All of the tinware is from catalogues of American manufacturers and individual tinsmiths and dealers.

TOP ROW: Brass mold for pewter spoons, seventeenth century; pewter ladle by Palethorp, Philadelphia, 1826; pewter medicine spoon with sipper through handle, *c.* 1800; spoon mold, and spoons made from it, *c.* 1770. CENTER: Advertisement of Sellew & Company, Cincinnati, 1839; pewter plate by Meriden Britannia Company, 1852; pewter plate, *c.* 1750; pewter spoon marked "P.R.," attributed to Paul Revere; bronze spoon mold, *c.* 1750. BOTTOM: Pewter coffeepot, *c.* 1825; pewter teapot by Josiah Danforth, *c.* 1825; pewter tea caddy, late eighteenth century, probably French. All pewter wares courtesy New York Historical Society.

Advertisement of Fletcher & Gardiner, Philadelphia, 1820, and a collection
of superior Sheffield plate, a ware imported from 1790 and sold in tremendous quantities. All pictures from the original catalogues of Love, Silverside, Derby & Company, and other English makers.

Henſhaw & Hamlin,

BRAZIERS & PEWTERERS,

HEREBY inform the Public, that they have lately ſet up their Buſineſs, at the Shop of the Widow Hooker, near the North-Meeting-Houſe, in Hartford, where they make, and have for Sale, Pot Kettles, Tea-Kettles, Coffee-Pots, Quart and Point Potts Baſons, Plates, Diſhes, Platters, Porringers, &c. on the moſt reaſonable Terms, for Caſh, Country-Produce, old Pewter, Braſs, or old Copper. 33 10w

N. B. They mend all Sorts of Copper, Pewter, and Braſs Wares.

Frederick Baſſett,

MAKES and ſells all kinds of PEWTER WARE, wholeſale and retail, where Country Merchants and others may be ſupplied on as low terms as in New-York.

The Houſe in which the ſaid Baſſet now lives, with the Lot of Ground, ſituated in Weſt Street, is for ſale. Enquire as above.

Hartford, December 20, *1784.*

TOP: Advertisement by Henshaw & Hamlin, pewterers, Hartford, Conn., 1767; advertisement by Frederick Bassett, Hartford, 1784. CENTER and BOTTOM RIGHT: Block tinware and plated tinware, including toasters, sitz baths, colanders, hot-water heaters, cake pans, and coffee roasters, offered by various shopkeepers from 1825 to 1850. BOTTOM LEFT: Advertisement by Harvey Lewis, manufacturer of silver-plate and jewelry at Philadelphia, 1820.

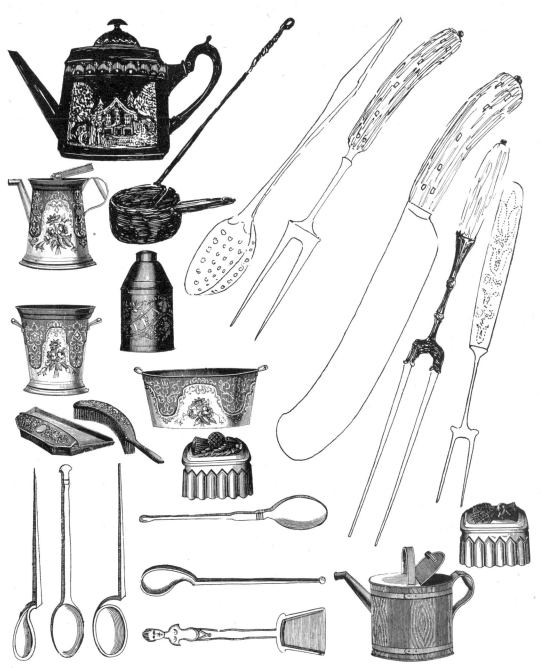

TOP LEFT: Fine painted tinware, rejoicing in the name of "Pontypool," because it was made at that place in England, c. 1790, and imported as an elegancy. CENTER, and downward to RIGHT and BOTTOM: A collection of painted tin toilet ware of the 1850s—an elaborate pudding mold; pewter pot for melting and pouring into bullet; button and spoon molds; strainer or "mote" spoon, c. 1760; pistol grip knife and fork of steel with buckhorn handles, c. 1750; Dutch and Swedish two-tined table forks, c. 1660 and 1700; tin water bucket simulating oak and walnut staves; decorative pudding mold of block tin. BOTTOM LEFT: Steps in the evolution of the spoon, from the fifteenth to seventeenth centuries, with some ideas worthy of the attention of today's silverware manufacturers.

American silver. TOP: Sugar urn by Freeman Woods of N.Y., *c.* 1790. From Robert Ensko, Inc.; tankard by Chaudron's & Rasch, Philadelphia, 1825, marked "Ster. Ameri. Man.," meaning sterling of American manufacture; Queen Anne footed creamer by Charles Hall of Lancaster, Pa., 1760. CENTER: Silver beaker by Joseph Goldwaithe, Boston, 1766-1780. From Robert Ensko, Inc.; mug by George Ridout, N.Y., *c.* 1745. From Robert Ensko, Inc. BOTTOM LEFT: Huge silver tankard by Loderwyk Heck of Lancaster, Pa., *c.* 1750. Courtesy Los Angeles County Museum. BOTTOM RIGHT: Spout cup by Allen & Edwards, Boston, 1700. Spout cups are excessively rare objects in silver. This outstanding example bears the arms of the Wadhams family and the initials "C.B.M." From Robert Ensko, Inc.

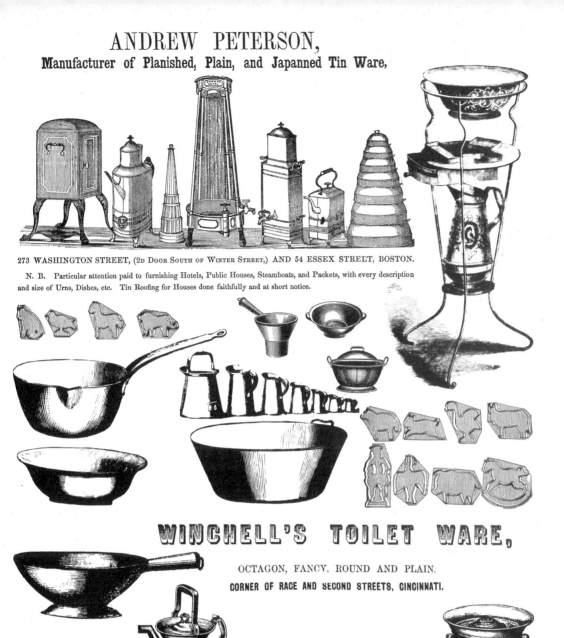

ANDREW PETERSON,

Manufacturer of Planished, Plain, and Japanned Tin Ware,

273 WASHINGTON STREET, (2D DOOR SOUTH OF WINTER STREET,) AND 54 ESSEX STREET, BOSTON.

N. B.   Particular attention paid to furnishing Hotels, Public Houses, Steamboats, and Packets, with every description and size of Urns, Dishes, etc.   Tin Roofing for Houses done faithfully and at short notice.

WINCHELL'S TOILET WARE,

OCTAGON, FANCY. ROUND AND PLAIN.

CORNER OF RACE AND SECOND STREETS, CINCINNATI.

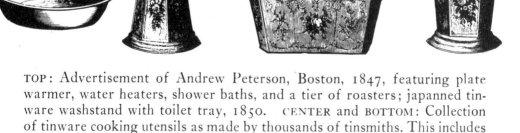

TOP: Advertisement of Andrew Peterson, Boston, 1847, featuring plate warmer, water heaters, shower baths, and a tier of roasters; japanned tinware washstand with toilet tray, 1850.   CENTER and BOTTOM: Collection of tinware cooking utensils as made by thousands of tinsmiths. This includes pots, pans, bowls, cookie cutters, and elaborately decorated toiletware, including a footbath as advertised by Winchell of Cincinnati, 1850.

GORHAM AND COMPANY

MANUFACTURING SILVERSMITHS,

12 Steeple St.

PROVIDENCE, R. I.

THE STOCK OF SILVER & SILVER-Plated GOODS AT THEIR WARE ROOM, COMPRISING NEARLY EVERY ARTICLE DESIRED FOR ORNAMENT OR UTILITY, CANNOT, FOR BEAUTY OF DESIGN, QUALITY AND WORKMANSHIP, BE SURPASSED BY ANY CITY IN THE UNION.

PLATED WARE.

A SMALL confignment of well afforted Plated ware, confifting of tea waiters, urns, tea pot, cadie, fugar and cream bafon, cheefe toafter, fruit bafket, difh ring, egg frame, toaft rack, gilt falts, fcollop fhells, difh crofs, foup ladle, branches, tankards, two ounce cannifters, cream jug, candle-fticks, &c. with a genteel affortment of plated buckles, gilt and plated buckles, received per the laft arrivals from Briftol; to be fold at a reafonable advance by the cafe, for cafh or approved notes, by
JOHN HASTIER, 78 Water-ftreet

ROGERS BROTHERS
MANUFACTURING COMPANY,
HARTFORD, CONN.
OFFICE FOR EXHIBITION OF SAMPLES AT
No. 17 Maiden Lane, - - - - - - **New-York.**

AMOS SANBORN,
MANUFACTURER OF
SILVER PLATE,
SPOONS, FORKS,
KNIVES, LADLES,
BADGES AND MEDALS,
WHOLESALE AND RETAIL.

Post Office Corner,

CENTRAL STREET, LOWELL, MASS.

Claim to be unequalled in Variety, Style and Quality of Plated Goods of their Manufacture. In their assortment may be found Tea, Coffee, Dessert, Table, Salt, Mustard, Egg and Bar Spoons—Dessert, Medium, Table, Oyster, Pickle and Beef Forks—Sugar Shovels, Tongs and Lifters—Butter, Fish, Pie, Cake, Crumb and Ice Cream Knives—Asparagus and Ice Tongs—Cream, Gravy, Oyster and Soup Ladles, &c., &c. Plated on fine Albata which is hard,

TOP: Advertisement by the famed firm of Gorham, 1852, and a collection of the sterling and plated silver they offered in that year. CENTER: Plated ware advertised in New York City, 1794. BOTTOM: Advertisement of Amos Sanborn, Lowell, Mass., 1854, and of Rogers Bros., 1856.

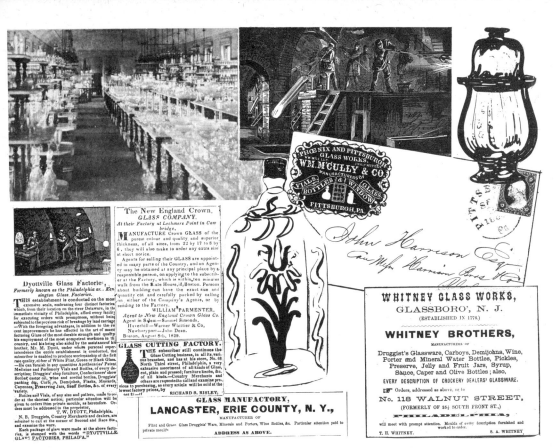

Because glassware would require a full volume to do it justice, the pioneering efforts at producing glassware in the colonies and the federal states is not made a chapter of this book. *The ABC's of Old Glass,* a volume now in preparation, will contain most of the story that should be a part of any recital of our pioneering efforts at producing glassware, both fine and common, by the offhand process and by mass production. TOP LEFT: A showroom of the New England Glass Company, Boston, 1850. TOP CENTER: Manufacturing window glass by the blown-tube method, Pittsburgh, 1850. TOP RIGHT: A sugar basin of amethyst glass blown at Pittsburgh *c.* 1820. Pictured at bottom are advertisements of the Dyottville Glass Factories, Philadelphia, the New England Crown Glass Company, the Lancaster Glass House, the Whitney Glass Works, established 1776 at Glassboro, N.J., and the glass-cutting establishment of Richard Risley, Philadelphia, 1833. Pictured also is a toilet bottle in the Swiss tradition, probably made at the Stiegel Works near Lancaster, Pa., 1769; and envelope trade card of M'Cully & Company, Pittsburgh, 1856.

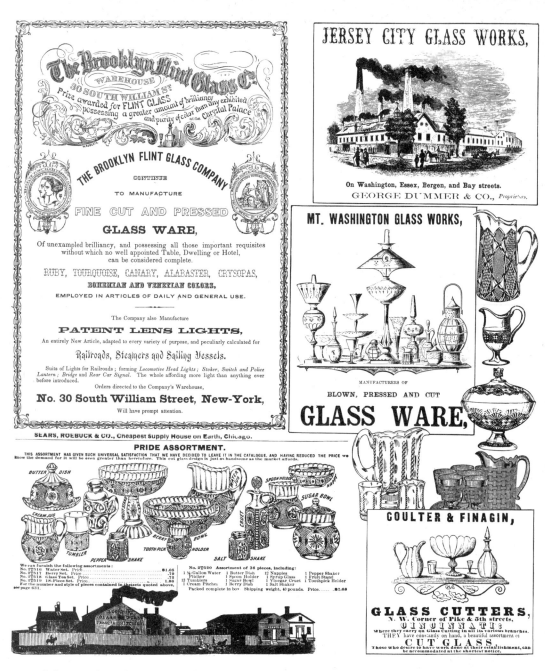

More advertisements of American glassmakers and vendors. Brooklyn Flint Glass Company advertisement, 1853; Jersey City Glass Works, 1854; Mt. Washington Glass Works, 1871; Coulter & Finagin, Cincinnati glass cutters, 1839; and a view of the Lockport, N.Y., glassworks, 1860. Glasswares illustrated are all pressed wares, dating from 1850 to 1900. Sears-Roebuck advertisement featuring pressed glasswares sold in huge quantities.

TOP: Bottle blowing on a mass-production basis, 1860; making goblets, *c.* 1855. Note the lady assistant! CENTER: Child's book on the art of glass-blowing, 1836; trade card of the American Glass Company, Boston, 1853; advertisement of Dorflinger's cut glass, 1890; blown-glass paperweight of a type avidly collected today. This example is of New England production and dates from *c.* 1850. BOTTOM: Advertisement of Nathan Sampson, who sold glass at wholesale and retail, Cincinnati, 1829; original advertisement of M'Cord & Shiner, glass cutters and engravers of Philadelphia, 1829; title page of Gleason's *Pictorial* for November 8, 1851, featuring the New England Glass Company's works at East Cambridge, Mass., in story and pictures.

CHAPTER XVIII

Flowerpots, Stands, and Garden Pieces

THAT knowledge of the care and growing of flowers, formal gardening, and the arrangement and display of flowers was a heritage enjoyed by many of our pioneers is a matter of record. Probably some of the pioneers had experience as gardeners and nurserymen. Even in the sixteenth century, in England and the Netherlands, the growing of plants, shrubs, and flowers was a business. All of our royal governors arranged for gardens around their palaces. Perhaps the Williamsburg Palace gardens were the finest in the land. But wherever there was a fine garden it was seen by people who, if they liked, could emulate it on a patch of their own land.

In the late eighteenth and early nineteenth centuries, trained fruit trees of dwarf size were advertised. In light of the fact that this elegancy of fruit culture was known in our mid-eighteenth-century gardens, it is quite likely that nurserymen grew them and sold them then. It is also certain that early potters made flowerpots and that vases for cut flowers and the forcing of Dutch bulbs were used in some eighteenth-century homes.

The great wave of floriculture that made this nation flower conscious did not break until the early years of the nineteenth century. David Landreth, who established a nursery at Philadelphia in 1784, can be characterized as our first commercial seedsman. In 1832 his firm began publication of a magnificent catalogue under the title *Floral Magazine & Botanical Repository*. This publication was embellished with lithographed color plates from drawings by American artists. Benjamin Gibbs of Boston advertised his services as a landscape gardener in the 1820s. He maintained a greenhouse for the growing of exotic and common flowering plants and for the safe storage of tender plants during the winter season.

Our first important flower prints in color appear in a drawing and painting instruction book, published in 1818 by M. Thomas of

Philadelphia. This book contains very beautiful, hand-colored aquatints of jonquils, carnations, apple blossoms, moss roses, tulips, and auriculae. In 1837 E. C. Biddle of Philadelphia published *A Drawing Book of Flowers and Fruit* by Mrs. Anne Hill, containing hand-colored lithographic plates. Currier & Ives and other lithographers issued flower prints in some variety. Mention should also be made here, even if it is reiteration, of the drawing book of flowers issued by Bishop Hopkins of Vermont. Bishop Hopkins's prints are medium folios and seem to be our first large flower prints. Dr. A. B. Strong's *American Flora,* a magazine in imitation of Dr. Thornton's *Temple of Flora,* was published in the 1840s and republished in 1850. This publication contained many prints, examples of which are pictured in this chapter.

So much for the pictorial part of our flower story. There are innumerable flower prints and a good many flower paintings still obtainable in shops dealing exclusively in this form of antiques. Many second-hand bookshops have portfolios of flower prints extracted from books not worth saving for their text. These prints, in many cases, are priced from five cents each up to five dollars. Really good American flower prints and paintings range in price from $25 upward to as much as one's pocketbook will stand.

For the collectors of flowerpots—and according to the editor of *House & Garden* this *is* a category of collecting—America, between 1825 and 1890, produced an array of pots, jardinieres, pans, and boxes for flowers the like of which no modern producer can match. Along with the pots produced or imported we had flower vases, crocus pots, bulb vases, fernery dishes, hanging baskets, and a lot of other oddities and elegancies for flower lovers. There is no need to recite what they offered. We can display here pictures of the actual objects in sufficient variety to exemplify the lines of goods our ancestors chose from the shops and stores of florists and seedsmen. Also, it should be noted, more than half of the customers for these objects didn't only buy the goods in stores and shops; they also ordered by mail from catalogues of the vendors.

Historically, flowers in the home and pioneer habits of flower arrangement are revealed by early objects made as elegancies. There are the "boughpots" and the "crocus pots" of Staffordshire, Chelsea, Worcester, and Bow, designed for the forcing of apple blossoms, forsythia, pussy willows, witch hazel, and other boughs, and to serve as delightful little gardens for the forcing and bloom of crocus and saffron bulbs. We have elegancies in this category dating from 1750.

Hyacinth vases, usually of glass, for growing hyacinth bulbs to full flower in water, seem to have come into favor about 1840. These were made in great quantities by American glassblowers and also imported from Belgian factories in considerable quantities. That many of them were once attributed to the factory of Henry William Stiegel is merely an episode in the parade of misconceptions about our own antiques. Most American-made hyacinth vases were blown at Boston, Sandwich, Philadelphia, and Pittsburgh. Some may have been produced at Baltimore. Pressed glass troughs in a variety of shapes for the assembly of centerpieces to suit the fancy of the user were made at Pittsburgh and Wheeling factories. Flower vases of glass—blown, cut, flashed, pressed, and in every other style and form of *décor* known to glassmakers—were produced in American glasshouses.

Many vases were imported from Switzerland, France, England, and the Vallerysthal works in Lorraine. Vases comparable to the famed French glass, Lalique, popularized in the 1920s as rich, rare, and modern, were imported in the 1850s. Vases were also made of Parian, majolica, mud pottery, Britannia, pewter, brass, and cast iron. The same holds true for jardinieres.

Cast-iron garden furniture in the 1870s included so many items that special catalogues of it were issued by iron founders. Fountains, statuary, chairs, benches, urns, and flower-bed fencings and edgings in a great variety of styles were offered at prices that compare favorably with the antique prices of the same objects today. The once tremendous public interest in town and city parks (sometimes called politicians' smoke screens) is today proved by the fact that almost every community in the United States has its quota of common land, landscaped and embellished with flower beds, fountains, and benches. Public interest and pride in water works, cemeteries, and the like may perhaps have been an almost unique American vagary. These spots, to our immediate ancestors, were a prideful outgrowth of the old village green or commons. They wanted the places neatly kept and properly furbished. Much of what was used to aid in this effort is now in the classification of antiques.

GREEN HOUSE—*Cambridge-Street*.
B. GIBBS'

INFORMS the Ladies and Gentlemen of this city, that he has for sale at his GREEN HOUSE, No. 99, *Cambridge-street*, a variety of *GREEN HOUSE PLANTS*, in good order, and at very moderate prices—which he will deliver to purchasers at any part of the city, free of expense.

Those who have stored Plants in his Green House, for the past season, are informed that they are just coming into bloom, and are respectfully requested to call and give their orders to have them removed as soon as convenient.

He attends to laying out Gardens, in a superior style—Sodding Lawns, Yards, and transplanting Trees, Shrubs, &c. &c. He will also take the care of Gardens in any part of the city, for the season and see that they are kept in perfect order.

Constantly on hand for sale, the best of virgin earth, for re-potting Plants.

Three pages from the *American Flora,* published by Dr. Strong in 1850. The pages here reproduced are one fourth actual size. The columbine print appeared, full size, in full color, in *House & Garden* for May 1948; advertisement by B. Gibbs of Boston, 1830, offering greenhouse plants, landscape gardening, and superior trees and shrubs.

TOP: Fern settee of bronzed cast iron, c. 1850; Victorian cast-iron settee, c. 1860. SECOND ROW: The grapevine settee. This design also made in garden chairs, c. 1840; wire plant stand and wirework chair, 1875; one of the seven dwarfs holding a huge platter, as a base for a vase of growing plants and flowers, c. 1855. THIRD ROW: The Palo Alto flower vase of cast iron, c. 1850; cast-iron garden vase, 1855. BOTTOM: Three elegant fountains, produced by the Mott Iron Works of New York from 1850. The smaller fountains were for home gardens. The large fountain was designed for public parks. Some of these are still standing and in operation, especially in the parks surrounding small-town reservoirs.

TOP: Two prints from *The Art of Flower Painting in Water Colors,* published at Philadelphia, 1818; hyacinth vase, 1875; hanging flower basket, 1870; triple hyacinth vase, 1875. SECOND ROW: Four decorative vases of glass, American and imported, *c.* 1870; pottery flower holder imitating section of tree limb, 1874; crocus hill for sprouting crocus blossoms indoors, 1870; decorative flower pot, 1865; single hyacinth vase, 1870; three fancy glass vases, 1870s. THIRD ROW: Decorative flower pot from China, *c.* 1855; four fancy glass vases, 1870s; pottery flower pot with portrait of Zachary Taylor, *c.* 1850. BOTTOM: Five decorative flower pots by American potteries, 1860s and 1870s.

TOP LEFT: One of twelve plates from America's little known but important portfolio of large-size flower prints, issued as a drawing instruction book by Bishop Hopkins of Burlington, Vt., *c.* 1848–1850. Bishop Hopkins made the drawings, transferred them to stone, and printed them with the aid of his family in the basement of his Burlington home. TOP and CENTER RIGHT: Prints from drawing instruction book, 1844. BOTTOM ROW: Fruit print and title page from Mrs. Hill's *Drawing Book,* 1844.

CHAPTER XIX

Lighting, from Betty Lamp to Electricity

SOME collectors, and many average American citizens, still have a deep-seated conviction that candles were the first lights of the pioneers. It is doubtful whether this was the case. Most likely the betty lamp and the rushlight, with the occasional use of pitch-pine splints, were the most generally used lighting devices of our first pioneer settlers. Candles were very expensive in the seventeenth century. Not until the pioneer could make his own candles in quantities did he turn from use of the cheaper and more readily made rushlight.

Examination of the betty lamp and its various relatives-in-form reveals that any expressed fat or oil could be burned, and indubitably was burned, in these simple metallic holders. The form is as old as Greece and Rome, as old as Egypt and Babylon. Lard, bacon fat, bear grease, fish oil—anything that was oil or fat—were burned in the betty lamp. Similarly, any fat or oil could be used to impregnate the stripped rush pith that made a rushlight. The pith of rushes is like a long pile of vegetable sponge. When dried, it will soak up oil as readily as absorbent cotton. Our pioneers gathered rushes by the bundle and bale, stripped off the outer shell, leaving only a spine to hold the pith firmly together. Then the rushes were cut in lengths and soaked in hot fat or oil. They were next wiped and stored in readiness for insertion in a rushlight holder for burning. They made a much brighter light than a single candle and as much smoke as half a dozen candles. A rushlight trough, dip or grisette, and numerous rushlight holders are among the pictures of this chapter.

By 1660 rushlight holders seem to have been made with a candle socket as a part of the ensemble. There is a clue of considerable interest in this addition to the rushlight fixture. A rushlight holder made also to serve as a candleholder is evidence that our pioneer was in a position, at times at least, to choose whether to burn a rushlight or a candle.

Candlemaking was encouraged by the early discovery of acres of bayberries, which grew profusely not only in New England but throughout the New Jersey coast, in New Sweden, Maryland, and Virginia. The vegetable wax of the bayberry was easily obtained by immersing vast quantities of berries in boiling water, which melted off the wax. Upon cooling, the water bore a crust of bayberry wax on its surface, like a coating of gray-green ice. This was removed and remelted in deep pans. Stiffened wicks were dipped in the hot wax repeatedly until candles of sufficient size were built up. One of the scarce things was candlewicking. Not until this simple need was filled by the importation of wicking or his own production of tow linen could the pioneer make candles, no matter how much wax he could gather.

As the years rolled on beeswax, beef tallow, bayberry wax, and other fats went into the making of candles. By 1685 professional chandlers were in Boston, New York, and Philadelphia, keeping shop and getting very pretty prices for their tapers. When the pioneer made his candles for a season, he may have dipped a thousand or more. When he cast his candles in molds, he may have poured 4,000 for a year's supply. That sounds like a lot of candles. Let us examine it in terms of light. Divide 4,000 by 365 and we discover we have a quota of less than eleven candles a day. For a five-room house that is about two candles per day, per room. That comes pretty close to living in the dark, so to speak. Of course they didn't ration candles at the rate of so many per room per day; they may have used from six to ten candles per day just to light the keeping room.

The antiques of candlemaking are few in number. Dipping wands and frames, drying racks, candle molds, and dipping vessels about cover the field. The molds, however, are known to have been made of glass, pottery, china, stoneware, tin, pewter, iron, and wood, and in sizes to mold from six to sixty candles at one pouring. There are some rotary candle dippers of a quite complicated character, and some pouring vessels with peculiarly shaped spouts.

Sticks or holders for candles are recognized everywhere as lighting fixtures. That they are not complete without a candle to burn in them is obvious. Our pioneers owned candlesticks of so many kinds, fashioned of so many materials, that we cannot, even at this time, say we have listed every material ever used. Potstone, soapstone, slate, and talc were turned and carved into candlesticks. Every known wood was used. There are wrought-iron sticks, cast-iron sticks, silver, brass, tin, pewter, glass, china, stoneware, and pottery sticks, copper sticks and sticks of papier-mâché. It is said that jet, a form of coal, was used in making candleholders; cattle horn, whalebone, and other materials were used in fashioning sticks. Multiple candlesticks, known as candelabra, and suspending fixtures or chandeliers holding many candles, were used in America after 1700.

The tools of candle care were quite simple; a snuffer to trim the wick was the one most generally used. The extinguisher, a cone-shaped metallic device, was not commonly used until, in the late eighteenth century, it was made a part of bedroom candlestick ensembles.

Oil-burning lamps seem to have been imported about 1750, but these were never popular. Apparently they were an elegancy, with too much trouble attending use. Not until the Swiss scientist, Argand, in the 1780s invented the center-draft lamp burner did domestic lighting take its first important step forward in twenty centuries of time.

It is claimed that our own pioneer philosopher, Benjamin Franklin, invented a two-wick candle that made more light than two separate candles. The draft of air between two closely spaced wicks did the trick. But a candlewick, at best, is not over a tenth of an inch wide. Argand developed a wick more than three inches wide, made it circular, compressed it into a ring not more than an inch in diameter, arranged for center draft, and lo! there was a lamp as brilliant as ten times three candles, or thirty candlepower.

We were not slow to accept the Argand lamp or to enter into lampmaking. After the Revolution individual lampmakers began laying the foundations of a great industry to come—the production of good lamps for the people at prices all people could afford. Many of the first efforts at lampmaking were just a reservoir and a burner. The reservoir had a peglike protuberance at the bottom which could be inserted in any candlestick, and thus make a complete lamp. This cute pioneering trick has been followed ever since in nearly all lampmaking. The reservoir, whether meant for oil or just for appearance (as in electric lamps), is made with a peg for its juncture with column or base.

The discovery that petroleum could be pumped out of drilled wells resulted almost immediately in that superior cheap fuel, kerosene. In spite of the fact that many people imagine that oil was discovered at Titusville, Pennsylvania, in 1859, this just isn't so. Oil was discovered in Pennyslvania before 1750. What the good Colonel Drake did was pioneer in going after the oil by deep well drilling and then finding uses for the product which gushed from the ground. This at once started a score or more of new pioneering efforts. There was one by-product of petroleum refining for which there was no use. So much of it was wasted that it "griveled the souls" of many pioneers. This product was gasoline. When this volatile hydrocarbon was first advocated as a domestic fuel for cookstoves, oil companies gave users the stoves free in order to develop customers for gasoline. And so it was, until Henry Ford put the nation on wheels. The first Ford cars ran on good gasoline that cost just eight cents a gallon—at the corner grocery store. Most grocers kept the stuff in sheet-iron drums in a shed back of the store.

The exposition of lighting equipment and fixtures pictured in this chapter includes some examples taken directly from the catalogues of American manufacturers, and from a catalogue of the Shelton Lamp Works of London and Birmingham, England. The latter catalogue was once used by an American importer who supplied thousands of the lamps to retailers. Some of the large lamp manufactories of America are among our pictures. So also are the kerosene lamps of the Centennial period, the ever-so-sweet eighties, and the gay nineties. Others are from catalogues issued as late as 1910. All of these lamps are considered antiques today although we know full well that many of them are quite late in the scene. What does it matter? The pioneers of Nebraska, buying new and better kerosene lamps in 1919, were doing exactly what the pioneers of 1660, 1710, and 1810 were doing in their day—making progress in lighting and in all else.

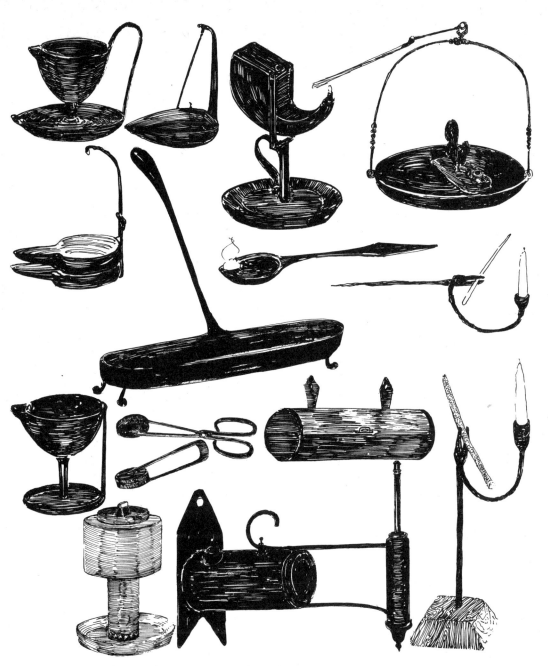

TOP ROW: Cup-and-saucer lamp, Swedish, *c.* 1660; crusie or Phoebe lamp, *c.* 1660; canting lamp, eighteenth century. As oil was consumed, lamp canted automatically to bring balance of oil to wick; rooster Betty lamp, seventeenth and eighteenth centuries.   SECOND ROW: Double Phoebe lamp, *c.* 1660–1790; handled trough for dipping rush in hot fat; spoon lamp with bayonet handle, *c.* 1700; combined candlestick and rushlight holder with bayonet end, *c.* 1680.   THIRD ROW: Slut lamp with handle, *c.* 1660; candle "d'outers." These are not snuffers. They were used to pinch out the flame, *c.* 1680–1780; candle box, used in seventeenth, eighteenth, and nineteenth centuries.   BOTTOM: Excelsior lard lamp with flat wick, *c.* 1860; camphene-burning wall sconce, *c.* 1840; combination rushlight and candleholder on wooden base, *c.* 1670–1700.

UPPER SECTION: St. Germaine student lamp introduced *c.* 1840; bayonet candlestick, *c.* 1800; rushlight holder on trammel, Swedish, *c.* 1650. It is five feet high; beaker candlestick with pierced base and glass shade, *c.* 1800; candle lamp in air-twist stemmed glass. Used from 1765 to 1850; rushlight holder on Queen Anne tripod stand, *c.* 1710. LOWER SECTION: Combination rushlight and candleholders on stands, dating from 1680s; Cornish "chill," a four-wick open lamp affixed to heart-shaped bracket; cone-shaped lantern, *c.* 1770; candle lamp, *c.* 1760. The candle is of white pottery with flat wick; tower or lighthouse lamp, with flat wick, *c.* 1810; eight-light chandelier on turned maple hub, *c.* 1810; hanging candle lamp with glass bowl, *c.* 1790.

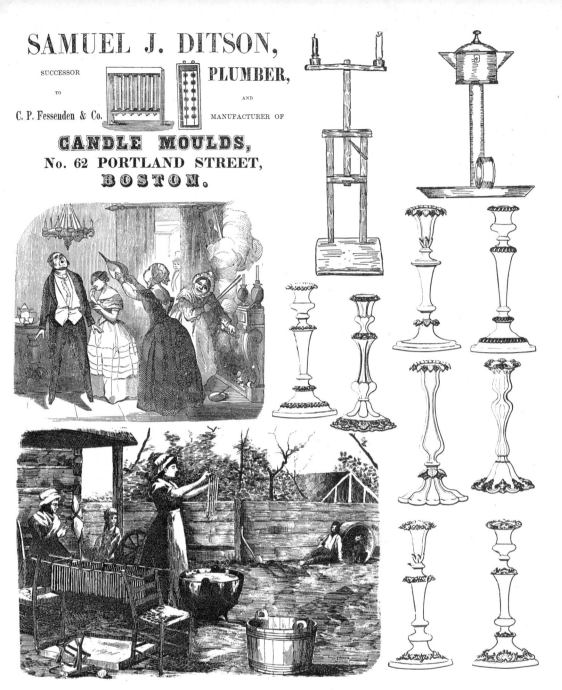

TOP: Advertisement of a candle mold maker, 1848. The firm was in business from c. 1800; adjustable candlestand, eighteenth century; can lamp with two wicks, c. 1800. CENTER: Caricature showing lady attempting to blow out candles with bellows; eight different designs of candlesticks in Sheffield plate, c. 1790–1840. BOTTOM LEFT: Dipping candles, c. 1850. Sometimes as many as 2,000 candles were made at one time.

Five pages from the catalogue of Cornelius & Baker, lamp manufacturers of Philadelphia, operating on a mass-production basis before 1830. Courtesy Arthur Sussel.

Five more pages from the Cornelius & Baker catalogue of the 1840s, picturing types of lamps made by the thousands in this mass-production lamp factory at Philadelphia. Courtesy Arthur Sussel.

Lanterns from the catalogue of Dietz & Company, mass-production lamp-makers of New York for over a century, and still in active business. All of these Dietz lanterns were designed for use on farms, on shipboard, on railroads, and for street and lane lighting. The first lantern in the second row is a pocket lantern patented in 1875.

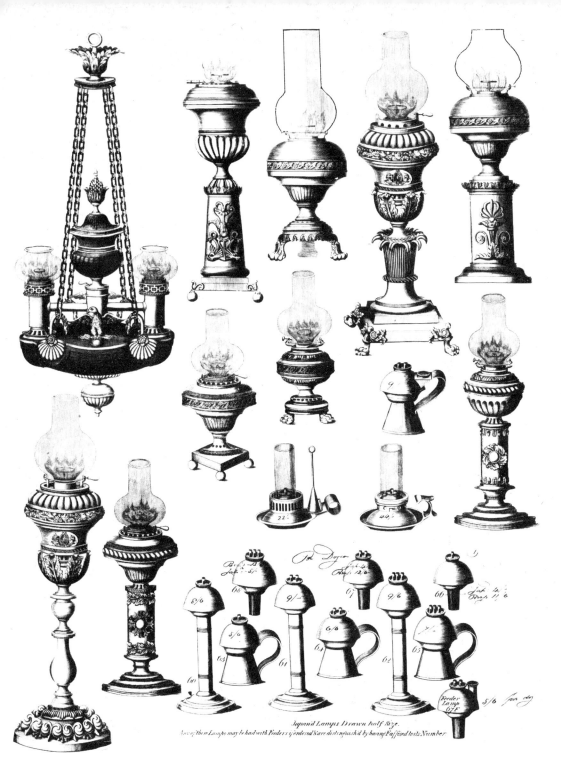

Lamps from the catalogue of the Shelton Works, London and Birmingham, showing lamps made from 1773 to 1840. Figures on the small lamps at bottom are the prices in shillings per dozen. These lamps were imported by a New York firm from 1790.

TOP ROW: Grand prismatic ceiling fixture with 500 prisms! Date is 1850; gas-ring ceiling fixture, 1850; gas chandelier with many prisms, 1850. SECOND ROW: Prismatic chandelier, 1850; advertisement, 1860, of a lamp that made its own gas. Read it, and be amazed! THIRD ROW: Argand burner St. Germaine student lamp, 1876; Dietz & Company advertisement, 1860; reflecting street lamp, Nicholas Kohlenkamp advertisement, Philadelphia, 1830. Lamps of this type lighted Chestnut Street from 7th to 11th in 1828. BOTTOM: Tom Thumb lamp with automatic lift to chimney, 1859; advertisement of patented safety parlor lamp, 1856; three lamps of the type now called "Gone with the Wind," produced in the 1870s by the hundreds of thousands.

TOP: Pierced globe lamp of iron, *c.* 1750; five barn lanterns of early nineteenth century. Shown courtesy of Thoreau MacDonald; arm lantern for railroad brakeman, 1855; gas-generating lantern, 1881. Naphtha was the fuel.   CENTER: Advertisement of Starr's Lamp Manufactory, 1848.   BOTTOM LEFT: Safety lamps with caps, and pressed-glass reservoirs and stands, 1850.   BOTTOM RIGHT: Advertisement of Spalding of Boston, showing the interior of his magnificent lamp store with thousands of lamps ready for sale, 1855.

Lamps as advertised in the 1890s and 1900s. Collected today as antiques, these lamps are scarcely older than our parents. Among them are several of the once-famous "Rochester" burner type.

212

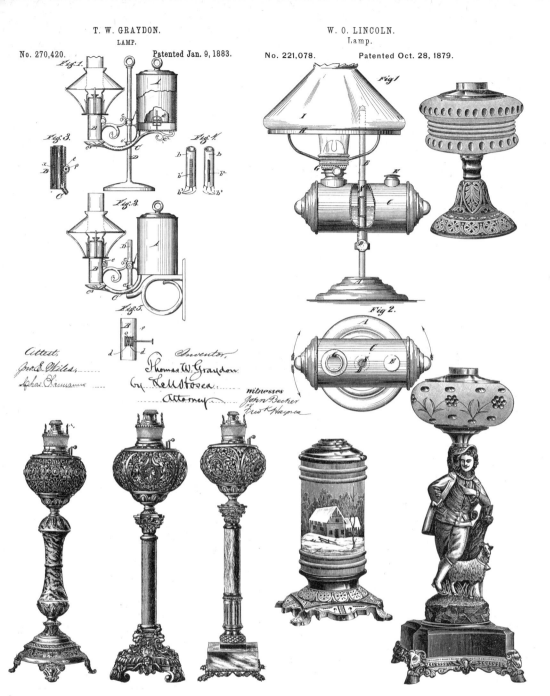

TOP: Patent papers for unusual St. Germaine student lamps, dated 1883 and 1879; lamp with cut-glass reservoir and bronze and onyx base, 1891. BOTTOM: Three onyx-and-bronze table lamps of the 1880s; bronze and painted porcelain lamp base, 1876; bronze lamp with figure of goatherd and with cut-glass reservoir, 1880.

TOP: Carriage lamps of the 1890s. These are all silver mounted; hanging
hall lamp with glass shade and kerosene burner, 1891.   BOTTOM: One
expensive ($5.00) and one cheap (50¢) decorated glass lamp of 1910;
decorative wrought-iron floor lamp, 1890.

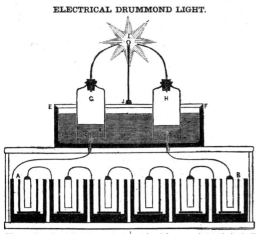

We sometime since intimated a promise to give an explanation with illustration, of the newly invented apparatus for producing the intense and brilliant light, known as the Drummond Light, and that by means of the combustion of water only, by the aid of galvanic electricity. We now present a sectional representation of the apparatus arranged to illustrate the principle in a compact and simple form. It is well known to all who are conversant with blast furnaces, that when any solid substance is intensely heated it becomes incomparably more brilliant or luminous, than the most intense flame : and it is well known to chemists that a more intense heat is produced by the combustion of oxygen and hydrogen gas,—a jet of each burned in conjunction,—than by the combustion of other fuel. The most intense light is therefore produced by heating some solid substance by the combustion of these two gases, and that in the same proportion in which they are combined in the composition of pure water. No common substance is found to be less fusible, nor capable of becoming more luminous by heat, than pure lime. Hence the Drummond light is produced by burning the oxygen and hydrogen gases in contact with a small piece of lime. These gases are produced in a pure state, and in due proportion, by the decomposition of water, which is readily effected by a current of galvanic electricity : for when water is made to constitute a part of a galvanic circuit, if the action of the batteries is brisk, these gases are liberated and produced at the poles or ends of the wires which conduct the electric fluid to and from the water. The best batteries for this purpose consist of plain cups cast of pure zinc, and amalgamated inside with mercury. Within each cup is placed another and a smaller cup,—usually called cells by way of distinction—of unsized porcelain or artificial stone ; and within each cell is placed a strip of platina plate about as thick as common letter paper ; and each plate is connected by a copper wire to the zinc cap of the next battery ; but the last plate of the series is connected via the circuit, to the *first* cup of the series. The most common and conveni-

ent size of these cups, is 2 1-2 inches in diameter inside, and three inches deep ; and each plate should be 3 inches long, 3-4 inch wide. It is not yet satisfactorily ascertained what number of batteries connected consecutively in each series, are the most economical for this purpose : but one series of six batteries only is represented in the engraving, though several sets are required to produce the gases in sufficient quantity to support a brilliant light. The batteries are charged for operation by filling the cells with nitric or nitrous acid, and the zinc cups with a mixture of one part sulphuric acid with twelve parts water. This series of batteries is represented from A to B. in the engraving ; A being the positive and B the negative poles ; but at the termination of the two wires, where they enter the vessel above, the poles are reversed, C is the negative and D the positive poles.. These terminations consist of narrow and pointed slips of platina plate. The vessel E F, is made of glass, porcelain or wood, and is nearly filled with water acidulated with one part sulphuric acid to 100 parts water. This vessel or font as it is termed, is covered with a lid of wood, which supports two glass jars G H, both of which are open at the bottom where they approach nearly to the bottom of the font, but the tops thereof are closed with perforated corks, in which are inserted two small metallic tubes through which the gases escape from the jars, and are thrown upon the lime I.— The piece of lime is cut in a conical form, with the point downward, and supported by a socket of platina, attached to a wire extending up from the lid at J. When the battery connections are made, the electric current passes from B to D, producing bubbles of oxygen gas which rise into the jar H, displacing part of the water, while the electric fluid passes through the water to the point C, where it produces a proportional quantity of hydrogen gas which rises in the jar G, while the current returns to the battery at A. The gases being thus produced and ignited at the point of contact, an intense light is supported by the action of the galvanic battery. The apparatus complete will cost $50.

TOP LEFT: An electric lamp of 1847, operated by six batteries which decomposed water and provided oxygen and hydrogen for combustion. TOP RIGHT: Hanging lamp of 1810 and hanging lamp of 1890. CENTER: Cross-wick lamp made at New Orleans, 1860; bracket lamp, 1890. BOTTOM: Electric street-lighting fixture, 1898; bracket lamp of 1880.

CHAPTER XX

Education

THE antiques of education are seldom placed in their proper category except by scholars whose interest is almost entirely academic. The majority of us are sometimes not even aware of the educational purpose of many antiques, such as battledores, horn books, New England primers, A.B.C. blocks, globes, pioneer art objects, drawing and painting instruction books, memory books, and so on. A few years ago the F.A.R. Galleries of New York City reproduced a series of delightful little pictures by Eveline Willis, done in her school memory book in the year 1828. There is much to be said about Eveline's efforts at portraying her surroundings, her friends, and her family, but when all is said, there remains this one fact—she did her work at school. If Miss Willis's work was unique her little pictures would be priceless treasures. It would seem, however, that no less than a hundred thousand other American girls and boys did precisely the same thing at school, and most likely as part of the tasks imposed by the curriculum.

Paul Svinin, the Russian diplomat who between 1810 and 1815 made some very engaging drawings of American scenes, was impressed by the fact that in our schools which, unbelievably, were open to everyone, art study and drawing had been made a part of school work! These little art exercise books are antiques of genuine value. In fact, so valuable are most of them that, when found, they are broken up and the pictures sold individually at almost fantastic prices. They are not sold as educational antiques but as pioneer or primitive art, or as miniatures.

Similarly, most of the objects used in early educational efforts are classified either as toys, scientific antiques, or simply as collectibles. School chairs and desks, benches, slates, inkwells, writing exercise books, blackboards, atlases, maps, dissected maps (the first jigsaw puzzle), magic lanterns, animated lantern slides—in fact almost all of the things used in schools are to be found in antique shops. Several years ago the Parke-Bernet Galleries sold a small table desk and basket swivel chair of Windsor type. This was school furniture. In some shops there are little desks with cast-iron frames and wooden tops and shelves. These desks were made in tremendous quantities to furnish thousands upon thousands of schoolrooms in the ever-increasing number of school structures erected by our pioneer public school boards.

The growth of education in our colonies and federation of states has engaged the interest of many writers since 1825. There are histories of education, books of designs for schoolhouses, plans for classrooms picturing and recommending all sorts of paraphernalia from desks and chairs to athletic exercise equipment for boys and girls. Before the establishment of public schools maintained by local taxation and fostered by state aid, practically all schools were supported by paying the master a fee. Some masters simply set up a schoolroom in a private house and advertised their services. Subjects taught varied from reading, writing, and arithmetic to lessons in sewing, spinning, fancywork and lacemaking, to Latin, Greek, philosophy, chemistry, and higher mathematics.

Many religious groups maintained schools. Notable in this category were the Moravians. Two of their schools for girls, established before the Nineteenth Century still function as educational institutions at Bethlehem and at Lititz, Pennsylvania. There were numerous Episcopal academies, some of which were established and maintained under most difficult conditions. Bishop Hopkins of Vermont has contributed much to the category of American flower prints because he engaged in the publication of flower prints as drawing exercise books for the pupils of his Episcopalian academy.

The bishop did not begin his active life as a minister. He was a lawyer at Pittsburgh until he assumed the pulpit as a layman after the death of the pastor of his church. He was elected rector, studied theology, was called to minister to ever-larger congregations, and finally was elected Bishop of Vermont. There, at Burlington and other points, he established parishes and schools. The bishop preached, acted as administrative officer of the diocese, published drawing instruction books, wrote and illustrated them, acted as architect for the construction of many churches, and taught school. If that isn't pioneering, we must invent another term for such dynamic creative activity.

Not all educational pioneers were males. In fact, as many schoolmarms as schoolmasters seem to have been engaged in educational work. Emma Hart of Berlin, Connecticut, born in 1787, was teaching school in her native town at the age of sixteen. She became principal of the Berlin Academy at the age of seventeen. In 1807 she was called to Westfield to head the female department of the academy, and from there to Middlebury, Vermont, where she was head of the Female Academy. At Middlebury she married Dr. John Willard and published a monograph titled *A Plan for Improving Female Education.* This was read by Governor Clinton of New York, who called it to the attention of the New York State Legislature. Some influential men incorporated a school on Mrs. Willard's plan at Waterford, New York, and called Emma Willard to take charge of it in 1819. From there Mrs. Willard moved the school to Troy. The work she started, as a pioneer, continues as one of the most highly regarded girls' schools in the country today.

Of course the established or dominant churches of colonies, regions, and states sponsored the founding of many colleges and institutions of higher learning. Harvard, Yale, and Princeton, were founded as sectarian colleges. The purpose, primarily, was to insure the education and creation of more ministers of the persuasion. The school for the education of Indians at Dartmouth became a famed college. In Virginia and North Carolina are many large colleges founded by religious groups to insure their continuation by the simple process of creating more and better ministers. The Crown established colleges such as Columbia and William & Mary. In the mid-1750s, largely upon the motion of Benjamin Franklin, a group of public-spirited gentlemen of London subscribed a sum of money to establish schools for the education of poor, ignorant immigrants in Pennsylvania. Several Dutch gentlemen also subscribed to this scheme. The schools were set up and most of them became colleges. They are the colleges that dot the Lehigh Valley. Franklin himself aided in the establishment of a college named for him at Lancaster, and was there to help lay the cornerstone of the first building.

Among the illustrations for this chapter are pictured a few schools, some school furniture, and a few advertisements of schools. The chapters on toys, elegancies, et cetera, carry other pictures of what were, actually, educational aids and objects used to inculcate knowledge in and out of school.

TOP: Receipt for contribution to the Union Schoolhouse of Germantown, Philadelphia, dated 1760; battledore with ABC's and numerals, used in schools of eighteenth century; New England primer, printed at Philadelphia, 1797. CENTER: A metamorphosis or series of transformation pictures, with cross-stitched patterns of alphabet and numerals. BOTTOM: Oak-horn book, so-called because the lesson was protected under a sheet of thin, transparent horn. Shown courtesy *Instructor Magazine* and Mr. George Rumage; engraving after an original picture by J. Louis Krimmel, titled "Departure for Boarding School." This scene depicts an American interior of c. 1815. Father is emptying the family purse to send daughter off to boarding school.

TOP: Linden Hall Seminary, founded by the Moravians, 1765, at Lititz, Lancaster County, Pa.; obverse and reverse of the Franklin medal awarded to Boston school children, 1792.   CENTER: Yale College, New Haven, from an engraving c. 1850; the Albany Select School, 1845, and the Normal School of Salem, Mass., 1850.   BOTTOM: Barre Academy, at Barre, Vt., 1850; Harvard University, from a woodcut of c. 1840.

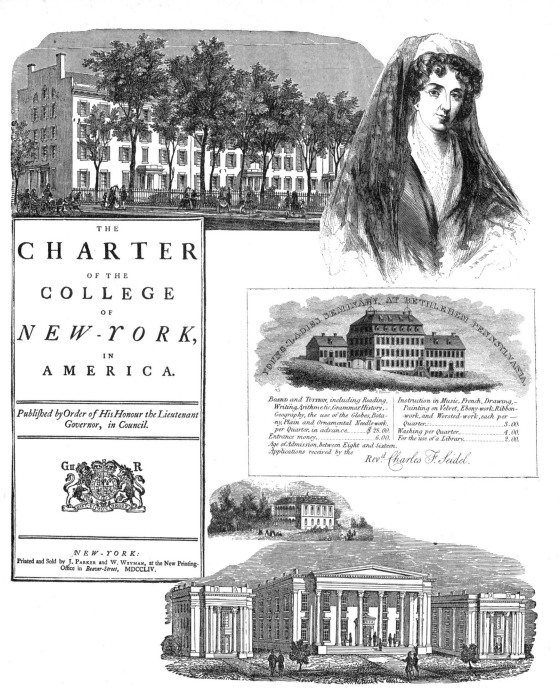

TOP: Troy Female Seminary, as it appeared 1858, and its founder, the eminent Emma Willard, one of the foremost educators of the first half of the nineteenth century. CENTER: Charter of the College of New York in America, then known as Kings College, 1754, and now Columbia University; engraving of the Young Ladies' Seminary founded at Bethlehem, Pa., 1760, by the Moravians. The rates of board and tuition will make many parents envious of other days. BOTTOM: University of Louisiana as it appeared in 1856; above it, the Normal School at Framingham, Mass., 1850.

Advertisement of Packard's Business College, 1867; Ohio Dental College, Cincinnati, 1856.   CENTER: View of the main buildings of campus of Amherst College, 1839, American Medical College, Cincinnati, 1856 BOTTOM: Franklin College, founded 1801, at Athens, Ga., as it appeared in the 1850s.

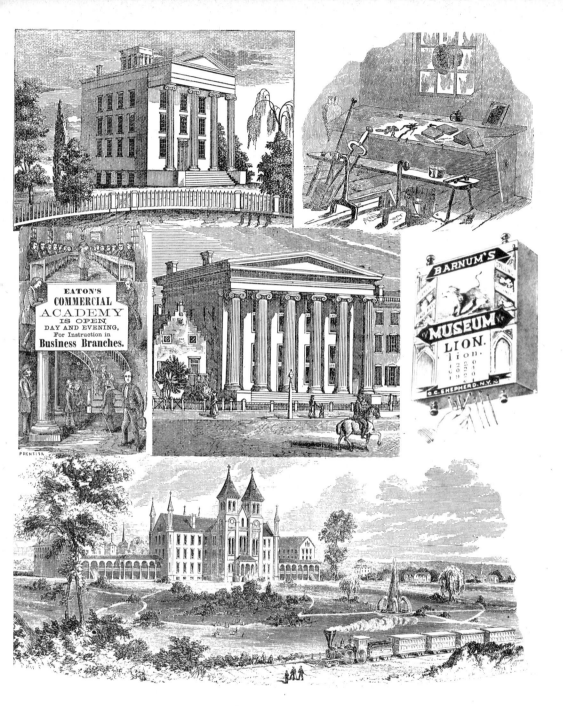

TOP ROW: Dutchess County Academy for Boys, 1839; interior of a district school, showing accessories, *c.* 1765.   CENTER: Eatons Commercial Academy advertisement, 1857; Albany Female Academy, 1839; Barnum's Museum, used in education, 1876. You had to pull the proper cords to get the right answers!   BOTTOM: View of the buildings and campus of Antioch College, Yellow Springs, Ohio, 1877.

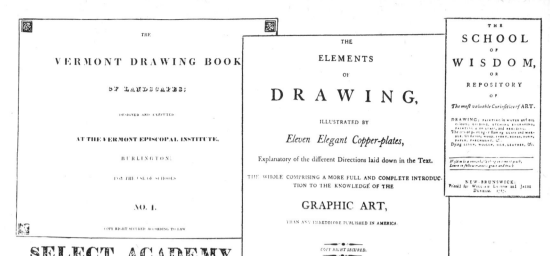

Aids to instruction in art, spelling, and morals. TOP ROW: *The Vermont Drawing Book of Landscapes,* published by Bishop Hopkins, 1841; *Elements of Drawing,* published by John Low, New York, 1804; *School of Wisdom and Repository of Art,* published at New Brunswick, N.J., 1787. CENTER: Advertisement of an academy of drawing and painting for ladies, New York, 1820s; reward of merit for a good scholar, 1840s. BOTTOM: Word builder composed of three circular and three square columns set upright in a frame. Date is 1876; Word builder, operating something like an early typewriter, used as an aid in school work, 1880; slate, 1880s; "The Burning of John Rogers," from the New England *Primer* of 1760.

WALES' BOSTON
SCHOOL FURNITURE MANUFACTORY.

Wales' American Chairs and Desk.

Wales' Teachers' Chairs.

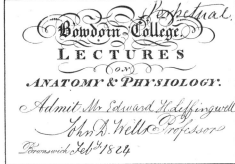

Wales' Single Desk and Chair.

Wales' Teachers' Desk.

Teachers' Desk.

Wales' Normal Desk and Chairs.

Wales' Basket Primary Chairs.

EVERY DESCRIPTION OF
SCHOOL FURNITURE,
Manufactured from ORIGINAL DESIGNS,
and constantly for sale, or made to order
and warranted by
SAMUEL WALES, Jr.
No. 14 Bromfield Street, Boston.
Communications by mail, or otherwise, promptly answered.

J. L. ROSS,
**Dealer in OAK, ASH, CHERRY, BLACK WALNUT, BIRCH,
MAPLE, WHITE, and BASS WOOD, &c.**

MANUFACTORY FOR SCHOOL FURNITURE.
JOSEPH L. ROSS, Practical Manufacturer of **DESKS** and **CHAIRS** for Schools.
Hawkins, corner of Ivers Street, Boston.

TOP LEFT: Advertisement of school furniture, 1850. BOTTOM LEFT: Advertisement of school furniture, 1855. Right hand group: School desks and chairs dating from 1830 to 1870, and ticket to anatomy lectures at Bowdoin College, dated 1824.

CHAPTER XXI

Quacks and Cures

THERE is an unbelievable quantity of antiques which actually belong in the subtle category of relics of quack doctors and patented cures. Every bitters bottle belongs in this classification, every bear's oil bottle, every ox-marrow jar, and scores of little boxes of metal, horn, paper, and wood which, without their labels, are imagined to be just boxes of antique status. At the 1945 meeting of the Early American Industries Association one of the members displayed a turned wooden goblet. "What is it?" is the question often asked by the members of the association at a regularly scheduled session at annual meetings. The turned cup was one of the items put up for identification. The answer put that wooden goblet right into the category of an antique "cure." It was a "quassia cup," turned from quassia wood. This wood imparts a bitter medicinal flavor to water permitted to stand in it a few hours or overnight. It does it over and over again. Our ancestors who thought they needed a morning dose of bitters were advised to buy a quassia cup, fill it every night, let it stand, and drink the draught in the morning. Cheap bitters, enough for a full year of dosage, was guaranteed before the essence, or virtue, of the cup was exhausted.

Because of the gullibility of many people there was wide use of patented nostrums, some perhaps harmless but most of them alcoholic. We cannot blame the people for this phenomenon. Early medicine in the colonies was so crude a practice that many people preferred physic administered by herb doctors, and the use of home-brewed simples and remedies.

For centuries the Chinese have fed powdered ants and other insects to sufferers from tuberculosis. In the twentieth century some remarkable experiments were conducted at Paris; certain natural acids were discovered to have a very good effect on sufferers from tuberculosis.

Then the powdered ants used by the Chinese were analyzed. They were found to contain the same natural acids!

Most of the tonics offered as cure-alls in the nineteenth century were really hard liquor for use by opponents of strong drink. Some of our most vociferous temperance advocates took a slug of whisky or rum four to ten times a day in the form of this or that bitters or tonic. One of the cutest tricks in this category has to do with the use of tobacco. Snuff was advocated as a dentifrice, and therefore the chewing of snuff was made a health habit rather than just a filthy habit—as reformers were wont to call it. It is also a matter of record that many of the tin, brass, silver, and iron pocket nutmeg graters, so popular in New England from 1750, were nothing more than snuff graters used in secret by those who publicly denounced the use of tobacco.

The notorious Dr. Dyott of Philadelphia who, among other activities, pioneered in glassmaking, was neither a doctor nor a medical man, in spite of his assumption of the degree of M.D. Dyott was a bootblack who made his own blacking. Then he became a vendor of shoe blacking. Then he mixed up nostrums and bitters—physic. Then he opened a drug and medicine store, and finally purchased a glassworks to produce bottles for his nostrums. That Dyott used child labor is not a fabrication of jealous competitors; he put orphans to work in his glass factory and enjoyed the fruits of their labor for a few pennies a day, plus board at a communal table and bedding on cots in barracks. Dyott finally started a bank, built up a great business fabric on false credit, and came to an end that was just plain ruin. But in his life's work he left behind him a trail of bottles and flasks, most of which today are avidly collected as antiques.

Wherever in this volume the activities of one or more individuals is mentioned, it should be remembered that the personalities are not selected as unique. They are exemplary only. Almost every city and town can produce another example. At the Hostetter sale of American glassware, where the greatest collection of privately owned Stiegel glass was sold, a Peruna bottle brought approximately eight dollars, as an antique. Peruna was a form of hard liquor—cheap whisky spiked with herbs and bitters. It was once known as "Gold & Sodium Tonic" and was made by a brewer and liquor dealer of Lancaster, Pennsylvania, named Mischler. A fellow townsman named Hartman bought the tonic business, renamed the liquor Peruna, and made a million dollars out of it. He moved the plant to Ohio, not for economic reasons but because he could no longer abide living in the town where his only son had died. The marvelous cure, Peruna, had failed to save his scion from an early grave.

The pictures here displayed are exemplary of the bitters bottles, pillboxes, and nostrum containers that are now antiques—some rich, some rare, some common. A few gadgets are pictured, and some advertising of other gadgets. The nationwide sale of artificial legs and arms from 1825 on and the many patents granted inventors in this field are not a part of this story. But the plastic surgeons who would change a face, or make a new nose or ear to replace one bitten off in a bear hunt, a fight, or shot off in war or fracas, are a part of this story because most of the practitioners were amateurs or, if you prefer, pioneers—in bloodless plastic surgery.

In this field of quacks and cures are many printed books and pamphlets having to do with surgery, faith healing, hexing, and of holdovers of medieval superstitions of the medical profession. One of the hex-cure books, titled *The Long Lost Friend,* published by one Hohmann in the 1840s, contains the weirdest collection of spells and remedies printed on this side of the Atlantic. Most of the simples, remedies, and superstitions of the cults of Yggdrasill and other Nordic groups, together with recipes from the Saracens and the ancient Hebrews, and the laboratories of alchemists of the Dark Ages are in the *Long Lost Friend.* It was printed in at least two early editions, one in English and one in German. Amazingly, it has been reprinted at least three times in this twentieth century. The "Witch Trials" of York County, Pennsylvania, in the 1920s had to do with a murder committed while two men were attempting to get a lock of hair from a suspect. They wanted the lock of hair to use in a rite that would remove a "spell" from a flock of chickens. The recipe for the trick came from Hohmann's book.

MARRIED LADIES

Who have for years lived without the blessing of having children, have, time after time, addressed letters for advice to Dr. Roback; and, from their grateful replies, his advice and Astrological calculations have invariably secured the gratification of their wishes. The above cut is the copy of a daguerreotype taken of a HAPPY FAMILY, where the mother had lived seventeen years without children.

☞ All letters, post-paid, strictly attended to, and the utmost confidence observed.

DR. C. W. ROBACK.

Can be consulted daily, from 9 o'clock A. M. to 9 o'clock P. M. at his OFFICE No. 7 HIGH STREET, BOSTON.

The subscriber has just returned from New York with a full ASSORTMENT OF

DRUGS & MEDICINES

which he will sell as low as can be purchased at any other establishment in this state. H. L. SCRANTON.

Bair Haven, Sept. 11, 1841.

In cases containing twelve twenty-four ounce white glass bottles.

AMBREINE CREAM!

FOR THE TOILET & THE NURSERY.

Use Crary's Ambreine Cream, and your skin will be as fair as mine is. | Why! what did you use to make your skin so fair? You were so dark as I am.

"An ounce of preventive is worth a pound of cure."

Yes, Ladies, use Crary's Ambreine Cream, which is prepared with great care expressly for beautifying the skin, and giving you a fair, clear complexion.—It is effectual in removing Pimples, Sun-Freckles, Tan, Morphew, Sallowness, Sun-Burn, and all diseases of the Skin.

WE would again call the attention of the Ladies of Newburyport and vicinity to the use of the Ambreine Cream, for the complexion in the Spring of the year, the worst time for the skin to become tanned, dark, sallow and harsh, and the best article to prevent these disagreeable appearances is the Ambreine Cream. In fact, no better recommendation is needed than the continued use of it by the most particular and observing Ladies, and the extensive sale of it at wholesale and retail by the proprietor.

N. A. Crary, 67 Merrimack Street, Lowell, Mass., And at retail by CHARLES WHIPPLE, Bookseller, State Street; Charles H. Hodge, Apothecary, corner of State and Charter Streets; Wm. W. Caldwell, Jr., Apothecary, State Street; and by Enoch W. Smith, State Street, Newburyport, Mass.

TILDEN & COMPANY,

MANUFACTURERS OF

PURE MEDICINAL EXTRACTS

FLUID EXTRACTS, PURE EXTRACT OF LIQUORICE,

LIQUORICE LOZENGES, &C., IN VACUO.

98 JOHN STREET, NEW YORK.

UPPER LEFT: Quack Dr. Roback of Boston advertises to the ladies, 1853. LOWER LEFT: Tilden & Company, ethical drug house at New Lebanon, N.Y., advertising in 1856. TOP RIGHT and downward: Pozzoni's Complexion Powder, 1892; Flowers of Petroleum Hair Tonic, 1879; Ambrosia Hair Tonic, 1850; Scranton's Medical Store, Fairhaven, 1841; Swayne's Wild Cherry Tonic, 1846; Livingston's "Rye & Rock," 1884; Ambreine Cream for a Clear Complexion, 1847.

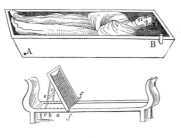

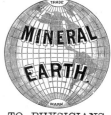

TOP LEFT: Hydropathy, or the "water cure," as advertised by ethical Dr. Trall, 1855. TOP RIGHT: Sloan's Family Ointment, Chicago, 1849. LOWER LEFT: Ozone generator for all sorts of ills, 1879. LOWER RIGHT: Mineral earth, a sort of penicillin of the 1880s. CENTER COLUMN: Drug jars from apothecaries' shops, eighteenth and nineteenth centuries; Marshall's Catarrh Snuff, 1833. CENTER LEFT: Digestive pills, advertised at Pawtucket, R.I., 1832; invalid's bed with hydraulic mattress and adjustable invalid's couch, both of 1840s; pill mold, 1850.

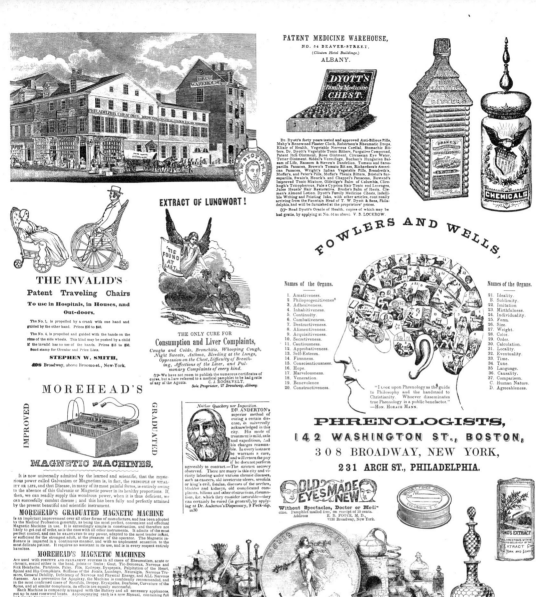

TOP ROW: Dr. Dyott's Warehouse and Store, Philadelphia, 1830; Dyott bottle, 1840s; Dyott medicine chest, 1845; Plantation Bitters bottle; druggist's jar, 1886. SECOND ROW: Invalid's chair, 1864; Lungwort Extract, 1845; Phrenology, 1855. BOTTOM GROUP: Magnetic machine, 1848; Dr. Anderton, quack on social diseases, 1819; old eyes made new, 1865; pillbox, 1890s; Pond's Extract, 1879; Ayer's Pectoral, 1855; fancy druggist's jar, 1880s; druggist's mortar and pestle, 1850s.

CHAPTER XXII

Stoves and Heating

SINCE almost every structure built in the colonies needed some kind of heating and cooking facilities, heating and cooking stoves constitute one of the largest individual categories of antiques. Andirons, and occasionally cob irons, were the usual fireplace equipment. Fireplaces were used for heating most rooms in cottages and mansions and, as long as wood was plentiful and cheap, there was no reason to find better methods of utilizing the burning of wood to provide heat for comfort or for cooking.

Stoves of stone appear to have been made in the seventeenth century. These were just iron-bound boxes made of six slabs of soapstone connected to a chimney with a length of clay or iron piping. The Dutch in the Delaware and Hudson valleys and the Swedes on the Delaware are now believed to have introduced the iron stove and the tile stove to the colonists. These were actually better heating devices than fireplaces. They permitted bringing the heating element forward into the room, from which point it radiated heat in every direction. A fireplace, even when fitted with a radiating fireback, conveyed most of its heat to the room through its one relatively small opening. Of course a chimney stack with eight fireplaces in it, all of them in almost continuous operation, was a sort of heating element in the center of a house. Some of these stacks, sixteen feet square at the base, would be heated to 80 or 90 degrees by continuous firing. This heat, in part at least, was imparted to the room; but most of it went up the chimney.

The cast-iron six-plate stove and its improvement, the ten-plate stove, were Norse inventions. They were used in Denmark, Norway, and Sweden from the sixteenth century. A few examples were brought to the colonies in the seventeenth century and some also were cast in that century in New York iron furnaces.

When Penn's invitation to European people was issued in 1682, there was an ever-growing influx of Dutch, Swiss, Huguenot, and

Palatinate settlers. By 1730 there were enough iron furnaces and enough immigrants wanting cast-iron stoves to foster the making of innumerable six- and ten-plate stoves in Pennsylvania. Many of these stoves were cast by Welsh and Cornish ironmasters, who made an effort to make the stoves acceptable to the immigrants. Therefore they cast biblical quotations in what they thought was the language of the natives—German. It is terrible German, wrongly spelled, abbreviated, and out of tense. But it sold the stoves. Most of the buyers probably couldn't read, certainly most of them couldn't write, but they did want stoves. The volume of business was good and continued good for almost a century. Then it got much better because new ideas in stoves, and a new fuel, anthracite, entered the scene of home heating.

Benjamin Franklin invented a combination stove and fireplace of cast iron which functioned as a stove but exposed the flame. This idea was promoted as the Pennsylvanian stove. Amazingly, there were more of these Franklin stoves cast in England than were produced in the colonies. In fact, a great number of them were imported by American stove merchants. We must look to the unwise and ridiculous rules, laws, and regulations of Britain's colonial authorities for explanation of this state of affairs in stoves. We could import bar iron, pigs, and finished ironwares but could not export them. That was the law. This collection of brash colonies was not permitted to compete with the vested manufacturing interests of England. Of course the politicians didn't explain their stand in that way. Their excuse was not to permit cheap colonial workmanship to enter England and deprive the honest British workman of his livelihood.

The story of stoves and stovemaking is admittedly dry, cold reading in spite of the connoted warmth of the subject. But the story of stoves and stovemaking, as told in pictures, is a sort of red-hot midway full of laughs, chuckles, guffaws, and not a little envy and desire to own a pictured example—if only for the fun of it.

Some of our nineteenth-century stoves are fearfully, wonderfully, and even beautifully made. Some of them have sold, as antiques, for five hundred dollars. We should forever keep in mind that although our stove production was tremendous we were also importing luxury stoves in considerable quantities. French, English, and Dutch stoves were imported from 1750 to 1850 by the merchants of Boston, New York, Baltimore, and Philadelphia. Stovemaking centers were Boston, Worcester, Albany, Hartford, New York, Newark, Philadelphia, Pittsburgh, Cincinnati, Lancaster, Baltimore, and Buffalo.

This, however, does not complete the geography of stovemaking. Wherever there was an iron foundry before 1860 chances are that stoves of a sort were cast and assembled. Reading, Pennsylvania, where once only charcoal iron had been smelted, became a stovemaking center when iron and coal were barged down the Schuylkill navigation.

American industries engaged in the production of modern heating equipment would do well to begin collecting the stoves and other devices which stand as signposts in the pathway to better heating. Perhaps the first modern producer of heating equipment to appreciate the significance of antique stoves was the Spear Company of Philadelphia. As early as the 1880s they owned a cannon stove cast by Henry William Stiegel at his Elizabeth Furnace, c. 1760. This type of stove, encased in a brick vault, from which copper ducts entered various rooms appears to have been the prototype of warm-air central heating as developed in the United States.

The following heating parade includes examples of nearly every type of stove once considered popular or elegant in our American scene. Captions include the bare facts, the approximate dating, and other pertinent information. Finding examples of like or similar stoves is a pursuit which is becoming more popular each year.

TOP: Ransom parlor stove, 1855; pot stove, 1820–1850; Franklin stove made by Hopewell Furnace, Pa., 1800s; Franklin's urn or vase stove, c. 1760; original bill issued by Charles and Andrew Pettit for one Franklin stove, dated November 25, 1785.   BOTTOM ROW: Beanpot stove of pottery, c. 1820–1850; original Franklin stove, c. 1750, and foot stove with container for charcoal or embers. Items of this type were used from 1650 to 1850.

A galaxy of oddities. TOP ROW: The Wilson Foolscap Franklin stove, 1816; Clute's Victorian urn stove, 1846; the Backus parlor stove, 1840; the Twin Oak stove by Beach of Philadelphia, 1840. MIDDLE ROW: Sheet-iron cookstove by Wright & Bridgeford, Louisville, Ky., 1850; six-plate stove, Pennsylvania, 1760; washboiler stove, 1840; gas stove in folding top mahogany cabinet, Cincinnati, 1858. BOTTOM ROW: Six-plate stove, 1850; parlor stove, 1850; cannon stove, 1850; bucket stove, 1850, and oval parlor stove, 1850.

TOP: Advertisement by Chilson, Gould & Co., Boston, 1850. The Trio stove
pictured is built in the form of a huge tuba. The same basic design was used
in the portable furnace, also pictured. Steam radiator of 1850s with ornate
cast-iron grille work on four sides, iron base, and marble top. Wood-burning
furnace of 1865. Many of these were used in cottages and homes of the
Midwest and Northwest. Advertisement of Prouty & Co., stove dealers of
Boston, 1850. BOTTOM: Enclosed furnace for installation in cellar, 1856;
advertisement of Baker & Smith, featuring their steam warming and ven-
tilating apparatus. This advertisement of 1850 features indirect steam
heating, considered a modern invention.

TOP ROW: Advertisement of Simpson's patent stove manufactory, 1817; Hessian andiron. In spite of antique appearance most of these date after 1790 and many of them are actually recasts made after 1900, usually decorated in full color; cooking stove as advertised by the manufacturer, Manchester, N.H., 1848.   CENTER: Oil stove by Dietz, the lamp manufacturer, 1870; advertisement by Wardell of Boston, 1829; improved tenplate stove by Benedict of Lancaster, Pa., 1825.   BOTTOM: Cooking ranges: left by National Stove Works, 1852; the one on the right by Hathaway, c. 1840.

TOP LEFT: Hub grate.　RIGHT: Hemisphere stove, 1876.　CENTER: Small modern Franklin stove designed by Harris & Zoiner, Cincinnati, 1854. BOTTOM LEFT: Laundry furnace holding eight irons, 1876.　RIGHT: The hot corn stove made in Connecticut, 1855, and cookstove named the Black Prince, also 1855. All illustrations from original catalogues of the manufacturers.

Benjamin Franklin, in his autobiography, mentions that a London iron-monger had taken the design of his stove and made improvements upon it that were really not improvements, sold great quantities and made a small fortune. This was the fireplace which our great philosopher is credited with inventing. First mention of such a stove is in *Mécanique de Feu* by Sieur Gauger, 1709. The ironmonger, not named by Franklin, was James Sharp, with manufactory at 133 Tooley Street, Southwark. He called his product the "Air Stove-Grate," "American stove" or "Pennsylvanian stove." His catalogue, issued in the 1760s, contains the above illustrations. Examples of all of these stoves were shipped to the colonies prior to 1776.

Stoves produced by J. F. Dudy of Leeuwarden, the Netherlands, in the 1820s, and shipped in quantities to the United States for sale through hardware stores. Dudy's stoves, whether the unique cookstove shown at upper left, the classic ten-plate stove shown at upper right, the modified "cannon" stove or modified Franklin stove, are classic in design and were, of course, in the category of elegancies when sold in the United States. Elegancy or not, our pioneers purchased them and used them.

Jewett & Root of Buffalo, N.Y., 1860, made the first six stoves here pictured. Names in sequence are the Eagle, Lark, Folding-Door Franklin, New Plate, Dwarf Franklin, and Drum, meaning the six-plate with heating drum—a very unusual and now rare type of stove. The large cookstove is by Shear, Packard & Co., Albany, 1850. Advertisement of John Mason & Co., Providence, R.I., 1853, specializing in the designing of stoves.

CHAPTER XXIII

Pioneer Furniture

THREE women, Esther Singleton, Alice Morse Earle, and Hudson Moore, and two men, Dr. Irving Whitall Lyon and Luke Vincent Lockwood, did most of the pioneer work in the field of American antique research. Then came Wallace Nutting, Esther Stevens, and Walter A. Dyer in the vanguard of amateur writers of popular treatises. R. T. Haines Halsey and other architects found good reasons for deep and abiding interest in American antiques. The American Wing of the Metropolitan Museum in New York, the Williamsburg Restoration, and Ford's great work at Greenfield Village are the natural results of academic and professional interest in this engaging phase of social history.

To pronounce the furniture of the seventeenth century our exclusively pioneer furniture is to miss the point of pioneering entirely. Duncan Phyfe pioneered in popularizing the Directoire tradition in our early federal days. In Philadelphia, as it is so unerringly revealed in *The Blue Book of Philadelphia Furniture* by W. M. Hornor, Jr., a group of cabinetmakers pioneered in the making of some of the finest furniture ever produced. These pioneers also planned a *Cabinet Makers' Director* that perhaps might have been better than Chippendale's *Director*. We must say perhaps because the work was never published. The Revolution put an end to the effort. After the Revolution we were in the mood to drop all Georgian and Chippendale styling without a single regret.

Pioneer cabinetmakers, emigrating to the Ohio country, created a cabinetmaking industry at Cincinnati more important to us historically than the famed industry of Grand Rapids. Actually, our furniture of antique and near-antique status, deserving of the term pioneer, includes everything we made and should not, in every instance, preclude furniture and other items imported by our pioneers.

Even the goods and chattels of the royal governors were here because of the progress of pioneering.

In this chapter the pictures have been selected as exemplary of all furniture of pioneers—the poor, the rich, the successful, the frontiersman, the cabin dweller, the artisan, the tradesman, and the soldier. Included are examples of great pioneering efforts at making chairs for the people—good chairs at low prices. There is as much pioneering behind the making of sixty thousand drop-leaf tables per year in 1877 as there was in making tulip-carved chests, one at a time, in the Connecticut River Valley in 1677. Of course, reflected in this showing of furniture is every one of the period styles from Charles I, and even Elizabethan or Tudor, down to the Louis XV revival that we persist in calling Victorian. There are examples of that once snobbishly promoted piece called a hunt board but which, in almost every case, was made for pioneering families as a sideboard for use in a combined kitchen, living, and dining room. There are some cute, queer, and quaint examples of furniture, some painted furniture, and an array of chests and boxes of all periods.

No effort will be made here to designate the high lights of any period style or to consider its fine points. The cavalcade marched from first to last in this fashion: Tudor-style furniture, the final gasp of the Gothic age in England; Carolean and Jacobean furniture of the various Stuart regimes; William and Mary furniture; Queen Anne and Georgian furniture; Chippendale's recordings of the Georgian styles and his adaptations of French and Chinese styles; Adam period classically styled furniture; Hepplewhite classic furniture motivated by Adam; Sheraton furniture copied from classic revivalists including Shearer, Cruckshank, and others; Directoire-styled furniture from designs by the great French artist David; Napoleon's made-to-order style known as Empire, and the Louis XIV and XV revival which began with the reign of Louis Philippe in France, in 1830, when the so-called "citizen king" put an end to the reign of the Empire style. It is this French-revival furniture that we made in America as French antique and which rejoices now in the name of Victorian.

One type of furniture enjoyed and often favored by our pioneers deserves special mention. This is corner furniture—furniture which utilized otherwise wasted corner space in a room. The most generally used corner piece was a corner cupboard, but in what variety! From the small walnut and pine corner cabinets of Dutch, Swiss, and Swedish ancestry to the "Beauffat" of built-in type, is a long, long story. In that story, like signposts, stand so many types of corner cupboards that a book could be illustrated profusely with no two examples alike. Mobile or portable corner cupboards were more favored than structural or built-in pieces. Among these are the corner wardrobe or *kas,* now called a coffin cupboard because the paneled door, reaching almost from floor to top, looks like a coffin lid. Bow-fronted corner cupboards and angle-fronted examples are far scarcer than the flat-fronted variety.

Corner chairs in the Windsor tradition, in slat-back and in fancy-chair type known as Hitchcock, were favored odd chairs of the pioneers. Later there is evidence of use of the quadrant chair, the seat of which is a precise quarter circle like a man-size wedge of pie. It is reported that these chairs were made in pairs and in foursomes, and that the height of something or other was to arrange four of them in a circle to provide a round seat for four people. This doesn't sound like a frontier vogue but it is within the category of pioneering as accepted in this book. The first people to buy and use chairs of this type were pioneers of high-style courage.

The corner sideboard appears to have appealed to pioneers in some sections of the country, notably North Carolina, western Virginia, Missouri, Louisiana, and Texas. Corner boards are reported from all these sections. There is a Hepplewhite example of great beauty now in St. Louis; it is a large board of perfect quadrant shape with a beautifully bowed front. Recently a corner board was discovered in New York State. It is one of a pair which could be used either in opposite corners or stood side by side against a wall to create a half-round or half-moon sideboard. The drawers of this piece are quite complicated examples of cabinetwork. They fit into angles so accurately that most people cannot get the drawers back into the piece until they are shown the secret. Pictured also is a corner board from Yancey County, North Carolina, which dates from *c.* 1840–50. It might be called a corner hunt board but it was made for a sideboard. It was fashioned by a carpenter, found in a mountain home, and is now privately owned.

Corner tables seem to have been used from about 1710. One unique type of Queen Anne period table is triangular in shape with a triangular top. Over this top and hinged to the edges are three flaps, each a trisected angle of the top proper. These unfold and enlarge the table top into a six-sided hexafoil or hex-square shaped top. The main top is pivoted to turn and bring the flaps over the corners of the triangle over each table leg. This could almost be called gadget furniture, but it isn't. It is pioneer furniture of highly inventive quality. Other triangular tables for corners have simple fold-over tops which convert the table into a square top. Some have a fourth leg which swings out like a gate; others have a folding bracket to support the fold-over leaf.

The space of years spanned by the furniture pictured in this chapter is from around 1650 to 1880. Other than this brief outline, the captions under the pictures or at the bottom of pages of grouped furniture must carry the story of this furniture of our people. All of it was made by pioneers, whether in one-man shops or in big factories. Nearly all those who bought and used it were pioneers, whether newly arrived in this country or descended from earlier settlers. The immigrants who poured in from 1849 to 1898 and later were seeking one thing above all—opportunity to be pioneers in the enjoyment of freedom, personal liberty, and further opportunity to earn a better living.

TOP ROW: New England carved chest, *c.* 1660; painted Huguenot chest, *c.* 1700, New England. At Metropolitan Museum; Pennsylvania wall cupboard, *c.* 1750, and Pennsylvania painted chest of Swedish type, dated 1764. SECOND ROW: Maple and pine console table, *c.* 1700; oak wainscot armchair and walnut side chair, *c.* 1660–1680, Pennsylvania. From Parke-Bernet; Spanish chest of oak, Florida, *c.* 1580–1600; table desk, William and Mary period, *c.* 1680. Topsfield Historical Society. CENTER: Queen Anne sofa, *c.* 1710. FOURTH ROW: Walnut wainscot settle, Pennsylvania, *c.* 1700; walnut armchair, Pennsylvania, *c.* 1685; walnut wainscot armchair, *c.* 1660; Walnut stretcher table, *c.* 1700, Parke-Bernet. BOTTOM ROW: Swedish chest, *c.* 1650; walnut-and-maple *kas,* Pennsylvania, *c.* 1700; Press cupboard, Pennsylvania, *c.* 1660–1670, Parke-Bernet.

TOP ROW: Six-board chest of Elder Brewster, *c.* 1620s. Wadsworth Athenaeum, Hartford; Walnut draw-table, *c.* 1660–1690. Philadelphia Museum; Pilgrim cradle, oak, *c.* 1650. SECOND ROW: Swiss-type extension table, *c.* 1700, Pennsylvania or Carolina; Swedish-type chest-on-frame with nail-studded decoration, Pennsylvania, *c.* 1670; New England cradle, oak, *c.* 1660. THIRD ROW: Pine trestle table, *c.* 1650; New England oak chest with extension top, *c.* 1680; Pennsylvania walnut turned chair, *c.* 1685. BOTTOM ROW: Pennsylvania painted chest, dated 1764; Extension table with falling leaves, New England, *c.* 1680; Dutch folding table with underside of top painted. The term for this type table is Hinderloopener Klaptisch used in many early Dutch homes in New York and Pennsylvania from 1650 to 1750.

TOP ROW: Single post bed. Anchored to supports in corner of room, this type bed was perhaps the earliest used in New England, *c.* 1620–1630; New England press cupboard, *c.* 1640–1650. Oak, with dyed wood bosses. MIDDLE ROW: Pine corner cupboard of type used in New England, New York, and Pennsylvania, *c.* 1680–1780; pine board chair on oak runner, used for pushing on ice of frozen streams, New York, *c.* 1750; oak press cupboard, New England, *c.* 1660. From American Antiquarian Society, Worcester, Mass. BOTTOM ROW: Chest-on-frame, William and Mary period. Decorative walnut veneer, twist-turned legs, and shaped flat stretchers, New York, *c.* 1690; William and Mary chest-on-frame, fashioned of cherry wood, Connecticut, *c.* 1710. Both from Parke-Bernet Galleries; Pennsylvania Swedish open wall cupboard of pine, *c.* 1680.

TOP ROW: Bowed New England meetinghouse settle of maple and pine, *c.* 1660; hooded fireside chair from New England, *c.* 1690; pine settle table, New England, *c.* 1700. Same type table made for cottage homes to 1880. CENTER: Walnut *kas* of Dutch type, used in New York, New Jersey, and Pennsylvania. This example dates from *c.* 1650 or later; chest bench and bedpost settee of types popular from 1680 to 1880. Found from Atlantic seaboard to Indiana; Flemish-Carolean type oak armchair, *c.* 1660, New York. BOTTOM: Oak desk-on-frame, New York, *c.* 1660. From Ginsburg & Levy: Queen Anne walnut desk-on-frame, Pennsylvania. From Arthur Sussel. Date is *c.* 1710; yellow pine slope-fall desk, Pennsylvania or Maryland, *c.* 1785. From Joe Kindig, Jr.

TOP: Virginia court cupboard, found near Petersburg. Fashioned of oak, this cupboard may date from 1610. Virginia had court cupboards before they were known in New England, a fact not generally appreciated by students and collectors; maple extension table with butterfly supports, New England, c. 1680–1700; Dutch chest-on-frame of walnut, Pennsylvania or New York, c. 1680. CENTER: Swedish court cupboard of pine, from Dalecarlia or Skane, c. 1650; "sawbuck" table of yellow pine. Swedish-type found in Pennsylvania. Date from 1650 to 1750; Virginia livery cupboard of oak, c. 1650. Courtesy Lurelle Guild. BOTTOM: William and Mary "S-leg" glass cabinet on frame, walnut and pine, c. 1690. From Parke-Bernet Galleries; French-type corner cabinet of walnut with bowed front, c. 1710. Oak cupboard and chest, c. 1660–1680. Parke-Bernet Galleries.

TOP: Pair of pine stretcher tables of Swedish type dating from c. 1660.
CENTER: Oak framed chair upholstered in Turkey-work. Date is c. 1650;
Swiss "Scabelli"—an all-wood cottage chair with carved back. Popular in
Pennsylvania from c. 1700 to 1750; triangular corner table with three
leaves which, when raised, make it a round table. Pine, dating from c. 1680
to 1710; oak and pine tulip carved chest, probably Pennsylvania, c. 1680
or earlier.   BOTTOM: Oak five-drawer chest, New England, c. 1660; Dis-
browe chest, c. 1660–1680. Courtesy Luke Vincent Lockwood, Esq.; Connecticut two-drawer chest of oak and pine, c. 1660–1680. Carved with tulip
and sunflower forms. Picture by courtesy of Thomas H. Ormsbee, Esq.

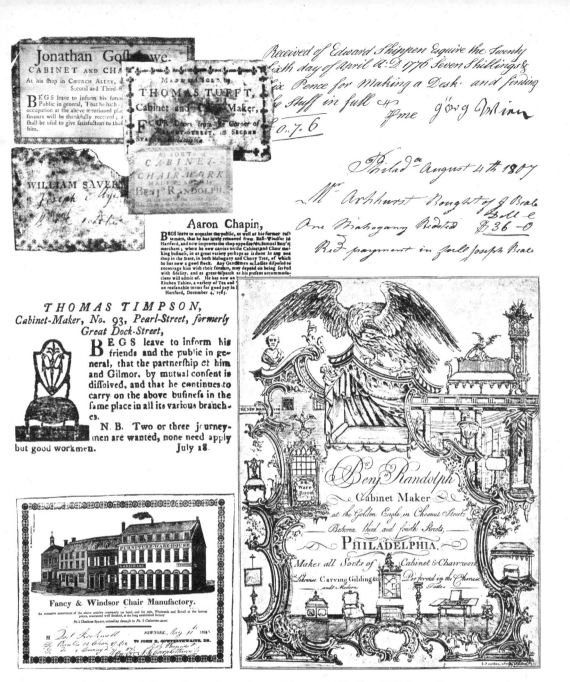

TOP: Labels of Jonathan Gostelow, Thomas Tufft, William Savery, and Benjamin Randolph, all master cabinetmakers of Philadelphia in second and third quarters of the eighteenth century. From Philadelphia Museum of Art; advertisement of Aaron Chapin of Hartford, dated 1783; bill of Gorg Miner, Philadelphia, for making a desk, 1776. Bill of Joseph Beale, Philadelphia, 1807, for one mahogany bedstead, priced at $36.   CENTER: Thomas Timpson of New York, advertisement dated July 18 (1787). BOTTOM: John Cowperthwaite bill for a dozen chairs at $12 and a sewing chair for 87 cents. Bill dated 1825; magnificent trade poster of Benjamin Randolph of Philadelphia. Pictured through courtesy of Philadelphia Museum of Art.

NORTH EAST CORNER OF SYCAMORE & FOURTH STS

CINCINNATI

MATTRESS MANUFACT'Y · CABINET WARE-ROOMS · CHAIR STORE

J.F.COATES BARTON WHITE JONA. MULLEN

J. F. COATES,
UPHOLSTERER & MATTRESS MANUFACT'R
Curled Hair, Cotton moss and Husk mattresses. Feather Beds &c Sacking, Brussels & other.

B. WHITE,
Manufacturer of CABINET FURNITURE SOFAS & CHAIRS.
Also for sale Mahogany Veneer, Hair &c

J. MULLEN,
Manufacturer of SOFAS & CHAIRS, CHAIRS MATRESSES &c.
Of modern fashion and good workmanship, &c.

CHAIR MANUFACTORY.

SAMUEL STIBBS,

RESPECTFULLY informs his friends and the public, that he still continues to carry on the CHAIR MAKING BUSINESS, in all its various departments.

His warehouse is on West Third Street, between Main and Walnut, where he constantly keeps a general assortment of WINDSOR, FANCY, CANE and RUSH BOTTOM chairs: Also, SETTEES of the latest, eastern improved FASHIONS.

He warrants his work to be equal to any in the western country. His long experience in his line of business, and the evidence which the patronage he has heretofore enjoyed affords him, fully justifies this assurance.

Orders from Steam Boat owners, and all others abroad or at home, will be thankfully received and punctually attended to.

Cabinet and Chair Manufactory.

ADAM GALER,

WINDSOR CHAIR-MAKER,
(Lately from Philadelphia,)
In Little Queen Street, next door to the corner of Great George Street, opposite HULL's tavern,
Makes and sells all kinds of
WINDSOR CHAIRS,
Any gentlemen or masters of vessels may be supplied with a neat assortment upon reasonable terms.

FANCY CHAIR STORE.

WILLIAM BROWN, Jún.

No. 50 Beekman-street, New-York, has constantly for sale, a large assortment of elegant, well-made and highly finished Fancy Chairs, Settees, Conversation, Elbow, Rocking, Sewing, Windsor, and Children's Chairs, of every description, on the most moderate terms.

*** Orders from any part of the continent will be attended to with punctuality and despatch. A liberal allowance made to shippers, &c.

††† Old chairs repaired, varnished and re-gilt.

JAMES R. HEATON.
FANCY & WINDSOR CHAIR MAKER,
Nº 240 GREENWICH STREET,
between Robinson & Murray streets.
NEW YORK.

ROGER PORTINGTON,
NO. 656,
Washington-Street,
HAS on hand, and is constantly manufacturing, of the best materials, and of the most fashionable patterns, a variety of CABINET FURNITURE.
He also manufactures Mahogany CHAIRS, SOFAS, and COUCHES, and the spring seat ROCKING CHAIRS, which have been so universally admired.   tf   nov 14

George Shipley, Cabinet Maker,
BEG leave to return hi sincere thanks to his friends and customers, for the many favours he has received, and hopes by a steady attention to business, to merit a continuance thereof; and as he has in employment a number of excellent workmen, he has no doubt of giving entire satisfaction to those that shall please to favour him with their commands. Articles in the cabinet business made in the neatest and most fashionable manner, and on reasonable terms and will take on them that he has at his cabinet manufactory, a large and warranted assortment of mahogany furniture, of the newest fashion, which he has now on sale very low, at No. 161, Water-Street, between Beekman and Burling slip.
MAHOGANY for sale, very suitable for stair cases and other uses.
LIKEWISE he has received from London, a quantity of satin hair leaving for chairs of the first quality, and Newest fashion, which he will dispose of on reasonable terms.
May 18.   eodm

THOMAS BURLING,

Cabinet and chair-maker, next the Chapel in Beekman-street, New-York,
GRATEFULLY acknowledges the many favours of his friends and the public, and takes this method to inform them, that he has now on hand, an assortment of most elegant Mahogany Furniture, such as he knows will do him credit, and give his customers satisfaction.
He served his time with the noted Samuel Prince and has now employed a number of his left hand, and means to use his endeavours to retrieve the credit of the buiness in this city, that has been greatly hurt by the sale of so much slight work at their workmen.
Bed Chairs for the sick, to let. 9th mo. 25th.

GEORGE J. HENKELS,
CITY
CABINET WAREHOUSE,
No. 173 Chestnut Street,
OPPOSITE INDEPENDENCE HALL,
PHILADELPHIA.

CATALOGUE
OF
FURNITURE
IN EVERY STYLE,
COMPRISING
Louis XIV, Louis XV, Elizabethan and Antique
WITH SCULPTURE CARVING,
AND
MODERN STYLE
In Rosewood, Walnut, Mahogany, Satinwood & Maple
ALL OF SUPERIOR CONSTRUCTION,
And Finished in the best Style, Equal to, if not Excelling in Quality the goods of any Establishment in the United States.

Employing none but experienced workmen (apprentices being positively excluded,) and using the best materials, the work cannot fail to give satisfaction to purchasers. Amongst the many advantages offered to purchasers is the Facility of Furnishing a House, either in Elegant or Plain Style, completely from one establishment; by which means all the articles in each room correspond in Style and Quality, and the IMMENSE STOCK always on hand being so various in design, enables purchasers to please their taste in a selection without the delay necessarily caused in ordering furniture.

To give an idea of the Finished Furniture on hand, I need only inform you that my Rooms are 175 feet long, by 27 feet wide, 4 floors in number; with Shops contiguous, sufficient to employ 200 hands, which is a guarantee that the work is all done under my own immediate inspection.

The Packing is all done in the Store, and Furniture warranted to carry safely any distance. Visitors to Philadelphia are respectfully invited as purchasers or otherwise, to Call and Examine the Goods.

FREDERICK DREER'S
Cabinet-Ware Room.
152
South FOURTH Street.
PHILAD.ᴬ

ALL ORDERS STRICTLY ATTENDED TO

TOP: Three Cincinnati firms issued this promotion piece in 1839; Adam Galer advertisement of Windsor chairs, New York, 1786; Roger Portington, cabinet and chairmaker of Boston, 1829; Thomas Burling of New York, 1788. CENTER: Samuel Stibbs of Cincinnati advertised thus in 1829; William Brown's chair store, 1818, and James Heaton's shop, 1810; George Shipley advertisement, New York, 1792; Reither, of Brooklyn, N.Y., trade card, 1856. BOTTOM: Frederick Dreer of Philadelphia trade card, 1800. Shown by courtesy of Historical Society of Pennsylvania; George Henkel's catalogue, Philadelphia, c. 1860.

TOP ROW: Oak chest, molded panels and one drawer, New England, *c.* 1660–1690; two-drawer chest of oak and pine with three painted panels, New England, *c.* 1690. From Shreve, Crump & Low, Boston; Pennsylvania open-shelved dresser or cupboard of pine, *c.* 1750–1800. CENTER: High blanket chest with seven drawers and deep top cavity. May be of Shaker production. Wood is dyed pine; open pine dresser, *c.* 1825, from Martin Schuster, Kansas City, Mo.; cradle bench of *c.* 1785. Painted pine. BOTTOM: Yellow pine dresser of unusual width, probably Maryland or Delaware, *c.* 1750; yellow pine kitchen cupboard of a type made in Pennsylvania, of cherry and walnut woods, dating from late eighteenth century; schoolmaster's desk of heart pine with lift-up writing board and small pencil drawer. This might be called "country Hepplewhite." Date is 1800 to 1825.

TOP ROW: New England table board of pine, *c.* 1750; true "hunt board," of inlaid mahogany, Virginia, *c.* 1790. Both from Parke-Bernet Galleries; corner sideboard from Yancey County, N.C., *c.* 1840.   SECOND ROW: High sideboard of yellow pine, from Memphis, Tennessee. Date is *c.* 1830; walnut side table, Pennsylvania, *c.* 1750, owned by George Hay Kain, Jr. THIRD ROW: Triangular sideboard, Hepplewhite style, *c.* 1790. These corner boards, while scarce, were made in many sections of the country; one of a set of four "quadrant tables." From Elizabeth Loebel.   BOTTOM ROW: Open and closed views of a unique folding table in the Queen Anne style. Walnut, *c.* 1730. From C. W. Lyon, Inc.; yellow pine corner cupboard, Pennsylvania, *c.* 1750. From Parke-Bernet Galleries.

TOP ROW: Spanish chair, *c.* 1660, once the property of Christopher Witt, Philadelphia; New York State Dutch chair, *c.* 1690; William and Mary period chair with trumpet turned legs and X stretcher, *c.* 1690; New England turned chair with split hickory seat, *c.* 1675. CENTER: Twist turned chair once the property of William Penn; Carolean-period chair with carved front stretcher, *c.* 1670; Queen Anne or Georgian "wide chair." Walnut frame. Date is *c.* 1710–1720. BOTTOM ROW: Queen Anne period corner cupboard of walnut. An exceptional piece, dating from *c.* 1710. From Arthur Sussel; Queen Anne drop-leaf table, walnut, *c.* 1750; Queen Anne chair with shaped and pierced splat in back. Philadelphia, *c.* 1735–1740.

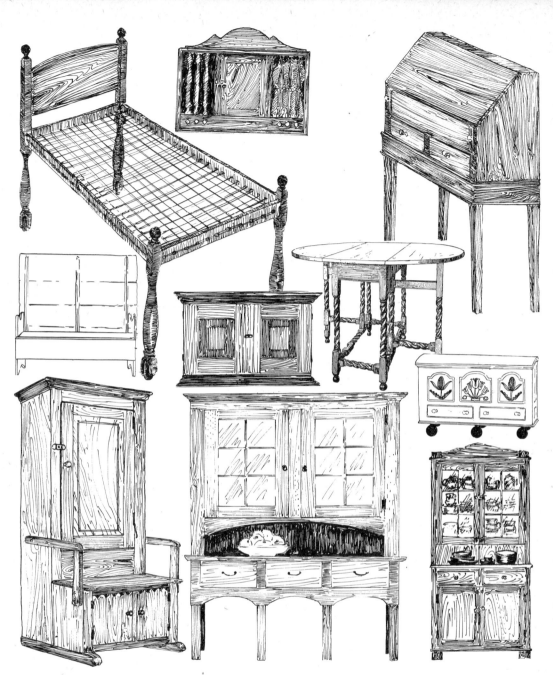

TOP ROW: Shaker-made high bed on rollers, *c.* 1830. Courtesy of Thomas H. Ormsbee; hanging cupboard for meat and bread, probably southern New Jersey or Delaware, *c.* 1725; yellow pine desk and sugar box on tapered legs, Kentucky, *c.* 1810.   CENTER ROW: Pine settle table, *c.* 1700; hanging cupboard of walnut, Pennsylvania, *c.* 1750; twist-legged gate-leg table of oak, *c.* 1690; Swedish chest with tulip decoration, N.J., Delaware, or Pennsylvania, *c.* 1725.   BOTTOM ROW: Bacon cupboard with seat, Tennessee. Yellow pine, dating from *c.* 1800; Welsh cupboard from Caernarvon, Lancaster County, Pennsylvania. May be eighteenth or early nineteenth century. From Mrs. Flickinger, Churchtown, Pa. Narrow pine cupboard of *c.* 1850. Made by the thousands for cottage and tenement use.

TOP ROW: Pioneer tilt-top table of yellow pine, *c.* 1840. From West Virginia; apple-drawer sideboard from Yancey County, North Carolina, *c.* 1850. SECOND ROW: Triangular table from California. It isn't Duncan Phyfe, but Spanish Directoire. Correct name for the piece is Rinconera. Mahogany, *c.* 1840; pine sink bench for cottage and tenement use. THIRD ROW: Pine settle, *c.* 1820; cherry cupboard, *c.* 1830, both from West Virginia; twin-seated mahogany settee, Directoire influence, Georgia, *c.* 1830. BOTTOM ROW: Hepplewhite-style sugar box on frame; mahogany with inlay, Kentucky, *c.* 1800; sideboard chest of cherry with twisted columns and glass knobs, Ohio, *c.* 1800; corner cupboard of walnut, Maryland, *c.* 1785–1790; small desk from West Virginia, yellow pine, *c.* 1825.

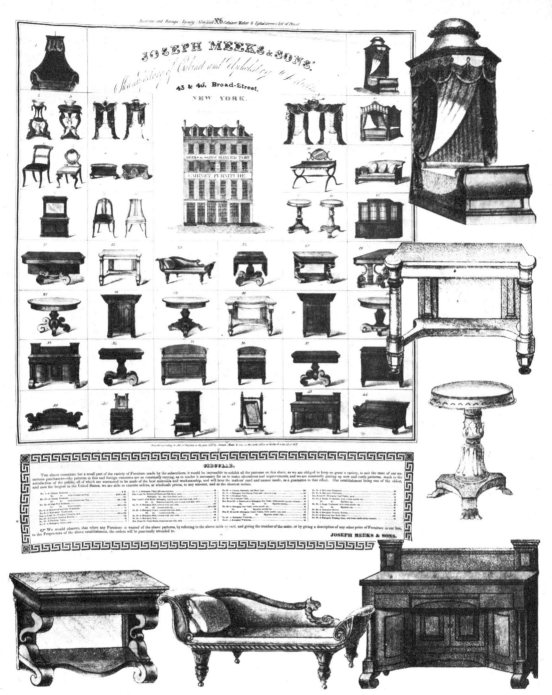

High-powered sales promotion for furniture in 1833; the elephant folio-size lithograph, hand-colored, produced by Endicott for Joseph Meeks & Sons to capture the export trade. From 1770 American cabinetmakers had an eye on the export business and sold furniture to Mexico and South America, where much of it is still to be found. Pictured with the poster are enlargements of six of the items advertised. The canopied bedstead, in the Empire style, was priced at from $300 to $500. The Meeks factory was in operation contemporaneously with Duncan Phyfe's establishment. Meeks probably had the larger factory. Both Phyfe and Meeks were making the same style and the same quality of furniture in the 1830s.

TOP ROW: French- or Swiss-type open corner cupboard of pine, *c.* 1750; angle-fronted corner cupboard of walnut, Pennsylvania, *c.* 1750; corner kas of Dutch type with ball feet, Delaware valley Dutch, often called Pennsylvania-Dutch. Walnut, *c.* 1700; shielded candlestand of walnut, *c.* 1750. CENTER ROW: Francis Trumble of Philadelphia, 1758, bill for a tea table and six Windsor chairs at eight pounds nine shillings; Queen Anne sofa with walnut frame, *c.* 1715. BOTTOM ROW: Chinese teakwood stand, brought to United States by clipper ships; Harlequin piano from collection of the late Bishop James H. Darlington. It is a combined desk, toilet table, and piano. Date is *c.* 1800; Connecticut banister-back chair with heart and star crest, *c.* 1690–1700; corner cupboard of cherry and walnut, *c.* 1770.

TOP ROW: Maple and cherry chest-on-chest in Georgian style, *c.* 1750, from Housatonic Valley, Conn.; cherry chest of drawers from Potomac Valley, Va.; yellow pine desk on frame in Queen Anne style, from Susquehanna Valley, Pa. CENTER GROUP: Corner cupboard of walnut from Conestoga Valley, Pa.; sideboard cupboard of cherry from Shenandoah Valley, Va., *c.* 1810; slant-top desk of walnut from Schuylkill Valley, Pa.; three-backed settee of maple from Mohawk Valley, N.Y., *c.* 1800; oak table, *c.* 1660–1690, from Merrimac Valley, New England. BOTTOM ROW: Swedish dough trough from Delaware Valley, *c.* 1660; Hudson Valley chest of drawers, walnut, *c.* 1700; Queen Anne lowboy of cherry, from Connecticut Valley, *c.* 1740.

TOP ROW: Baluster-backed corner chair of maple, *c.* 1730; pair of corner chairs of walnut, each having three turned and one carved and shaped Queen Anne leg, dating from *c.* 1740–1750; master corner chair of walnut with carved and pierced splats. From Parke-Bernet Galleries. MIDDLE ROW: Queen Anne period saddle-seated "stick chair" and settee. All such pieces were once considered of English make. Now we have reason to believe they were made in Philadelphia and that the American Windsor developed by the simple process of using turned instead of carved legs; camp bed used by Washington; Empire convertible sofa bed of mahogany, *c.* 1850 straight from Royal Street, New Orleans. BOTTOM ROW: Turned table and chair, *c.* 1720; turned gate-leg table, maple, dating from 1690–1720.

The most important item on this page is the broadside proposal to publish an American (colonial) *Gentleman and Cabinet-Makers' Assistant* at Philadelphia, 1775. Unfortunately, subsequent events prevented the development of the work. Among the advertisements of interest here pictured is an auction of Hitchcock chairs, 1830; advertisement of the Allegheny fancy-chair factory, Pittsburgh, 1837, and of Thomas Ash, Windsor chairmaker, New York, 1770. Early newspapers and directories of any city, of date prior to 1850, often yield advertising of cabinet and chairmakers, sometimes illustrated.

TOP ROW: Bill, dated 1769, for two Windsor chairs with mahogany arms; Adam-style upholstered chair, c. 1760. SECOND ROW: Directoire-style chair, c. 1790; Hepplewhite-style chair, c. 1785; Adam and Sheraton styled chairs, dating from 1765 to 1800. All from Parke-Bernet Galleries. THIRD ROW: Five chairs by J. W. Mason Furniture Company, 1840–1880; three rocking chairs made by the Shakers, 1870s. BOTTOM GROUP: Advertisement by Ward & Stokes, Louisville, Ky., 1832; early Windsor chair, c. 1760; Dewey's Furniture Warehouse, Connecticut, c. 1830; advertisement by A. H. Brick of Gardner, Mass., dated 1867, and bill of William Cox, Philadelphia, for twelve green (Windsor) chairs at six shillings three-pence each in 1791.

A PARLOR VIEW IN A NEW YORK DWELLING HOUSE.

TOP LEFT: High-toned parlor of 1854, furnished in what we call the high Victorian style, but which was really French antique revival. RIGHT: The young ruler for whom the period should *not* have been named. She had nothing to do with it. What we call Victorian was sparked as a revival by Louis Philippe, the citizen King of France, 1830. Under portrait of Victoria is an "antique" revival table designed by Conner, of New York, 1842. CENTER: Rosewood side table, rosewood extension table, *c.* 1850; iron chair of 1850s. BOTTOM LEFT: Advertisement by Aaron Shaw of Cincinnati, 1856. The French revival we call Victorian had captured the imagination of most people by 1850. BOTTOM RIGHT: Rosewood dressing table, 1850.

A fold up kitchen table.

Furniture of the 1840s, 1850s, and 1860s. At top a sofa by Belter of New York, a Grecian sofa, and a Louis XIV chair by Henkels' of Philadelphia. The bed at lower left is the true Jenny Lind. Henkels furnished her suite during her concerts in the Quaker City. Jenny fell in love with the bed. Smart Mr. Henkels said, "It is yours, if I may honor it by calling it the Jenny Lind." The singer agreed. Mr. Henkels sold a lot of beds just like it. The advertisement from Muscatine, Iowa, dates from 1860; the Smallwood advertisement is 1853. The fire screens on poles, box sofa with tubular cushions, the folding table, and the sewing stand are from *Godey's Lady's Book* of the 1850s.

DESIGNED, DRAWN AND PUBLISHED, BY JOHN HALL
ARCHITECT.
BALTIMORE

Issued in 1840, John Hall's *Cabinet Maker's Assistant* consolidated what we call the late Empire style into the production schedules of scores of American furniture factories. On this page are exemplary designs from Hall's book. Our factories made this kind of furniture on a mass-production basis. Now all of this furniture, whether we like it or not, is designated as antique and is an object of search by many collectors. It is the major period-style furniture of any state settled after 1840 and before 1860. Pioneers purchased it as the very best and the very newest in style.

CHAPTER XXIV

Woodenwares

THE woman who knows most about American woodenware has never, up to now, been mentioned. That woman is Mrs. Arthur Greenwood who, with her husband Dr. Arthur Greenwood, during the past twenty-five years has collected examples of all that with propriety can be called fine or notable woodenware, and authentic data about every piece of it.

Of course it is proper to designate as woodenware anything made of wood. You can buy modern woodenware today in dime stores, houseware shops, and hardware emporiums. As antiques, however, we must draw the line somewhere. We should, perhaps, come to a full stop with the woodenware made during the administration of Ulysses Grant. After that time the individual makers of woodenware were mighty scarce artisans. Some of them were working in pioneer villages west of the Mississippi, but factory-made woodenware was available almost everywhere and there were ships, railroads, and wagon trains to carry it even to the mining camps of California and Colorado.

Our choicest woodenwares are burl bowls, cups, and mortars. Cake molds, marzipan molds, butter molds; carved, painted, and plain band boxes; sieves, pails, tea caddies, chestnut urns are all delightful collectors' items. Historically, mazers, drinking cups, and similar objects have been turned on lathes since the Dark Ages. There are coopered examples—fashioned of staves after the manner of barrel and pailmaking—dating from the fifteenth century. The making of burl bowls was not learned, as a craft, from our native American Indians. Englishmen turned and shaped bowls and cups of burl before a single colony was planted in the New World. What our pioneers did learn from the Indians was the aborigine's way of hollowing or shaping a bowl without the aid of a lathe. The method was a laborious chipping, charring, grinding routine which was discarded as soon as lathes were set up. That our early artisans at the lathe turned burl bowls with thick walls can be traced to two causes: their lathes were not perfect tools and thinness of wall was not feasible. Next, burl is apt to split on a lathe when cut too thin by the forming tool. So bowls were turned, although crudely, and in years of use in which both interior and exterior were pretty well battered, they have taken on the appearance of having been hand-cut from the whole burl.

Trays and troughs—elongated oval or rectangular burl pieces— were probably made by cutting and shaping. There were no lathes to turn irregular shapes and forms until Thomas Blanchard invented the gunstock lathe in 1820. On this lathe were turned decoy ducks, shoe lasts, gunstocks, and woodenwares in any shape or form desired. It is not beyond the realm of possibility that some, if not all, surviving oblong burl vessels were turned on lathes of this type.

How old *is* a piece of woodenware? As old as so-and-so says it is? How old is a trencher, a wooden spoon, or what have you? As old as it looks? To attempt to date woodenware is extremely difficult. Families may have replaced their wooden plates with pewter only to discard the pewter for china or pottery; but other new families were starting the cycle again with wooden plates. Wooden tableware was on sale until at least 1825. It was made in the same old way, turned from logs on a lathe. It was cheap, non-breakable, and easy to keep clean. If there was no water the plate could be scraped with a knife to cleanse it. We still use wooden plates at picnics and at some luncheons. Now we use them and throw them away; our ancestors bought heavier ones and used them over and over again. In the dairy—a part of almost every farmhouse and rural home—woodenware was preferred for the handling of milk, the skimming of cream, and the making of butter and cheese. Milk bowls, churns, cheese presses, ladles, skimmers, molds, pats, butter workers—all were made of wood.

At various times butter molds have been promoted as a Pennsylvania-German contribution to woodenware. This has been because of the assumption that anything bearing a tulip, a heart, or a flower is Pennsylvanian in origin, no matter if painted, carved, stamped, cast, or scratched. Three major dairy traditions were followed in the colonies—the dairying of England, of Switzerland, and the Low Countries. What butter molds we have are either in the Swiss, the Dutch, or the English tradition. In the English tradition should fall also the Scotch, Irish, and Welsh utensils. England was influenced by Norse, Norman, Danish, and Swedish dairy practices of ancient tradition. Therefore, some of the butter molds here pictured fall within these traditional patterns. One, which at least a dozen authorities pronounced Pennsylvania-German at first sight, is actually Irish, made in Ireland, and brought to this country by Irish immigrants settling in New Hampshire and having a dairy. They made Irish butter which our ancestors considered the finest butter churned. Irish butter was advertised at premium prices in the markets of New York, Philadelphia, and Boston early in the nineteenth century.

Glee is the word for it—for the emotion we have when we delve into the history of the things made and the things used by our pioneers. The owner of this Irish butter mold is a museum official. She is busy, every day, studying the provenance and the history of the appurtenances of the museum in her charge. She has had as much fun with this butter mold as with any of the important accessions of her museum.

Again it is necessary to clip the words on a subject and resort to the pictures and captions which constitute the major reason for this volume's existence. Misinformation is usually traceable to words about our antiques. The objects themselves forever pose the questions: Who made me? Why? How was I used? When? Where? And by whom?

TOP LEFT: Footed walnut burl bowl, c. 1620–1640. TOP RIGHT: Wooden mortar and pestle, c. 1770. CENTER: Wooden spoon, 1660; ancient turner at his lathe, from a drawing dated A.D. 1260; wooden butter scoop, c. 1780. BOTTOM GROUP, LEFT: Burl bowl with handles, c. 1660; above it a quern scoop, c. 1750. CENTER: Burl dipper with hook handle, c. 1660. RIGHT: Wooden skimmer with pierced strainer bottom. The utensils here pictured are really important pieces of early woodenware, especially the footed burl bowl.

TOP ROW: Coopered or staved cup with handle, sometimes called a "quaich,"
Tennessee, *c.* 1825–1840; pair of scrubbing boards from North Carolina,
c. 1790. SECOND ROW: "Scheppel," a Dutch grain measure, with flat iron
bar handle, *c.* 1660; washboard with inserts of pottery scrubbing rods, *c.*
1810. THIRD ROW: Flour hutch, *c.* 1840–1890; coopered measure with
copper spout, *c.* 1700; pair of wooden measures, 1850–1900. BOTTOM
ROW: "Lade-gorn," a bucket for use in shallow wells, used from 1660 to
1860 and perhaps even later; "bow-beater," an early rotary whipper for
eggs and cream, *c.* 1750; laundry "dolly," used to agitate and stir laundry
in wash boiler, *c.* 1770; "cowl," or deep tub, usually suspended on a staff
carried by two persons. Hence "cowl staff." Date is from 1620.

TOP ROW: Marchpane, or marzipan mold, Pennsylvania, c. 1780–1790; kit, or milking pail with cover, c. 1820; dredging box—container for the flour or meal used in dredging or dusting roasting meat. Date is c. 1800. CENTER GROUP: Gourd ladle, used from c. 1750 to 1900; porringer-shaped maple wood strainer, c. 1750; chopping bowl with ears, or handles, c. 1750. BOTTOM ROW: Dredging box, c. 1750; valve-bottomed well bucket, c. 1780. The valve in bottom is a little trapdoor. When bucket is lowered in well it permits immediate entry of water through bottom. When withdrawn, the door closes and the bucket comes up full; staved bucket with one long stave for handle, c. 1810; birch broom in use c. 1785. The birch broom is still made and still used in many rural New England homes.

TOP LEFT: Five-piece Irish butter mold, *c.* 1825. From collection of Mrs. Provost; wooden funnel and three wooden measures, *c.* 1880; (under the measures) large wooden milk bowl, *c.* 1880. CENTER, RIGHT: Large marchpane, or marzipan mold in celebration of Greek Independence, *c.* 1830. BOTTOM GROUP: Butter scoop, 1880s; advertisement of wooden-ware manufacturer, 1876; round butter stamps, or molds, 1880s; spoon rack, Dutch or Swiss, eighteenth century.

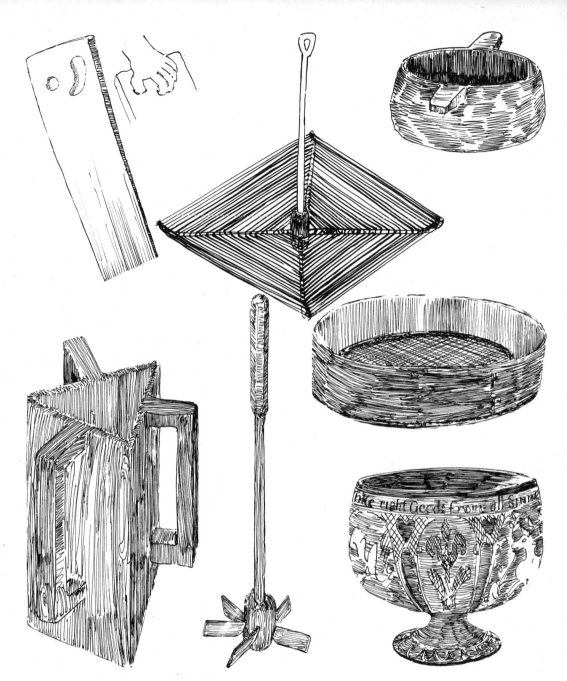

TOP LEFT: "Shake ladle" or spatula made from a shingle, with unusual handhold holes. Used from *c.* 1610 to 1800. RIGHT: Schist bowl. This object is a chopping bowl, carved from schist, or pot stone. Date is *c.* 1660. CENTER: Drying basket—a sort of four-ribbed umbrella hung upside down from ceiling and filled with cut fruits. The cross-pieced stuff is thin willow. BOTTOM LEFT: Triangular wooden mug with three handles, *c.* 1660; rotary whipper, *c.* 1740; mazer bowl, early seventeenth century, English. Above it a temse, or sieve, *c.* 1800. When a worker was diligent at sieving he was said to be "setting the temse on fire." Hence the often-misquoted term, "setting the Thames on fire." It was not the river Thames, but the temse, that got hot!

Woodenwares of the nineteenth century in an array too numerous for complete mention of each article. The large drawings from top to lower center are sketches of an herb basket with cover, a wooden trencher (of type used from 1610), and a flat basket for gathering fruits and herbs. Other items include scoops, twine holders, baskets of split hickory and willow, butter stamps, churns, steak-mallet, advertisement of Gideon Cox, woodenware maker, pictured at work coopering a bathtub (1833), women washing and churning, 1853, and a pair of coffee grinders of the sort used when coffee was either bought roasted in the bean or purchased in the green bean and roasted at home.

Philip's Samp-pan.

Woodenwares of the nineteenth century;   TOP: A rolling pin, a knife tray,
three flour buckets.   CENTER SECTION: "Engine" butter churn with elegant
decoration, milk bowls, butter stamps, butter tub, butter worker, butter
mold, and six wooden spoons.   BOTTOM SECTION: Butter scoops, wooden
bowls of oval shape, advertisement of N. & J. Howe & Co., Boston, makers
of all sorts of woodenwares.   LOWER LEFT: King Philip's "samp-pan," or
spoon. This seventeenth-century bit of woodenware is said to be of native
American Indian make.

CHAPTER XXV

For the Foibles and Frills of Man

EVER since man considered himself more attractive when clean-shaven, he has left behind him a trail of antiquities dealing with his primping and preening. The wig stand, powdering closet, shaving stand, bachelor's chest, gunrack, and other items of furniture, the cockfighting and sporting chair, the bill-yard or bil-liard-cue rack, and a veritable museum of Staffordshire sporting and other figurines are all a part of this story. In America the uncommon "common man" among our pioneers was seldom conditioned by birth and education to acceptance of, or desire for, niceties and elegancies. He just earned them and emulated, as he saw fit, whatever other fellow he felt like imitating. There are few collectors of razors, as such, within our company of antiquarians. There is, of course, the DeZemler collection of barbering items, but by long odds the most interesting part of that great collection to most people is the impressive lot of occupational shaving mugs it can boast. These, almost entirely, repre-sent an American phenomenon.

The shaving mug was not a new idea that sprang, full blown, into use in the nineteenth century. Some sort of mug to hold soap and hot water for working into lather with a brush was used, so it is said, in the seventeenth century. Some shaving bowls—in fact most of them—also served as containers in which lather was prepared. The person being shaved held the bowl under his chin while the barber worked on him.

Among the pictures illustrating this chapter is a drawing of a pewter shaving mug which is a perfect piece for this usage. The wide spout is a good brush holder. The date of this piece is c. 1775. In 1835 the master tinsmiths of Philadelphia sold tin-plate shaving mugs at twenty-five cents and sixty cents a dozen, depending on the type.

Shortly after 1800 several American soap chandlers (a term indi-cating they made both candles and soap) began packaging a better grade of soap for shaving. Their first wrapping was simply a piece of printed paper bearing their advertising and making many claims for the product. Usage proved that shaving soap, to be most effective, required packaging that prevented the drying out of the natural oils of the soap and the moisture that kept the soap in a condition of readiness for quick lathering. Our manufacturers, as they improved their products, also began to improve the package. By 1835 they were packaging shaving compounds in china or pottery boxes. Today these boxes are much scarcer than shaving mugs. The examples pictured represent six years of fairly active collecting. One of the users of this form of packaging, H. P. and W. C. Taylor of Philadelphia, in 1852 conceived the idea of packing soap in a china mug. It is doubtful whether the mug was designed for permanent use as a shaving accessory. More likely it was for use only until the soap was consumed, whereupon the mug became a coffee cup or a good drinking vessel for Tom and Jerrys.

The idea caught hold almost at once. A mug for shaving soap was made a universal practice. Within ten years personal shaving mugs, owned by the patrons, were appearing in barbershops. By 1870 almost every barbershop began building tiers of little niches in which these mugs were kept. They were used only when serving the patron. Almost at once there was an effort to personalize the mugs. At first only the name of the patron was lettered in gold. In some very exclusive shops only plain mugs with gold lettering were allowed. But in the rank and file of shops patrons' mugs were decorated with pictures indicative of the interests, profession, or trade of the user. These were considered the ultimate in barbershop elegancy.

This interest in shaving mugs added considerably to the activities of the vendors of soaps, powders, leeches, tonics, and perfumes who supplied the barbershop trade. They became also the suppliers of shaving mugs. Dealing in a pottery or china item was not exactly a new thing with them. Nearly all lotions were dispensed from fancy bottles; leeches were kept in leech jars; powder was sold in jars. It was the custom of the barber's supply man to furnish these.

The 1875 catalogue of the W. H. Sample Company of Albany, supplying barbers in New York, Connecticut, and Massachusetts, lists 415 subjects painted on shaving mugs, ready for hand lettering of the owner's name. The barber quoted the price to his customer, took the order, passed it on to Sample, and made a nice little profit on the transaction. Since the Sample list of subjects constitutes at least the beginning of a check list of occupational shaving-mug designs, the list is included in this chapter. Significantly, this paragraph was added to his list by Mr. Sample: "Emblems not mentioned here will be made to order if designs are furnished." One may wonder what trade or profession is not on the list. The first one noted is the profession of undertaker; but there is a coffin design and a hearse with horses! There is nothing for the doctor, the lawyer (unless the lyre was used), and the male midwife. Lodge emblems and symbols such as lyre, owl, and so on are not listed here although listed by Sample. The list most of us want in respect of shaving mugs is the record of occupations known to have been pictured.

Occupational shaving mugs and shaving soap boxes, together with other relics of the frills and foibles of the male pioneer, constitute most of the pictures of this chapter. This male used whisker dye, affected wigs and toupees and, sometimes, false whiskers. His cravats were something out of this world and his collar boxes were a delight—at least to him. His cigar cases, at times, approached the bawdy in character, but generally he was content with a discreet nude painted as a miniature on his cigar case. His cigar cutters, pocket lighters, jewelry, watch charms, and fobs are now collectors' items. What a man he was! Breadwinner, Indian fighter, trapper, farmer, cabin builder, artisan, rancher, miner, schoolteacher, highwayman, prize fighter, wrestler, politician, lawyer—all rolled into one. Of course you might never suspect we had men of this kind by the thousand in every age and generation, but we had. We only recognize the varied and checkered careers of our greats and near-greats as worthy of study. But there were thousands of Andrew Jacksons, Abraham Lincolns, and William Henry Harrisons who remain obscure only because they never reached the White House and never had fame thrust upon them.

The history of tobacco in our colonies begins with Jamestown, where the golden weed was grown in the streets because it had more money value, per ounce, than anything else that could be grown. To those desirous of studying the history of tobacco there are many noble, some hilarious, and some bawdy tomes waiting for them in the lanes and byways of bibliography. Also, it may interest many to know that among the New York Public Library special rooms is one housing the Arents Collection of tobacco data.

We derive the name tobacco from an instrument native Indians on the Island of Hispanola used in inhaling smoke from their dried weed. They called their three-pronged hollow tube a "tobago." The weed itself they called Kohiha. From the accounts of amazed observers, the natives inhaled the smoke of smoldering Kohiha through the tobago; they powdered the dry plant and snuffed it; they rolled the leaves into tubes and smoked it that way; and they chewed it, as food. The first observers thought the Indians were drinking the smoke. For well over a century all smokers were called tobago or smoke drinkers. It is fairly certain that the Aztecs and Mayans smoked long-stemmed pipes and used tobacco in the form of cigars. There are Mayan carvings of an undetermined age, but pre-Columbian by at least five hundred years, which show gods smoking things that look like modern Corona-Coronas.

Tobacco was a rich man's pleasure in the seventeenth century. That it was also the poor man's delight is owing in no small measure to the planters of Virginia who raised it in quantities and to whom tobacco was the most stable currency. Hundreds of inventories of old and noble Virginia families are reckoned in pounds of tobacco as the standard of value rather than in such a silly thing as hard money—in pounds, shillings, and pence. Tobacco, apparently, was introduced into England by Sir John Hawkins in 1565. Sir Walter Raleigh, the virgin Queen Elizabeth's favorite, took up smoking and made the habit popular with the gentry and also with the ladies. In the sixteenth century and through the seventeenth century to 1650 tobacco was worth its weight in silver. Some records of its sale, in England, are at the equivalent of three dollars (twelve shillings) an ounce.

King James I hated tobacco. He wrote a "counterblaste" against it and its use. He fostered laws against smoking and made it a punishable offense. The penalties were drastic: hanging on the gibbet was the penalty for smoking and having your nose cut off was a penalty for taking snuff. Dr. Cheynell of Oxford delivered a discourse in favor of tobacco, smoking a pipe as he lectured to an audience which included the King. By 1614 there were seven thousand dealers in tobacco, wholesale and retail, in London. It is no wonder that Virginia waxed rich on the weed. The first tobacco-store Indian of record was put up in the Netherlands as a sign in 1617.

By 1620 the potters of Staffordshire were potting clay pipes from the white clay that for several centuries has been designated as pipe clay, even when used for whitening buckskin breeches. These pipes were imported to the colonies. The Dutch were trading for tobacco, loved the weed as a habit, and perhaps made their bid for a place in the New World out of respect and desire for tobacco. The Dutch not only made pipes but fashioned brass and silver tobacco boxes, delftware jars in which to store smoking tobacco at home, and bigger jars for the use of retail tobacco merchants.

The antiques having to do with tobacco amount to a considerable number, categorically, and run into the millions, numerically. The rarest items are gold and enameled snuffboxes, some decorated with miniatures by famous artists and some studded with precious stones. We must remember that the first appurtenances of the weed were created for very wealthy people, both male and female, and that a snuffbox of, say, 1640, would be about as ornate and costly as the owner could afford. It was made to house the most precious balm out of Gilead. Snuff graters of most ornate character were used to make one's own snuff, fresh and sweet. Jars in which to store snuff and tobacco were made of delft, majolica, and Staffordshire redware, of stoneware, Bristol glass, and fine porcelain.

Pipes were made in tremendous quantities, mostly from clay. To attempt to estimate the annual production and then total it down through the years that link up two centuries is like looking at the figures of New Deal national budgets. Tobacco boxes for one's pocket, historical snuffboxes, leather pouches for chewing tobacco, match safes, lighters, china smoking pipes, silver, iron, copper, and tin smoking pipes, porcelain, stone, and meerschaum pipes, pipes as richly carved as a mandarin's chair—these are part and parcel of tobacco history. Cigar holders and cases, snuff bottles . . . But why continue? Again in this book there are pictures to tell this story far better than words can ever tell it. The only pity of it is that not one thousandth of the possible cavalcade of tobacco appurtenances can be shown.

A partial check list of occupational shaving mugs, showing the breadth and scope of this vagary and vogue. All of these were "stock" items with just one supplier in 1875

Anvil, Hammer, and Tongs	Barbershop
Architect Emblem, Plain	Barque
	Baseball Player
Baggage Master, Track and Car	Baseball and Bats
Baker Shop	Basketmaker at Work
Baker Wagon, Horse, and Driver	Basket of Peaches
Baker's Emblem, Two Lions and	Bass Fiddle
Pretzel	Beer Bottle and Glasses
Bakers at Work	Beer Brewer's Emblem
Barber's Implements	Beer Glass

Beer Wagon, Horses, and Driver
Bicycle and Rider
Billiard Playing
Billiard Table, Balls, and Cue
Billposter, Posting Bills
Blacksmith at Work
Boilermaker at Work
Book for Stationery
Bookkeeper and Desk
Bookbinder at Work
Bookbinder's Emblem
Boot and Shoe
Boot and Shoe, Fine
Bottle Blower at Work
Box of Cigars
Brass Horn or Cornet
Bricklayer's Emblem, Trowel and Square
Bricklayers at Work
Bridge Span
Brushmaker's Emblem
Brushmaker's Store
Buggy, Horse, and Driver
Buggy Maker's Emblem
Buggy Trimmer's Emblem
Buggy, Two Horses, and Driver
Bull
Butcher Dressing a Steer
Butcher Slaughtering a Steer
Butcher Dressing a Hog
Butcher Standing by Steer
Butcher Chopping Meat
Butcher Store
Butcher's Design, Steer's Head, Knife, and Steel
Butcher's Design, Bull's Head

Caboose
Calf
Caliper and Hammer
Caliper in Hand
Camera with Stand
Card in Hand

Carpenter at Work
Carpenter's Emblem
Carriage, Horses, and Driver
Chairmaker at Work
Chicken
China Dealer's Store
Cigar
Cigarmaker's Emblem
Cigar Store
Clock
Clothing Dealer and Customer
Clothing Store
Coach
Coach and Horses
Coal Cart
Coal Miner with Tools
Coal Wagon, Horse, and Driver
Coffin or Casket
Commission Merchant, Three Barrels, Port, Whisky, and Flour
Compass, Square, and Three Links
Conductor's Punch
Confectioner's Store
Confectioner's Pyramid
Confederate Flag
Cooking Stove
Cooper Making Barrel
Cotton Field with Darky Picking Cotton
Cowboy Horseman, Lassoing Cattle
Cylinder Printing Press

Dentist Drawing Teeth
Dentist Set of Teeth
Dog
Donkey
Dray
Dray and Horses
Dray, Two Horses, and Driver
Drove of Cattle
Druggist's Mortar and Pestle
Druggist with Mortar
Drugstore

Drum
Dry-goods Store

Eagle
Eagle Shield, and Flags
Eagle with Two Flags
Eagle with Spread Wings Above,
  Flowers Below Name
Electric Streetcar
Engine, Stationary
Express Wagon
Express Wagon, Horse, and Driver
Express Wagon, Two Horses

Farmer Plowing with Two Horses
Fire Engine (Steam)
Fire Engine (Steam) with Two
  Horses
Fireman's Emblem
Fireman's Hat
Fish Dealer's Emblem
Fishing Tackle
Fisherman
Fish Stand and Salesman
Flag, Sword, and Cannon
Flags, Two of Any Nation, Crossed
Flint Glass Blower at Work
Flint Glass Gaffer
Flint Glass Presser at Work
Flour and Feed Emblem
Flour Dealer's Store
Freight Car
Freight Propeller
Fruit Stand
Furniture Store
Furniture Emblem, Sofa, and Chairs

Gambrinus, Glass in Hand
Gambrinus and Keg
Gas Fitter's Emblem
Grocery Store
Grocery Wagon, with One Horse
Gunning Skiff

Gunsmith and Customer
Gun Store

Hand and Pen
Hand Car
Hand Printing Press
Hardware Store
Harness Maker at Work
Hat and Cap
Hat in Hand
Hatter at Work
Hearse, Horses, and Driver
Hod Carrier Carrying Brick
Hog Butcher
Hog's Head, Knife, and Steel
Hook and Ladder, Truck Only
Hook and Ladder, Two Horses
Horse Racer on Horseback
Horse Racer in Sulky
Horse and Wagon
Horseshoe
Horseshoer at Work
Horse Car and Horses
Horse Trainer, Training Horse
Hose Carriage, One Horse
Hose Carriage, Two Horses
Hotel Register
Hunter, Dog, and Game
Hunter and Dogs
Hunter Shooting Ducks
Hunter under a Tree
Hydrant and Hose
Hydrant and Tools

Ice Wagon, Horses, and Driver
Iron Moulder at Work
Iron Puddler
Iron Safe

Jeweler's Store
Jockey's Cap and Whip
Justice of the Peace Emblem

Lager Beer Wagon, Horses, and Driver
Ledger
Letter Carrier, in Uniform
Liquor Dealer Testing Wine
Livery Stable
Loaf of Bread
Locomotive and Tender
Locomotive and Train of Cars

Machinist at Work
Machinist Calipers
Mail Wagon, Horse, and Driver
Malt Shovel
Man Carrying Keg of Beer
Mantel, Grate, and Front
Marble Cutter at Work
Mattress Maker at Work
Mechanic's Emblem, Hand and Hammer
Milk Wagon, Horse, and Driver
Miller's Emblem
Miller Sharpening Millstone
Miner's Hat, with Lamp on It
Miner's Hat, Pick, Lamp, and Shovel
Miner with Pick on Shoulder
Mortar and Pestle
Musician, with Any Instrument

Nailer, Cutting Nails
Notion Dealer's Store

Ocean Steamer
Oil Dealer, Oil Barrel
Oil Derrick
Oil Derrick with Scenery
Omnibus and Horses
Oyster or Oyster Basket

Paint Pot and Brush
Painter at Work

Painter's Palette
Paperhanger at Work
Parlor Organ
Passenger Coach
Pen in Hand
Photographer at Camera
Photographer Posing a Lady
Photographer's Instrument
Piano Dealer's Emblem
Piano Player
Piano Upright, Square, or Grand
Pick and Shovel
Plasterer at Work
Plasterer's Trowel and Hock
Plow
Plumber's Emblem
Police in Uniform
Portable Engine
Porter Carrying Trunk
Power Printing Press
Pretzel Baker's Emblem
Printer Setting Type
Printer's Composing Stick
Propeller

Razor and Shears
Restaurant and Bar
Roller, Rolling Iron
Roller Skate
Rooster

Saddle
Saddler at Work
Saddler's Emblem
Sailor, Cannon, and Flag
Salesman behind Counter
Saloon, Bartender, and Customer
Sawmill
Schooner Sailing
Scroll Sawyer at Work
Scull Boat and Sculler
Set of Teeth
Sewing Machine

Sewing Machine and Lady
Sheep
Sheriff, Criminal, and Jail
Ship Sailing
Shirt and Collar
Shoemaker at Work
Shoe Store
Sign Painter at Work
Sledge in Hand
Sofa and Chair
Soldier and Flag
Sportsman and Dog
Stagecoach and Horses
Stake Wagon, Two Horses, and Driver
Stationery Store
Stationary Engine
Steam Hammer
Steam Passenger Boat
Steam Propeller
Steamship Sailing
Steer's Head, Knife, and Steel
Stonecutter at Work
Stove
Streetcar, Horses, Conductor, and Driver
Sulky, Driver, and Horse
Surveyor with Instrument

Tailor at Work
Tailor behind Counter, Cutting
Tailor Measuring Coat
Tailor Holding Coat
Tailor's Shears

Tanner's Emblem
Telegraph Instrument
Telegraph Key
Telephone Office
Tenpin Playing
Tinner at Work
Tinner's Emblem
Tinsmith's Furnace and Iron
Tobacconist Store
Tool Grinder at Work
Towboat
Toy Store
Trotting Horse and Wagon
Trowel and Hammer
Trunk
Truck Wagon
Truck Wagon, Two Horses

Umbrella, Open

Vial Blower
Violin and Bow
Violin Player

Wagon, Two Horses, and Driver
Watch and Chain
Whisky Barrel
Wheelwright
Windmill
Window Glass Blower
Woodturner at Work
Workmen's Emblem

Yacht Sailing

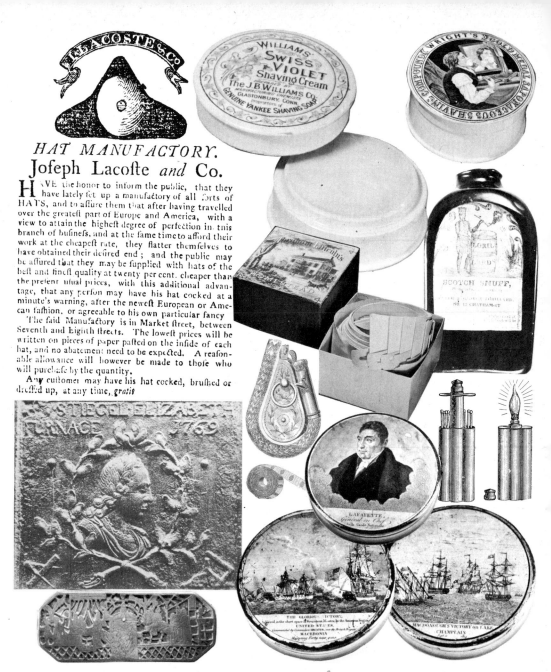

TOP LEFT: Advertisement of hat manufacturer, Philadelphia, 1786. TOP CENTER and RIGHT: Williams' shaving soap in box, 1870, and Wright's shaving soap in box, 1840. CENTER SECTION: Paper collars in box with view of President Lincoln's home, 1862; bottle of Lorillard snuff, 1796; the Eric pocket lighter and roll of paper caps which ignited the slow-burning fuse, 1880; pocket lantern or lamp, combined with matchsafe, *c.* 1870. BOTTOM SECTION: Stove plate from Elizabeth Furnace, Pennsylvania, dated 1769; oblong brass snuffbox, Dutch, *c.* 1670; snuffboxes commemorating Lafayette as General of the National Guard of France, Commodore Decatur's victory in the frigate *United States* over the British frigate *Macedonia,* and MacDonough's victory on Lake Champlain. These date from *c.* 1815. From Arthur Sussel, Philadelphia.

TOP LEFT: Pewter mug believed to have been designed for shaving, the spout to hold the brush. Probably an adaptation by a smart gentleman, as vessel originally was designated as a pouring mug. BOTTOM LEFT: Patented shaving mugs offered by J. B. Williams Company, 1876. Balance of page is a collection of occupational shaving mugs offered by the W. H. Sample Company of Albany, N.Y., established 1871. Occupational shaving mugs are today collected by many enthusiasts. J. Porter Ware of Sewanee, Tennessee, has a magnificent collection and is at present engaged in preparing an illustrated book on this engaging vagary of collectors' interest. The De Zemler collection of early barbering material is also rich in occupational shaving mugs.

Nath! Rockwell Jr.
Best quality cigars.

GENUINE
BEAR'S OIL

For promoting the
GROWTH & BEAUTY
of the
HAIR

TO COUNTRY MERCHANTS.

J. P. Mounier & Lallou,
WHOLESALE AND RETAIL ORNAMENTAL HAIR MANUFACTURERS,
Also, Importers of Artificial Flowers,
No. 28 South Fourth street, at the corner of Ranstead Court, and nearly opposite the Indian Queen Hotel,

HAVE the honor to inform the country merchants that they have constantly on hand the largest assortment of all the goods connected with their line of business.

Orders left with them promptly attended to, and the goods, packed up with particular care by them, are insured to arrive at their destination in perfect order, as when taken from the store.

Country Merchants will find it their advantage to call and judge for themselves before purchasing elsewhere; as, besides the quantity of the goods offered, they will find them cheaper than in any other similar establishment in the country.

J. P. M. & L. have invented and make Wigs of a superior quality to any thing yet seen in Europe, or imported into America.

Should any wig made by them not give entire satisfaction to the purchaser, it may be returned, and another will be made, free of additional expense, and according to directions. Transportation at the cost of the purchaser.

JOHN DOOLEY.
HAT MANUFACTURER,
IMPORTER AND DEALER IN

Hatters' Plushes, Trimmings,
and Manufacturing Materials,

No. 81 MAIN STREET, RICHMOND, VA.

Nᵒ 212 Broadway New York.
Corner of Fair Str.

GENTLEMEN'S FASHIONABLE WEARING APPAREL WAREHOUSE.
JOHN WILLIAMS
CLOTHIER

BUCKINGHAM'S DYE
FOR THE
WHISKERS.

TOP ROW: Early American cigar label, *c.* 1825, from the Bella C. Landauer Collection at New York Historical Society; pipe and tobacco box, *c.* 1765; Staffordshire figure of the Heenan-Sayres bare knuckle fight, 1860. Courtesy Paul Magriel Collection, Museum of the City of New York. CENTER: Tobacco pipe patented 1875, made as a souvenir for the Centennial of 1876. The bowl is a replica of the Liberty Bell; bottle of liquid bear grease for the hair, *c.* 1830; advertisement of a wigmaker, Boston, 1833. BOTTOM: Trade card of a New York tailor, 1817; advertisement of a hat manufacturer, Richmond, Va., 1856, and advertisement for whisker dye that would "change the beard to black or brown at discretion." Date is 1851.

TOP ROW: Pewter snuffbox, French, *c.* 1740; brass tobacco box, Dutch, *c.* 1780; brass tobacco box, *c.* 1650, picturing Suzannah and the Elders. CENTER SECTION: Copper and brass tobacco boxes, Dutch, *c.* 1680; pictorial snuffboxes, "Glory to the American Arms," *c.* 1815, St. Thomas Church, Broadway, N.Y., *c.* 1820, *United States-Macedonian* naval battle, *c.* 1815, portrait snuffboxes featuring Robert Fulton and Washington Irving, *c.* 1815; brass snuffbox, Dutch, *c.* 1785. BOTTOM: A pudding or pressed roll of tobacco leaf, containing eight stalks, corded and labeled, *c.* 1790 or earlier; violin tobacco box, Dutch, *c.* 1690. All brass and copper boxes shown courtesy New York Historical Society. All round snuffboxes from Arthur Sussel. Pudding of tobacco courtesy Lorillard Company.

TOP ROW: Clay pipe made at Newcastle-on-Tyne, *c.* 1720. Shipped to America by the crate—perhaps by the millions—in the eighteenth century; the last word in 1870—a decorative metal clip to affix to any coffee cup to make it a mustache cup; trade card of John Jackson, Cincinnati, hatmaker, 1839. CENTER: Matchcase with automatic device to ignite match and pop it out to light a cigar, *c.* 1884; Star safety razor, advertised 1887. BOTTOM: Razor box, *c.* 1725; leather-covered glass flask, *c.* 1835; advertisement of Christopher Tonge, manufacturer of bootblacking in cakes, balls, and liquid form, *c.* 1820.

CHAPTER XXVI

Buttons

THERE is considerable chitchat in print about buttons. Unfortunately, too much of it is a recital of who went where, saw whom and what, and a great deal of back- and front-door gossip. We should not blame the initial writers on the gentle mania of button collecting for this state of affairs. There was little organized research to begin with and there is still but little of it in evidence. Looking at a museum's collection, reading books on style and fashion, and talking to button wholesalers is not basic research.

What would be in order as a project is a checking of all city and town directories, all courthouse records, and all newspaper advertising to isolate the artisans and dealers who made and sold buttons in the colonies and after the peace that followed Yorktown. In the interim between colonial status and proved and recognized national status there was a lot of buttonmaking. If there is a researcher who cares to isolate the spots where Continental Army uniforms were made in quantities, there he will find that button production must have been carried on. Buttonmaking was the basic trade of John Fitch, that queer and morbid genius who built several steamboats, made clocks and watches, and who, before the Revolution, had a button factory at Trenton, New Jersey, employing up to twenty people.

Buttonmaking, as a trade, could be an ambulatory business. The buttonmaker could quite easily transport his few dies and hammers, molds, pots, and pans from place to place. His metals were tin, lead, antimony, copper, brass, and sometimes, if he was a master workman, silver. It is much to be doubted that buttonmakers, as such, made any gold buttons. That was the task or the privilege of the goldsmith and jeweler. It is quite certain, however, that many clockmakers made buttons. Caspar Wistar, the great Dutch glassmaker, had a button factory in Philadelphia in the 1720s and 1730s.

It is easy to refer to that blessed encyclopedia issued by Diderot of

Paris between 1750 and 1770, or to Dobson's American Encyclopedia issued at Philadelphia in 1798. Both contain information on the tools, practices, and methods of many trades and arts. Diderot is by far the more complete work and contains many pictures. In these and other encyclopedias of record we find illustrations of buttons and button-making. Also, it is easy to quote ponderous pronouncements about buttons—quips, jests, and clichés by greats and near-greats. But again this is not button research, and is not the approach to buttons that squares with the research dictum: "Who made what, and when, and where, for how much, and why?"

Buttons were not made in quantities in the colonies until there was demand from an increasing population requiring new clothing at more and more frequent intervals. The increase in the number of tailors from year to year—1625 to 1725, for example—would be a sure guide to the probable increase in button production or importation. Up to 1750, generally, it was the men who sported the buttons, not the women. It is not until we reach the nineteenth century that we note the phenomenon of women's styles creating a great popular demand for buttons. It is doubtful whether any fashion or style magazines for women ever reached these shores in quantities as general imports before 1790. It is with the Directoire in France, the Napoleonic Empire period, and the Bourbon Restoration in the person of Louis Philippe, in 1830, that the influence of French styling was appreciated and followed by our women in general. Most of the buttons collected today, except military and naval buttons of all kinds, are nineteenth-century buttons. Some of them are very late nineteenth century, and a great many are twentieth-century buttons.

Every art and craft, minor and major, fine and common, is found reflected in buttons. Every metal, be it cheap or precious, every animal and vegetable substance, every plastic, including glass in a wide variety, went into buttonmaking in the nineteenth century. Semi-precious and imitation gems, miniature paintings, cameos, the craftsmanship of Staffordshire potters from Wedgwood to Spode, went into buttons. In one button examined recently was found glass, brass, gold, hair, shellac, pewter, cloth, tin, paint, and paper. There was also a powder that may once have been a clay core. It should be fairly obvious that buttonmaking by factory methods called for the competitive pursuit of new design, price arrangement, discounts, distribution, and all else. Mass production was mandatory.

After 1825 buttons were not sold as common staples but as "lines" of goods for dealers to carry in stock. Fancy stores, of which every city had several dozen and every village of more than one thousand population at least one, were the prime source for the purchase of buttons. General stores did not, as a rule, carry fine lines of buttons, they carried the staples. Pack-a-back and cart peddlers vended buttons in towns, villages, and over country lanes. Even staples in buttons were made in so many minor patterns, and of so many materials, that the subject of buttons can display immense variety in staples alone.

At this writing there is in progress of compilation a sort of button dictionary that will, in all likelihood, be the first volume of a multi-volume series. Yet this book is scheduled to contain pictures of no less than five thousand, all different, buttons. We venture to predict that four thousand of these pictures will be of buttons made between the years 1820 and 1890. Fortunately, two well-qualified authors are at work on the book. Between them they represent the happy combination of scientific research, enthusiasm, and ability to organize their work.

In 1850 the clockmaking firm of Benedict and Burnham issued a salesman's catalogue of one of the by-products of brass clockmaking—buttons. This catalogue in all its glory, complete with two full pages of buttons, is pictured in this chapter. Note, please, that the catalogue is bound in gold stamped and tooled Morocco and that original, genuine buttons are mounted on its pages—not just pictures of the buttons. Other Connecticut clockmakers also made buttons. Brass companies made buttons. Glass companies made buttons. Horn and bone button factories are known to have been in operation. Woodturners made button forms that, covered with fabrics and with metal, added to the gaiety of women and their costumes. There is record of one button collector (a hard-headed business executive) who wants nothing but buttons from policemen's uniforms. Another is interested in livery buttons. Still another in buttons from firemen's uniforms.

It is possible to specialize on the buttons of streetcar conductors alone and assemble a button collection of enormous size. There were so many trolley companies that to look at the buttons makes one just a trifle dizzy. The same thing is true of railroad buttons, steamship-line personnel buttons, and so on. Military buttons almost without end are at collectors' beck and call; some of them at prices to cause one to think they are made of gold rather than brass or pewter.

Buttons made to aid a man in displaying loyalty to a political leader or hero were made in considerable quantities. There are buttons memorializing Washington, Lafayette, Jackson, Harrison, Lincoln, Buchanan, Grant, and other notables. Men were not forgotten, nor their love of display overlooked, in the nineteenth century. Cuff buttons for men in this period are a specialty standing in defiance of any collector to assemble the possible ten thousand, all different, that seem to have been made by just one company in some forty years of production.

These few leaves from the monumental story of buttons must suffice for this volume. Pictorially, the display is scanty. It would be scanty if we pictured several hundred more examples. But no book on the antiques of our pioneers can be complete without notice of buttons in some form or other for, whether we have recognized it or not, buttons were among the first "little things" made by artisans in our early colonial days. Buttons are one antique concerning which can be said, "They were made by the millions and the billions." Now there are perhaps more button collectors—whether they admit it or not—than any other type. Every woman, somewhere, has a button box or a button string. That makes her a button collector.

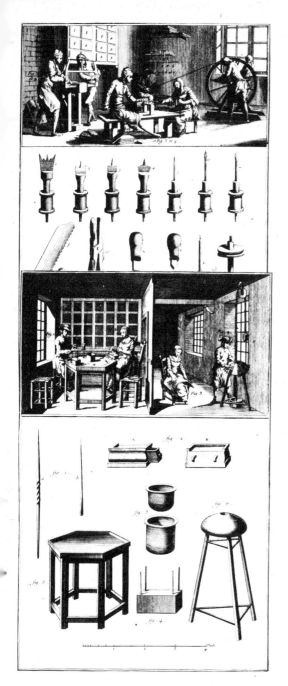

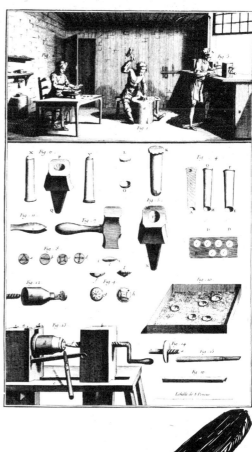

Three plates from the great encyclopedia of Diderot, picturing the making of buttons and the tools used in this art. The illustrations of operation include workmen sawing wood to produce molds for covered buttons, the making of button molds, and the finishing of metal buttons. We imported tremendous quantities of buttons from France prior to and after the Revolution and all through the nineteenth century. BOTTOM RIGHT: Mold for casting four pewter buttons, c. 1790–1820; George Washington President button of brass with a chain of original states, the initials "G. W.," and the motto "Long Live the President." Date c. 1790. Courtesy American Wing, Metropolitan Museum.

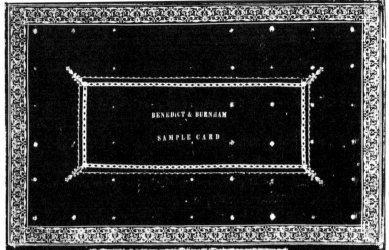

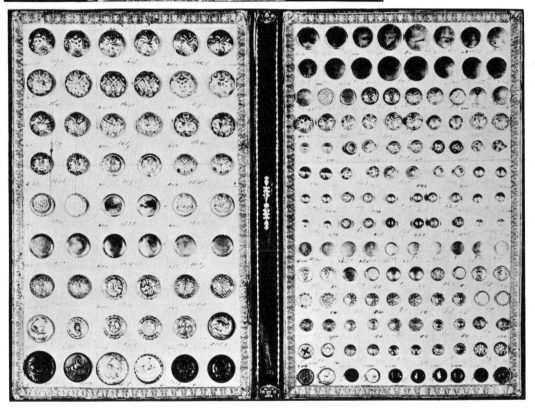

Buttons de luxe, as produced by Benedict & Burnham, Waterbury, Conn., 1850s. Morocco leather folder with gold stamping containing two pages of beautiful stamped and plain brass buttons. UPPER RIGHT: Sleeve buttons, sold as souvenirs at the Philadelphia Centennial, 1876. From C. W. Lyon, Inc.

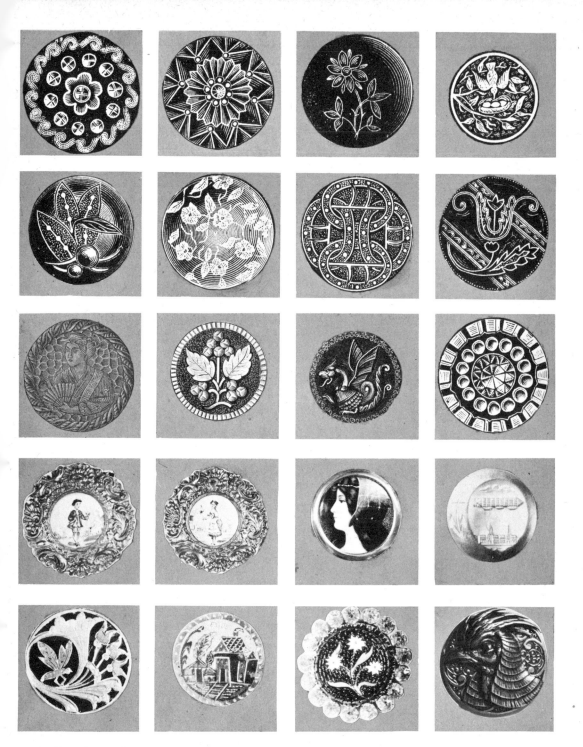

Preview of a page of illustrations from a massive tome on buttons, now being prepared by Lillian Albert and Kathryn Kent, scheduled for publication by Doubleday & Company in 1949. There will be 5,000 buttons illustrated in this forthcoming book.

CHAPTER XXVII

Transportation—Personal, Private, and Public

THE category of predilections of all pioneer Americans included a general desire to go places, probably because we always had so much room and so many places to go. We moved across the country at a fairly rapid rate even when horse, oxcart, or shanks' mare were the only means of transportation. The antiques of transportation, one would think, are mostly prints and pictures memorializing inventions, canal completions, railroad building, and so on. But when we survey this great field we discover the list includes many collectors' items, not only of transportation prints but also of every type and kind of relic of every type and kind of transportation. Among these are toboggan sleds, horse sleighs, skates, bicycles, tricycles, wagons, carts, carriages, stagecoaches, tickets, timetables, locomotive engine bells, whistles, headlamps, posters, manufacturers' advertisements, canal boatmen's horns, models of all sorts of transportation machines and vehicles, and books, pamphlets, memorial handkerchiefs, relics of canal travel, steamboats, ballooning, and heavier-than-air aviation, railroading, bicycling, and automobiling. In May 1937 one dealer issued a catalogue of books on transportation by air, rail, and road. Seven hundred and seventeen different books and pamphlets were offered at prices ranging from a few dollars to a few thousand dollars.

If we were to attempt even a short treatise on each of the major subjects touched upon by the array of pictures in this chapter it would be largely text and slim in pictures of the relics. It should be more fun to plunge directly into the story in pictures and captions. In our parade of pictures are some of the most delightful street cars ever built—relatives of the Toonerville—some of which traversed the streets of New Orleans in the days when the South was all magnolias, glamour, fried chicken, corn pone, *café brûlé,* and broiled pompano.

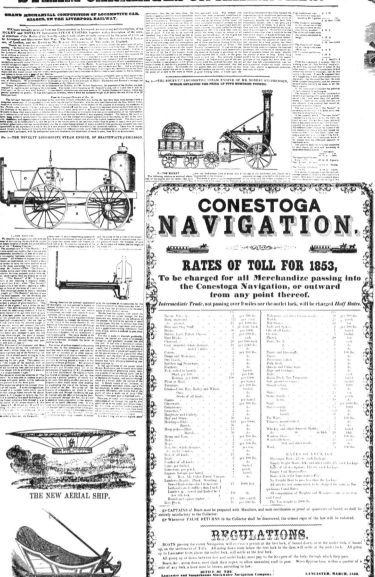

GRAND MECHANICAL COMPETITION OF LOCOMOTIVE CARRIAGES, ON THE LIVERPOOL RAILWAY.

No. 2.—THE ROCKET, LOCOMOTIVE STEAM ENGINE OF MR. ROBERT STEPHENSON, WHICH OBTAINED THE PRIZE OF FIVE HUNDRED POUNDS.

No. 1.—THE NOVELTY LOCOMOTIVE STEAM ENGINE, OF BRAITHWAITE & ERICSSON.

THE NEW AERIAL SHIP.

AIR BALLOON.

THE subscriber, who is the proprietor of the SPEAKING IMAGE, begs leave to inform the public, that he is perfectly acquainted with the nature and construction of AIR BALLOONS—that he constructed one at Bristol, and ascended with it on the 9th of April, 1785, at 9 o'clock at a place called St. Philip's, in the presence of many thousand spectators—and after being in the air about half an hour, he descended at a place called Chipnam, about 15 miles distant from the place of his ascent, though from the best computation he must have travelled (owing to contrary currents) upwards of 40 miles.

At the novelty of an exhibition of this nature may afford some amusement to the public, at the request of a number of respectable characters in this city, he proposes to open a SUBSCRIPTION for supplying the materials necessary for constructing and filling one of twenty-five feet diameter.—And in order that the public may not be deceived, the subscription money is to remain in the hands of Mrs. Bradford, at the Coffee-House, Mr. Bardin, at the City-Tavern, and Mr. Nortes, No. 165, Queen-street, (with whom the subscription book will be left,) and who are to advance the money from time to time as it may be wanted, for providing the materials, workmen, &c. which will cost about one hundred Guineas, including the expense of gas or inflammable air. The subscriber, who is to superintend the business, pledges himself to the public, that he will attend with it as soon as the same can be completed, which will principally depend upon the success of subscriptions; and none but those who have tickets, will be admitted within the inclosure, during the process of filling and ascent of the balloon.

The Subscription books will be opened at the above places, and Tickets given out to each Subscriber, at eight shillings each—and it is hoped such Gentlemen and Ladies, who wish to favor him with their subscriptions, will be as expeditious as possible, as most of the materials are already bespoke—and such as choose may see the Balloonmaking at the Exhibition-Room, No. 14, William-street.

N. B. The intent of the Subscription is only to raise as much Money as will be sufficient to pay for the materials. The subscriber's enticement (if any) he expects will arise from exhibiting the Balloon to public view after his descent.

June 11. tf .... JOSEPH DEEKER.

CONESTOGA NAVIGATION.

RATES OF TOLL FOR 1853,

To be charged for all Merchandize passing into the Conestoga Navigation, or outward from any point thereof.

Intermediate Trade, not passing over 9 miles nor the outlet lock, will be charged *Half Rates.*

☞ CAPTAINS of Boats must be prepared with Manifests, and such certificates or proof of quantities on board, as shall be entirely satisfactory to the Collector.

☞ Whenever FALSE RETURNS to the Collector shall be discovered, the utmost rigor of the law will be enforced.

REGULATIONS.

BOATS passing the entire Navigation will receive a permit at the first lock, if bound down, or at the outlet lock, if bound up, on the settlement of Tolls. All going down from below the first lock to the dam, will settle at the outlet lock. All going up to Lancaster from above the outlet lock, will settle at the first lock.

All going up or down between first and outlet locks, must pay to the Keepers of the locks through which they pass.

Boats, &c., going down, must slack their ropes, to allow ascending craft to pass. When approaching within a quarter of a mile of any lock, a horn must be blown, according to law.

OFFICE OF THE
Lancaster and Susquehanna Slackwater Navigation Company.) .... LANCASTER, MARCH, 1853.

RAILROAD HACK OFFICE.

PASSENGERS wishing to take the Cars can Book their names at the Stage Office, No. 119 Union street, and be called for and carried to the Depot.

Coaches will be in readiness at the Depot on the arrival of the Cars, to convey Passengers to any part of the Town.

Coaches will be on the Steamboat Wharf on the arrival of the Boat from Nantucket, to carry Passengers to the Depot, &c.

Fare to or from the Cars, 25 cents.

MITCHELL, SMITH & CO., take this opportunity to tender their sincere thanks to their friends and the public for the liberal and constant patronage which they have heretofore extended to them, and beg leave to assure them that no pains shall be spared, on their part, to merit their continued support.

They are now prepared and will at the shortest notice furnish Stage Coaches, Hacks, Cabs, Buggy Wagons, Carryalls, Clonses, &c. with first rate Horses and steady and careful Drivers.

Taunton, Boston & Providence

TOP LEFT: Broadside page from the Boston *Evening Gazette*, January 23, 1830, dealing with the new idea of steam locomotives for railroads, and reporting what England had accomplished. TOP RIGHT: America's first steam locomotive. It was an amphibian, equally at home on land or sea, built and operated, 1803, by Oliver Evans of Philadelphia. CENTER: Rates of toll on the Conestoga Navigation, 1853. CENTER RIGHT: Aviation, as advertised in New York, June 19, 1789. BOTTOM: Aerial ship, a dirigible, built at Hoboken, N.J., 1851; hand sled, Dutch, *c.* 1750; advertisement of the Railroad Hack Office, Boston, 1843.

America is on wheels! TOP LEFT: Velocipede, 1865. TOP RIGHT: The Rantoone, excellent for invalids, 1865. CENTER: Wooden velocipede with spool pedals, 1869; the cantering horse that actually cantered on three wheels, 1864; group of four unusual American inventions—the ice velocipede with spiked wheel, the single wheel for acrobats, steam velocipede advocated in 1856, and the monocycle with low center of gravity, 1869. BOTTOM: Advertisement of the Pearsall Velocipede, 1868; Columbia high-wheeler, 1870, sometimes called a "boneshaker"; two-wheeler of 1845, and a slick, streamlined bicycle built for two, 1890.

The streetcar comes to town. TOP LEFT: First car on Baltimore City Street Railway, 1859. TOP RIGHT: Advertisement of omnibuses by John Stevenson, New York, 1855. CENTER: Advertisement of the Troy & Albia streetcar as a suburban line, 1867. BOTTOM: The first streetcar, made in 1831 by Stevenson of New York, and five streetcars made by the same maker in the 1880s; advertisement of the Maryland stage wagon, running between the Elk River, Md., and Philadelphia, 1778.

By land, air, ice, and water, in fact and in fancy. TOP LEFT: Fisher's steam carriage, 1859. TOP RIGHT: The Great Steam Duck, advocated at Louisville, Ky., 1841. CENTER: Cover of the *Balloon Almanac*, 1787; caricature inventions of rocket propulsion, steam operated helicopter, and batwing glider, 1860; United States mail line on monorail, advocated 1827; early American steam railroad. BOTTOM: Caricature poking fun at the United States mail, 1848; steamboat to operate in water or on ice, designed, 1859, for operation between Prairie du Chien, Wis., and St. Paul, Minn. Immediately above the ice boat pneumatic underground mail car, proposed, 1856, and tubular pneumatic railroad at American Institute, 1867.

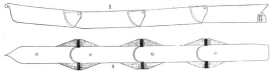

COMMERCIAL LINE STEAM PROPELLERS

BETWEEN

NEW YORK AND PROVIDENCE

TRI-WEEKLY,

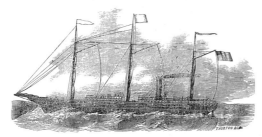

FROM PIER THIRTEEN, NORTH RIVER.

TOP LEFT: Jointed steamship of 1857. The rear unit pushed three units ahead of it. Designed to ride the waves like a dolphin, 1857. TOP RIGHT: Pressing half-sections of all-steel boats, 1853; buggy-boat with two side paddles under stern operated by hand cranks, 1860. CENTER: Advertisement of the Providence Line, 1852; advertisement of clipper line to San Francisco, 1862. BOTTOM: Robert Fulton and a view of his successful steamship, the *Clermont;* the Philadelphia-Camden ferry, operating in 1853.

THE STUDEBAKER WAGON.

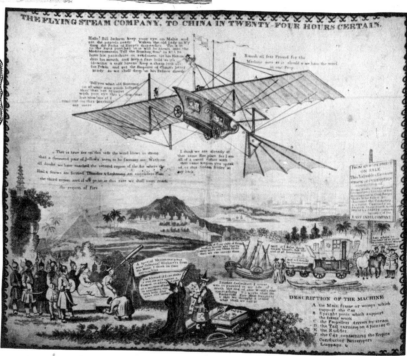

THE FLYING STEAM COMPANY, TO CHINA IN TWENTY-FOUR HOURS CERTAIN.

DESCRIPTION OF THE MACHINE

TOP LEFT: Balloon ascension by John Wise, Lancaster, Pa., 1854.   TOP
RIGHT: Conestoga wagon, c. 1810, shown carrying DuPont powder to Lake
Erie on the 100th anniversary of Perry's victory. Under wagon, a tar
bucket from which lard and tar were ladled to lubricate the axles; George
Washington's state coach, 1785.   CENTER: New York sleigh, dated, 1788;
John Fitch's steamboat, 1796; Studebaker wagon, 1880.   LOWER RIGHT:
Handkerchief memorializing Henson's steam carriage in flight. Courtesy
C. M. Keys.   BOTTOM LEFT, from top down: Bob sled, 1890; trade card,
1860; Kinsey's Express, 1851; coachmaker's advertisement, 1833.

TOP LEFT: Clipper ship cards of the *Great Republic* and *Young America*, 1857. TOP RIGHT and CENTER: The Studebaker Works, 1880, and the Cook Carriage Works, New Haven, Conn., where the mass production of carriages was inaugurated. CENTER: Caricature of pioneer travel over the plains, 1850s. BOTTOM: Canal boats on the Erie and early steam trains, 1845; advertisement, 1860, featuring carriages and the self-propelled land-regatta carriage, which was self-propelled if you continued to turn the cranks. This was the last word in sporting equipment.

CHAPTER XXVIII

Tools

THERE are today perhaps half as many tool collectors as once there were tool makers and manufacturers in our colonies and states. There is evidence that the latest vagary in tool collecting pays attention to the tools of early motoring; the things that were in the tool boxes of the early Pierce Arrows, Locomobiles, Simplexes, Stevens-Duryeas, Pope-Toledos, and Fords. Collecting the tools of a specific trade and art has intrigued many specialists for a number of years. The late Dr. Henry Mercer, tilemaker of Doylestown, Pennsylvania, collected a notable lot of shoemakers', candlemakers', clockmakers', blacksmiths', carpenters', and cabinetmakers' tools which today are on display, in miniature shops, in the Bucks County Historical Society Museum. Dr. Mercer's book on early carpenters' tools is an almost definitive book on the subject. The tools of agriculture are covered at least in part in a chapter of this volume. To attempt to do even partial justice to all the other tools of production would require several large volumes.

The general subject of tools offers many categories of possible interest for those who wish to indulge in the sensible pastime of purposeful collecting. The tools of the art of writing, for example, embracing everything from a stylus to a typewriter, should engage the interest of creative writers. The tools of printing, engraving, button making, pewtering, silversmithing, clockmaking, gun-making, and so on, are a very logical part of collecting prints, books, pewter, silver, and firearms. In the gunroom of a famed collector of rifle-barreled firearms there is a tool: a barrel-rifling engine. It attracts more attention from casual visitors than any of the racks of guns. A collection of inkwells can be a joy forever, or just as long as the collector doesn't have *all* the types and kinds of inkwells ever made. One of our American furniture factories has assembled a great col-

lection of cabinetmakers' tools. A representative collection of ironworkers' tools is owned and displayed by a steel company. The tools
of all artists and artisans, the tools of the barber surgeons, the tools
used in weighing and measuring, are all objects not only worthy of
preservation but also worthy of collecting, tabulating, and display.

Tools, as a subject, is deserving of first place rather than last place
in any parade of accomplishment for without tools there would be
little accomplishment about which to write. Tools, as a subject, is
made the last subject of this book in order that all of us can say, "Of
all that has gone before, there would be nought, save for the tools
by which we achieved all that we have."

Roy T. Bramson, editor of *Production Engineering & Management,* in 1945 published a short *History of Mass Production in
America* that deals in part with mechanics' tools. Thoreau Mac-
Donald's *Tools of the Pioneers* has many delightful drawings by the
author, certain of which are pictured in this chapter with his permis-
sion. The few pages of tools making up this, the slimmest of this book's
chapters will, it is hoped, whet the appetites of collectors not at present
interested in the subject. Real tool collectors will skip the chapter as
puerile and not even elementary. The time is not yet ripe to attempt
publishing detailed information on tools for popular consumption.
Those who are interested need no urging to become members of
Early American Industries Association and to peruse the bulletins
of that group of enthusiasts. Perhaps in another decade interest in
these antiques will be so general that a book, or books, on the subject
will be forthcoming. Until that day we shall say no more, specifically,
on the subject of early American tools—the aids to production and
artistry used by our pioneers.

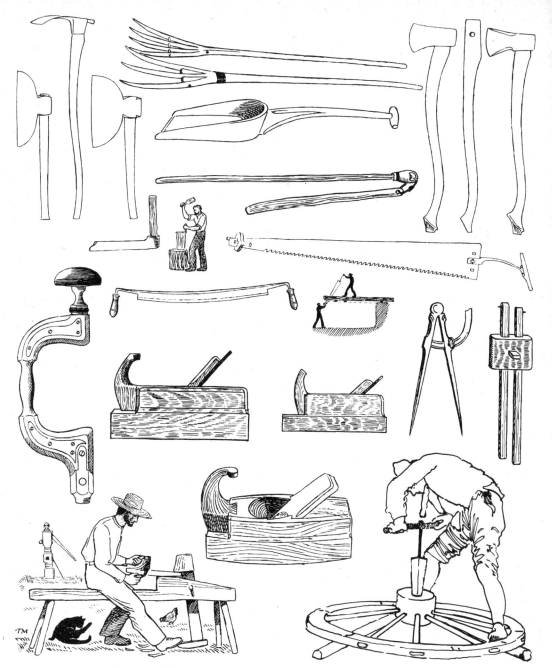

TOP ROW: A pair of broadaxes and an adze; hay forks, scoop shovel, and grain flail, all of wood; pair of axes and axe-handle pattern. Drawings by Thoreau MacDonald, from *Some Tools of the Pioneers*. CENTER: Auger brace; drawknife; pit sawyers at work; planes, calipers, and scribers, from drawings by Thoreau MacDonald. BOTTOM: Artisan at work on shaving horse; smoothing plane, 1820s; workman boring and tapering the axle hole in a wheel hub, from a Dutch painting, *c.* 1710.

A Quaint, Antique Chair.

Now that antique forms in furniture are popular, we give a design of a chair which may be easily made. If the pattern is not exactly reproduced, it will suggest the putting together of a chair that will be both useful and ornamental, in the farmer's hall, or "front entry," on the piazza, or, if neatly made, even in the parlor. Those who have the use of a lathe can easily turn the parts, or, in the absence of this, such a chair would be pleasing even if made in rustic work, of such material as the limbs of the Red-cedar, or roots and branches of the Mountain Laurel. The pattern is taken from the President's Chair at Harvard University, Cambridge, Mass. The history of the chair is lost in antiquity, but it has been in use for more than a cen-

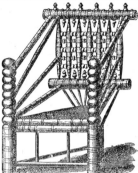

tury, and is still occupied by the President of Harvard when he confers the degrees at the annual commencements of this old University.

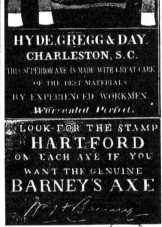

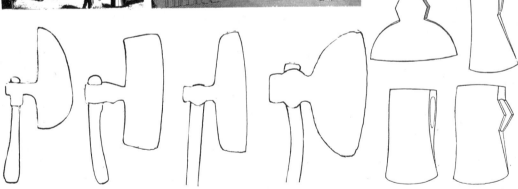

TOP LEFT: The *American Agriculturist*, in 1883, featured this turned chair, known as the President's Chair of Harvard University, and dating from *c.* 1600, as a chair any amateur turner could duplicate. TOP CENTER: The "Steakgreith," a cube steak tool advertised in 1883. RIGHT COLUMN: Advertisements and labels of edged tools, 1840s and 1850s. CENTER: Blacksmith's forge, *c.* 1810. BOTTOM: Interior view of Diamond file works, 1856, and row of axes as follows: broadaxes, 1600s; broadaxes, 1700s, and four axes of 1800s. Many edged-tool works started with a single waterpowered trip hammer and grinding wheel and developed into factories producing as many as 1,000 axes a day.